TURNING BLUE:

A LIFE BENEATH THE SHIELD

LAWRENCE HOFFMAN

PAGE PUBLISHING, INC.
New York, NY

First originally published by Page Publishing, Inc. 2015

ISBN 978-1-68289-104-9 (pbk)
ISBN 978-1-68289-105-6 (digital)

Printed in the United States of America

Contents

Introduction

In the 1650s, a civilian watch organization known as the Rattle Watchmen patrolled New Amsterdam. They were armed with a rattle which made a loud and distinctive sound that warned colonists of any dangerous or threatening situation. Because there were no streetlights, the watchmen carried a lantern with green glass sides to allow the community to recognize them. After patrolling the area, the watchmen would return to the watch house and hang the green lantern on a hook outside the house. This would let the people know that the watchmen were inside. Adult male citizens were required to be on watch on a rotating basis. If someone could not perform their duty as scheduled, they would have to pay a substitute. In 1658, widespread fears of Indian raids and slave uprisings initiated the establishment of a paid rattle watch that consisted of a captain and eight men.

In 1664, the English conquered New Amsterdam from the Dutch and renamed it New York after the English Duke of York and Albany. The military had the responsibility of keeping the peace until 1684 when, for twelve pence per night, a paid citizen's watch was established. The watch consisted of a constable and eight watchmen for each ward.

Young New York was expanding at an alarming rate. As increasing immigration population forced its borders north, crime rose at an almost impossible pace. In the 1820s, the first street gangs rose up in the area around Columbus Park known as the Five Points. Gangs such as the Forty Thieves, Roach Guards, Dead Rabbits, and Yankee Bowery Boys roamed the streets making this one of the most feared and lawless places in the world. The gangs used different markings to identify each other. Named after Ted Roach, the Roach Guards gang wore a blue stripe on their trousers, while the Dead Rabbits wore red stripes. Modern-day gangs still honor this tradition into the current century with the Bloods wearing red and the Crips defined by blue.

Early forms of policing were ravaged by political influence and corruption. The police were compensated by fees rather than a salary which led to only the jobs of greater value being considered. Calls went out to the governor's office for reform. In 1844, Governor William H. Seward passed legislation that abolished the night watch and created a unified full-time police force of eight hundred men. The law didn't go into effect until 1845 because of fighting between the city and state over control of the police. Governor John King maintained the Metropolitan Police, while Mayor Fernando Wood, who fought the Metropolitan Police Act in the Court of Appeals, controlled the Municipal Police.

An arrest warrant was issued for Mayor Fernando Wood after he refused to grant Governor King's appointee access to city hall. The mayor had the bearers of the arrest warrant physically removed, only to have them return with fifty Metropolitan Police officers. The fifty were met by five hundred Municipal Police officers loyal to the mayor, and the two forces went to battle. At this time, the Seventh Regiment of the National Guard happened to be marching down Broadway en route to embarking on a ship to Boston. General Sanford, the head of the Seventh Regiment, ordered the troops to come to the aid of the Metropolitan Police.

The two camps agreed to coexist until the Court of Appeals made its decision. The opposing forces continued to fight for custody of prisoners and police buildings. Once again, General Sanford's troops were called in to maintain the peace. On July 2, 1857, the Court of Appeals decided by a six to two vote to uphold the Metropolitan Police Act. In response, a disgruntled Mayor Wood disbanded the Municipal Police.

In 1870, the Metropolitan Police came to an end. The smaller separate departments such as the New York Watch Police, Brooklyn Police, Long Island City Police, Park Police, and Morrisania Police were later merged on January

01, 1898 when the five boroughs were officially consolidated into the Greater City of New York. Not long after, the smaller police departments joined over six thousand police officers in the larger New York Police Department (established in 1844). A reform called for abolishing the police board, and in 1901, Mayor Van Wyck appointed Colonel Michael C. Murphy as the first police commissioner.

Today, policemen wear an eight-point hat issued in 1928 that symbolize the original eight watchmen who patrolled New Amsterdam and early New York. Green lights adorn the entrance to police precincts to honor these early watchmen and to symbolize that the "Watch" is present and vigilant.

Prologue

I do solemnly swear that I will support the Constitution of the United States, and the Constitution of the State of New York, and that I will faithfully discharge the duties of Police Officer in the Police Department of the City of New York according to the best of my abilities.

I took that oath on February 3, 1984 and embarked on a twenty-year journey that would take me to places within myself where many, thank God, will never have to go. On so many levels, I was forced to expose and reevaluate beliefs that governed my own life.

It's amazing what you can see with your eyes closed. I sat with my fingers poised on the keys, not knowing where or even how to begin telling my story. I hoped to relive my past experiences looking through life's rearview mirror more commonly known as memory. As I directed my internal sights to a particular event or stage in my life, images started becoming clear. At times, it was almost an out-of-body experience; I hovered above myself, while an inner dialogue narrated intense actions and feelings. I navigated through my personal history, my fingers working the keys like a Ouija board.

I was so proud to be a member of the New York City Police Department with all its glorious traditions and history. But just as passing an exam and wearing a stethoscope won't, by themselves, make you a doctor, putting on that uniform won't make you a cop. It's what you do and how you react to unimaginable human circumstances that will make you an officer.

Somewhere within that twenty-year span, I had transformed from a skinny kid from Long Island into a veteran New York City detective. And with this transformation comes the ability to separate the daily exposure to the dark side of human nature from your own life sustaining core beliefs. Many will fail to acquire this ability and fall victim to drugs, alcohol, divorce, crime, and even suicide. This is a process which I have come to call Turning Blue.

This is my story of how I was drawn to the "job" by a strong psychological undertow. Not only what I had to go through as a New York City police officer in some of the toughest neighborhoods during a tough time but also how these incidents affected my life on a personal basis. How I dealt with these experiences at home, while my gun belt and uniform hung safely in my locker.

It is written from my point of view and to the best of my recollection, with all the flaws and blemishes included. At times, it can get downright ugly, and my mistakes are brought to the surface. Whenever possible, other people involved have been contacted to ensure accuracy. In some cases, names and physical descriptions were changed in order to protect their identity.

This job I have chosen has allowed me to see people at their worst. Over time, that perspective can make people jaded. I have written this as if you were right there alongside of me. You (the reader) are my partner. I want you to feel how I felt. I want you to see what I saw. I want you to experience all the sounds and smells with me. What would you have done as my partner? Would you act the way I did, or would you have chosen a different path?

Some of the decisions I made were sketchy, and you won't find them in any patrol guide. When you have less than a second to decide a course of action, you go with your first impulse and hope for the best. What would you have done in that split second? I consider myself to have been truly blessed throughout my career, and I definitely had a guardian angel watching over me. At any given time, any one of these incidents could have gone in a different direction.

Many people have often said to me, "You must have seen a lot of bad things, huh." When I tell them some of the situations I've been involved in, they have a "better you than me" attitude. I am in no way unique and do not claim in any fashion to be a super cop. Any cop could fill volumes with incredible stories.

I believe that it takes a special kind of individual to do what we do, but we're still human beings. We're capable of making mistakes. We feel pain. We hurt. We cry. We bleed. We get scared. Have you ever truly feared for your life? I can honestly answer that question with a resounding yes. What does fear look like to you? What does it feel like? What taste does it have?

More importantly, could you separate the job from your personal life? Could you go back to work after a night spent crying yourself to sleep, reliving your partner's screams as he lay bleeding to death in the backseat of your unmarked car, the only thing keeping your heart in your chest was your department-issued bulletproof vest?

I invite you to strap on a gun belt, pin on a shield, and walk with me, partner, on my journey of "Turning Blue" and experience "A Life Beneath the Shield."

to the corner, the driver looked in the rearview mirror and yelled, "Post four. You're up."

I backed out of the van, put boots on the ground, and laid claim to my territory. At this early time in the morning, Nostrand Avenue was quiet. But I knew, as the sun traveled across the sky from east to west, this place was gonna be jumping. I would soon find out that this day would change my life forever and make me question my career choice.

I squeeze the transmit button on the side of the radio, and in what I hope is a calm voice reply, "Post four is on the corner, Central. I will check and advise."

"Are you a one-man post, post four?"

"That's affirmative."

Central transmits, "Any Seven-Seven units available to back up post four on this ten thirty-four (10-34) on Sterling Place?"

The patrol sergeant responds back, "Seven-Sergeant on the back."

The second building off the corner is 721. Chilling screams drew my attention upward as I step to the front door of the address. A woman desperately hung out of a third floor window. The hair on my neck stood at attention. The woman's screams and the wail of the siren on the approaching police car seem to merge into one.

The entrance is locked, so I ring every bell until someone buzzes, breaking the magnetic lock. I held it open, allowing the sergeant and his driver to enter behind me. I race up the stairs, taking two at a time. I still remember unlocking and removing my gun from the holster, being conscious of pointing it in a safe direction. To me, it was like unlocking the Holy Grail. The magnitude of power and the responsibility of drawing your weapon are both exhilarating and overwhelming at the same time.

I'm charging up the stairs with my Smith & Wesson .38 caliber revolver in my right hand. I remember that it felt extremely heavy. Its weight is a symbolic reminder of the immense burden of accountability that comes with releasing and drawing your firearm from the safe haven of your leather holster.

As we get closer to the third floor, the sergeant grabs me by the arm and stops me mid-step saying, "Slow down, kid! You just can't go running in there! You're gonna get yourself killed! You gotta look…you gotta listen…you gotta smell…use them all." I looked at him wide-eyed, nodding my head as I tried to catch my breath. I inhaled deeply, tugged on my hat, and continued more cautiously up the stairs. I started to come out of my tunnel vision. I have often heard that time appears to slow down at moments like this, and I could honestly say that this is true, along with the fact that everything happens so quickly.

On the third floor landing the woman's screams became deafening. There was an open door with an orange extension cord snaking out of the apartment, running into the hallway. As we made our way closer, I could see that the lock had been kicked in and hung off the partially opened door. I looked at the sergeant and said, "Looks like we're in the right place." I turned the corner into the doorway letting my gun lead the way. I could see there was a short hallway adorned with family photos opening up into a larger area which was the living room. Peering over the barrel of my gun, I inched my way in. My eyes were as wide as possible, afraid to blink, for fear of missing some movement which could cost me my life. I could see two closed doors ahead and a kitchen on the right. My gun felt like a giant magnet as it pulled me into the living room. Screams were coming from the closed door on the left. I made my way into the kitchen area near the second closed door.

The sergeant and his driver positioned themselves behind the couch with their guns trained on the door where the screams were coming from. The boss pointed to the door near the kitchen area, indicating he wanted me to clear the room. I nodded and grabbed the knob and pushed it open. My magnet pulled me in.

What I saw remains as vivid today as it did when that door opened twenty-four years ago. It will stay with me forever, along with hundreds of other haunting images which I have collected over my twenty-year career. They have conveniently tucked themselves away in a part of my mind which, with any luck, will be rarely visited. As I write this story, I carefully peer in, being careful not to disturb the other sleeping ghosts.

The opening bedroom door reveals a boy, maybe five years old, staring at me with these wide-open wet brown eyes. Our eyes met for what seemed like an eternity, but I'm sure was just a second. He was standing over a female about twenty-five years old, his mom, who was laying face up on the floor with a large wound to the left side of her forehead. My eyes darted around the room quickly and determined the room to be clear. The boy looked to me for answers. I had none. I was in full police mode now. This was no exam or test. This was as real as it gets, and my life was potentially on the line. I indicated to the sergeant that we had a confirmed female shot, and the room was clear.

I motioned to the boy to be quiet and to get under the bed. I backed out of the room and closed the door behind me. I stepped into the kitchen and turned the table over and used it for cover with my gun drawn on the last closed door. My body was fully engulfed in the moment. I was ready. Game on. I was making sure I was going home tonight. With the door covered from three points, the sergeant commanded, "Open the door slowly and show us your hands."

The screaming subsided for a moment, and the knob jiggled and slowly turned. I closed my left eye, allowing my right to align the sights on my gun as I waited for the devil himself to emerge. An elderly woman stepped from the room and collapsed onto the floor yelling, "He shot her, he shot her!"

We determined the apartment to be safe, and the sergeant got on the radio and notified the dispatcher that there was a confirmed female shot and requested an ambulance forthwith. I holstered my gun, pushed the table aside, and slowly opened the door near the kitchen. I got down on one knee and peered under the bed. Those brown eyes came back to mine. I gave him a soft smile and grabbed him by the hand and lead him out of the room. The boy's grandmother leaped from the living room floor and smothered him in a protective hug.

The sergeant maneuvered the grandmother and child into the opposite room, out of sight of the boy's mom. The sergeant's driver and I went into the small bedroom where the woman was laying face up. Her eyes were half open and amazingly she was still breathing. The hospital was nearby, and because of the severity of her injury, we decided it was best to transport her in the RMP (radio-mobile-patrol / police car). Every second could make a difference.

I pulled the bedsheet off and laid it on the floor next to her. We gently rolled her on to her side and slid the sheet under her. I grabbed one end of the sheet, and the driver grabbed the other, as we picked her up and carried her into the living room. I said to the sergeant, "Boss, we can't wait for a bus (ambulance) we're gotta take her in the car." He nodded to us, and we exited the apartment. We stepped over the orange extension cord and carried her down the three flights of stairs in the bedsheet stretcher. We struggled as we awkwardly snaked down the narrow stairwell.

We got to the car, and the driver opened the back door. I slid in first while pulling my end of the homemade stretcher. The other officer pushed from his end and closed the rear door. Her limp legs were bent up against the rear passenger door, and her head rested in my lap. I moved the sheet away from her face as the driver started the car, sounded the siren, and pulled from the curb. I looked at her, and I could now clearly see a large entrance wound on the left side of her forehead. Her breathing was horribly erratic. I could feel her fighting for life. I looked for any encouraging sign in her unfocused, half-opened eyes and gently began to talk to her. I leaned in close to her face and whispered, "Don't give up on me… please. You're gonna be okay. Just hang in there." The white bedsheet slowly turned crimson as her blood eerily creped down before my eyes.

I can't recall any of the ride. I just remember talking to this girl and see-ing those same brown eyes that I saw when I first opened that bedroom door. I was jolted back to reality when the car door suddenly flew open, and we arrived at the hospital. The process was reversed as we removed her from the car. Doctors and nurses greeted us at the emergency entrance. They put her on a gurney and shuttled her into the hospital, yelling in medical language I couldn't understand. I stood at the door for a moment looking at my blood-smeared hands. My pants felt cool and sticky where her head had rested in my lap. I stood out of the way, taking deep breaths as I tried to comprehend what had just happened in the last ten minutes. The driver returned to the scene to lend assistance to the sergeant.

I knew my job didn't end here. It was my responsibility to gather information and make notifications. I walked into the hospital bathroom and washed my hands and face, trying to remove any personal connection to the girl. I couldn't allow my emotions to interfere with my responsibility of handling the shooting on Sterling Place.

I phoned the Seven-Seven precinct and advised them of my location and was told to keep the detectives updated. I asked the hospital staff where the victim was taken and made my way toward a makeshift operating room. She was surrounded by ER workers, all dressed in blue, as beeping machines converted her condition into ever changing numbers.

I noticed her clothing was balled up on the floor and grabbed a pair of plastic gloves from a dispenser on the wall. I knelt and started to go through her belongings to see if there was any identification or papers to indicate who she was. As I was doing this, the doctors started working frantically on her. Her chest was cut open, and the doctor began to massage her exposed heart. I felt like an intruder kneeling in the corner, as I sifted through her blood soaked personal property.

After a few minutes, they stopped and turned off the machines. The beeping machines gave way to silence. A nurse pulled up the sheet as the blue staff snapped off their gloves with a pop. The doctor announced a time through his facemask, and it was all over. Nothing more to do. She was gone. I got the doctor's name, time of death, and phoned the detectives. The case was now classified as a homicide.

Later, after signing out, my tour of duty was over. I went downstairs into the Seven-Nine locker room with the rest of the new jacks. There was always an excitement in the locker room at the end of each tour. Everyone seemed to magnify and boast about the incidents that took place on their posts. Although I clearly owned the bragging rights for the day, I just didn't feel like talking about it.

In slow motion, I removed my gun belt and laid it across the hard wooden bench in front of my locker. I noticed that my handcuff case and my memo book holder had light green paint smeared across them. I sat for a moment and tried to figure out where it came from. Then it hit me like a ton of bricks. I carry my memo book holder in my rear pants pocket, and my cuff case is located on the back of my gun belt. I remembered that the paint in the narrow stairwell on Sterling Place was that same color green. I visualized myself and the sergeant's driver carrying the gunshot victim down the stairs and recalled having to brush against the winding stairwell walls as we hurried out of the building. That paint was a daily reminder of what I might be exposed to on any given day.

I later found out from the Seven-Seven detective that caught the case that the incident stemmed from an ongoing dispute between the girl and the superintendent. He chased her with an electric drill until the orange extension cord pulled out from the wall and then decided to finish the argument with a single gunshot to her forehead. He changed many lives the instant he pulled the trigger, including mine. To this day, I don't know his name, if he is black, white, Hispanic, how tall he is or how much he weighed. But I will never forget him. He was later arrested in Puerto Rico and brought back to New York to stand trial.

Today, I looked death in the face. I wondered how many more times in the next twenty years we would meet again, on what terms, and who would win. I also wondered if I had what it took to do the job.

I realized that I would have to learn how to separate my personal life from the job in order to protect myself and my relationship with my loved ones from emotional destruction. I knew that I had a long way to go before I became a veteran police officer.

I still thought of myself as a skinny kid from Long Island, who loved life, friends and laughter. What happened that day was so completely different from the life I lived just 25.4 miles from here. It was as if I had crossed the border into an entirely different country.

ask about "him." However, he has managed to thrive inside of me, like a parasite slowly devouring its host, leaving me eternally injured and always needing to find a way to heal myself on many different levels.

My mother was the youngest of twelve children (one of whom died shortly after birth). God bless my grandparents, Mary and John. I can only imagine the fun and conflict that must have coincided in a home with that many people colliding with each other on a daily basis.

My mom was raised in Lynbrook, Long Island where she was a very popular and athletic girl. My aunts and uncles were all good athletes in their own right. One uncle I particularly remember is Uncle Nick. He was voted First Team All-American for two years (1939–1940) at Cornell University. He was drafted by the Cleveland Browns in 1941 and inducted into the College Hall of Fame in 1981. My mother's sister Vera was a great golfer, who, during her golfing career, had three hole in ones. She hit the last one when she was well into her eighties.

Being a single parent back in those days was very difficult and not well accepted, which caused friction with my grandparents. Somehow, my mom was able to do what needed to be done, and I am grateful for her sacrifice and struggle.

At the age of three, I met an angel. This angel went by many names: Jack, John, Jake, Jake the Snake, Mr. P. Brojack, Uncle Jack, Hun, Honey, Sweetheart, Dear, Grandpa, Dad, and my personal favorite: Pop. To me, he was a giant of a man who had balding slicked back black hair and a perfectly groomed handlebar mustache that looked like you could do pull-ups on it. He had the largest hands and wrists that I have ever seen, and they were as smooth as silk. He could give you quite a swat with his huge hands or be as loving and tender with his smooth touch.

He was so many things, to some many people, and one of the most caring, giving and unselfish people to ever walk the earth. God absolutely has a special place for this man in heaven with an ice cold beer at the ready. Other than the small detail that we don't have any of the same genetic makeup, he is my dad.

But realizing how great a man he is was not an overnight process. Being a step-parent is a very difficult job. I don't want to undermine the job of a natural parent in any way, but to fill the shoes of a father or mother is a challenging and demanding job. In my case, there were no shoes to fill, so his were just right. At times, he was able to fit his size twelve's in my ass when needed although our opinions for what those times were may have differed. Looking back, I'm sure his judgment was clearer than mine.

Pop had a biological son named Jay, who was four years my elder. When I was about three years old, a decision was made for my mother and me to join forces with Pop and Jay and become a family. We left our Lynbrook apartment and moved into a one family house in North Bellmore. The transition was not easy for me at first. I went from being an only child to the youngest child in a matter of minutes. I did get my own room though, which was sweet.

Although we were a modified condensed version of *The Brady Bunch*, minus the girls and a maid, my upbringing was like any normal middle-class family. Domesticated pets were always a huge part of my early life. Over the years, any combination of rabbits, fish, birds, gerbils, turtles, and dogs could be found inhabiting the property.

My stepfather had a soft spot for strays and dogs that were being given away. For a short time, nine dogs called my house home. We had a German shepherd named Satan, and a Belgium shepherd named Duchess. Both of these dogs were acquired from other families. Duchess was mated with a full-bred Belgium shepherd stud and gave birth to six puppies. After a family visit to Brooklyn one day, my father spotted a white German shepherd running loose along the Belt Parkway. We stopped and rescued the dog from certain death and brought him home. We called him Bullet and added to our ever growing animal kingdom. My parents placed an advertisement in the newspaper stating the location and type of dog that we found. About a month later, Bullet was returned to his grateful owners.

In an odd way, I see myself as one of those strays taken in by my step-dad. Maybe he viewed me as a future asset. As you could imagine, nine dogs generated a lot of poop, and it became the job of yours truly to clean up that mess before the neighbors had the house condemned. And let me tell you, I could shovel shit with the best of them. It was all in the wrist baby. Bag 'em and tag 'em, Johnny! Our house was unquestionably the safest on the block and a mailman's nightmare.

THREE

You Want to Know My Winning Secret?

A blue and yellow Cub Scouts uniform replaced my army outfit as I started to sprout. I became a member of a pack, complete with our very own den mother. In no time, I was a highly decorated Cub Scout, fulfilling my task requirements at the speed of sound. One of my favorite events was the Pinewood Derby. Each cub was given a small block of wood which he had to shape and mold into a racing car with little plastic tires that were held in place by nails. We would race these cars down a twenty-foot pitched race track against the other Cub Scout packs in the area.

I think my stepdad loved this event even more than I did because he couldn't wait to get his hands on that block of wood. He brought the small rectangle piece of pine down into the basement like Dr. Frankenstein, where he would bring it to life. I was afraid to go down there after hearing sounds of evil, deep-throated laughter, woven between vibrant bolts of electricity sparking off metal objects. He would come up days later holding this perfectly shaped wooden race car. One swipe of the hand and the four wheels would spin frictionless for minutes.

On race day, I proudly walked into the gymnasium of my school, Newbridge Road Elementary School, where the event was held. I carefully carried my race car in both hands as if it were a priceless Tiffany lamp. Scouts from neighboring packs tugged on their father's shirt sleeves as I strutted by them with the Pinewood Derby's equivalent of Secretariat in my outstretched hands.

I found the folding table with our pack flag draped across it. I gently set the car on the felt covering and surveyed the gym for signs of competition. Apparently, other dads had decided to make attempts at producing winning cars. Although some appeared to be remarkable specimens, they all paled in comparison to the champion, which sat temporarily motionless at my side. I couldn't wait to unleash the wrath of my stepfather's aerodynamic creation on the unsuspecting visiting packs. Not in my house!

There were always those one or two kids, whose dad either worked two jobs or had no desire to participate with the scouts, who shaped their own car using just a dull Cub Scout folding knife. For safety reasons, those knives couldn't cut through air without difficulty, let alone whittle a sports car out of pine. Their cars looked like they had already been in a horrific crash on the way to the event. But to their credit, they still participated in the race.

My car made it easily through the qualifying heats. I cheered my fellow scouts as their cars roared down the track. As the night went on, the slower cars were eliminated from the competition.

The main event had arrived with only two cars remaining. The final showdown included my car and one from a neighboring rival pack. The excitement grew as the cars were released at the top of the track. Both cars surged from the gate with equal speed, but his was no match for mine. My car hit the halfway mark and quickly distanced from its enemy. Secretariat thundered across the finish line to claim first prize.

It was a joyous occasion, and our pack celebrated my victory over sundaes at the Friendly's Ice Cream Shop just up the block from the school. We were all smiles as we bounced around in our booths, talking over each other, sticky ice cream and toppings smeared all over our faces.

As soon as we parked in the driveway, I ran from the car eager to tell my mom and Jay the outcome of the competition. My mother fed off my excitement, while my stepbrother could give a rat's ass. He was four years older and thought the Cub Scouts were for little boys. He had been a Cub Scout himself but never had a winning car, so I believe jealousy played a big role in his reaction. After creating several losing cars for Jay, my stepfather had finally perfected his skills.

Pop walked in behind me carrying our gladiator. He was very proud of his creation. My mom was very happy for the both of us. My stepfather asked my mom, "You want to know my winning secret?"

Mom said, "Secret? What do you mean secret?"

Pop proceeded to turn the car over and scraped the paint off the bottom to reveal a little trap door. He pried open the tiny vault, shook the car, and a hunk of lead fell from the car's belly onto his hand. The wood had been hollowed out, and a piece of lead had been inserted into the hull, giving the car added weight and an unfair advantage over the other much lighter cars. He stood there with the hunk of lead in his hand and a devious smile on his face.

My mother stared at him momentarily and said finally, "You cheated."

My stepfather answered with a shrug of his shoulders, as both my mother and I turned and walked away. He stood alone in the dining room with his monster, calling out after us, "Nobody said you couldn't do it."

Cub Scout regulations stated that a competing car could not weigh more than five ounces. Mine could have doubled as a bowling ball, being just a couple of ounces short of requiring its own trailer and license plates. I had won illegally but was too embarrassed to tell anyone. My victory will be forever prefaced by an asterisk, a footnote indicating: "Achieved with the use of illegal performance-enhancing metal."

FOUR

She Was the Enemy

My neighborhood was rich with playmates, and we competed in every sport we could imagine. We created our own leagues for everything. We had a basketball league divided up into two-man teams. Our stadium was at Danny O'Neil's house where we kept score and tracked rebound statistics from a little hut off the side of the house. I would offer a jump shot (minus the jump) from the top of the cement which was usually followed by my yelling, "Off" alerting my teammate Neil Carboy that my shot was off its target. Neil would battle Danny's partner Jerry Lenze under the boards for the rebound, as Danny and I would await the victor's outlet pass. This was our Madison Square Garden, where Danny's Aunt Mimi sometimes sang the national anthem for us before the game, as we stood still, our hands over our hearts. If we could, we would have charged admission. Many years later, my alert of "Off" was changed to a real health warning in the form of "FORE" as many an errant tee shot would go horribly off course.

My stepfather was the coach of my little league baseball team, so we had all the equipment. On the off days, our front lawn became Yankee Stadium. The catcher wore all the gear. First base was a designated cobble stone, second base was an actual base at the back of the driveway, third base was the stoop, and we had a real home plate. The lawn was worn out in a diamond shape that provided the base paths. Looking back as an adult, it amazed me how small our field was but at the time it seemed just right.

My stepbrother and I had a large collection of NFL team helmets plus a couple of pairs of shoulder pads. Of course, we had to have our own neighborhood football team. The kids would come over to pick the helmet of their favorite team on a first-come-first-serve basis. As we got a little older, we became a traveling football team that played other nearby neighborhood teams. We would ride two on a bicycle wearing our helmets and pads. Luckily, we lived one block from Mepham High School, which we took full advantage of whenever we could. Sometimes, Jay would be the official quarterback, and we would play one-on-one or two-against-two. I had no problem burying my helmet into my opponent's gut and stepping over their crumpled bodies.

I looked up to Jay in many different ways. One was his size. He was much taller than I with a sturdy athletic frame. I had a lot of talent and enormous heart but was built like a walking X-ray. Jay was always lifting weights and studied karate. He would blend protein drinks containing raw eggs and bananas and suck them down while he pounded a bucket of rice to harden his knuckles. He liked to crush my head like a walnut while flexing his eighteen-inch biceps, which he measured weekly. I, on the other hand, watched TV at night, while drinking Schaeffer beer and eating Saltine crackers in hopes of gaining a single ounce.

It is because of Jay, that to this day, I cannot stand the smell of peanut butter and jelly sandwiches. He would pin me on my back and hold my arms down under his legs. Then he would take a large bite of his peanut butter and jelly sandwich, lean over and huff in my face. He would cackle with delight as I wiggled in total disgust.

But revenge is bittersweet. One holiday, we were lying among the guest's coats that were piled up on my Aunt Kay's bed, watching a small black-and-white television. But as any kids of our age, we started messing around, and yours truly delivered a deadly strike to Jay's lower spine area that left him flattened like an empty Coke can for the rest of the afternoon. That'll teach him to keep his stink breath to himself.

Sports were the dominant interest in our lives. Every neighborhood had that one person who hated the kids on the block, ours was no exception. We had "The Keeper of the Ball" lady. Her house was on the corner, and it was painted prison gray with a gray metal fence that cordoned off the property. The bottom of the fence curled up in places revealing menacing fangs. Twisted metal snaked around the fence, ending in a "Y" at the top, daring young boys to cross its boundaries, ready to shred flesh from the bone. She patrolled the yard with her white guard dog.

When she wasn't out on patrol, she stood watch from her kitchen window guard tower. We would be totally engulfed in our own World Series game or Super Bowl when suddenly, a misguided ball would enter the forbidden zone. Everyone would stop in their tracks and not say a word. "The Keeper of the Ball" lady would charge out of nowhere to scoop up the ball with her guard dog leading the way. They would both bark at us as they slowly withdrew back into their hiding place rejoicing over a new capture.

The Keegan brothers across the street were very daring and occasionally hopped the spiked metal fence risking life and limb, retrieve the ball and hustled back over before the monster could strike. I believed she had one room completely filled with every type of ball imaginable, and I pictured her jumping around on them, laughing demonically, like it was the plastic ball pen at McDonald's. I can't tell you how many times our World Series or Super Bowl games were called off due to lack of ball. As kids, we despised her. She was the enemy.

My parents were extremely sociable and always had parties and friends over for cards. As I got older, my perspective changed, and pickup street games slowly gave way to thoughts of girls. "The Keeper of the Ball" lady became an occasional guest, and I later realized that she actually had a name, Hazel Lyle. My childhood enemy stood about four foot eight inches tall, and her vicious guard dog was actually a cute little Yorkshire terrier that had since died. She had been a widow for many years with no immediate family to speak of. She was a very lonely old lady who turned to caring for her lawn as her only outlet and focus of her life.

My perception of her patrolling was really only her tending to her lawn that she loved so much. Now with open, maturing eyes, I could see that she maintained her property like it was the Pebble Beach Golf Course with beautiful flowers accentuating the perfectly trimmed grass. As I grew older, her intimidation factor weakened. She was usually invited over for Christmas and would show up with a baseball that I had hit over her fence six years earlier as a peace offering. She was actually a very nice person who just needed someone to talk to. This was something you didn't realize when you're ten years old, and the game you're enjoying comes to an abrupt halt.

FIVE

Its Bras, Ladies and Gentlemen!

My room was upstairs to the left, and my stepbrother's was to the right. A white louver door guarded my fortress from the outside world even though it had no lock. It was like a large wooden venetian blind that you could never shut all the way. Light green walls angled toward a white ceiling like a tent. A dark, blue-green, indoor/outdoor carpet covered the floor. Years later, a wine spill commemorating my loss of virginity, would leave a stain on the carpet like a bruise.

STOP, ONE WAY, and NO PARKING street signs that once commanded motorists to obey their written voice or risk fines hung silent on my wall in retirement. A hand-painted orange bed frame sat against the wall on the right, and my dresser was positioned to the left of the door. Dusty baseball and bowling trophies stood atop any available flat surface. A matching small desk and chair occupied the space below the window. I spent many years gazing through that window with a view of the neighbor's backyard. As time passed, the desk seemed to shrink, not allowing my legs to fit comfortably underneath; all the while, the neighbor's tree branches seemed to reach out toward my window, trying to get a glimpse inside my life like probing paparazzi.

My friend's home had an attic that had a small pull-down ladder you used to gain entrance like you were going topside in a submarine. My attic was inside the wall on both sides of the room, as if the house had somehow continued to grow, pushing the attic off to the side. I remember as a kid growing up, an older gentleman explained to me that he wasn't going bald; he was just outgrowing his hair, and I believed him. So when I looked at my attic, I thought to myself, *Is my house suffering from structural male-pattern baldness?*

A half-sized door marked the entrance to one of the sideways attics in my room. This door was perfect for an elf. As I grew older and taller, I also grew to despise this mini-me door. You could never fully open the door because my dresser was positioned against the adjoining wall. There was a permanent dent in both the door and the dresser, where they painfully came together. I considered this their tender spot, that special spot on your shinbone you always manage to bang on stuff as if it were aiming for you like a kamikaze pilot.

As a child, this small attic area had a sense of mystery and danger. It was dimly lit by a bare, unprotected, low wattage, pull-chain bulb. Once the door was opened, I would reach along the inside of the wall with my left arm, while the left side of my face smashed up against the outside wall. Risking electrocution, I fumbled to find the bulb's socket and then felt my way down to the chain. A short tug on this three-inch chain simultaneously illuminated the filament and allowed my face to return to normal as if the two were somehow connected. The bulb didn't really light up the cave as much as it brought the shadows to life. At the mouth of the cave, my clothing hung from a wooden bar suspended from the low angling interior wall by metal screw-in hooks. Below the clothing was an array of items ranging from footwear, books, and sporting equipment to things I thought had been lost years ago. Beyond the hanging bar was an area I considered the abyss. A four-foot, red-and-white sailboat without the masts lay diagonally, separating my safe section from the chasm. Past the boat were piles of boxes. After the boxes was Japan, or somewhere like that for all I knew. It definitely wasn't China because as a kid, I was told that you could only get there by digging.

Christmas is usually a very joyous holiday. Growing up, I had a different view of Christmas: I hated it. Don't get me wrong, I love December 25 and what it represents. It's the unusually excessive preparation and decoration that my mother would become absorbed in that I hated. I always dreaded that day shortly after Thanksgiving when my mother would make the announcement, "Okay, boys. Do not make any plans on Saturday because we are decorating the house." Those words pierced my head like a rusty pitchfork.

You're probably thinking, "Oh my god, don't be such a Scrooge and get in the Christmas spirit." You don't understand. My mother's definition of decoration was to apply some sort of bulb or tinsel to everything in the house. If you stood still long enough in front of the open refrigerator deciding what to eat, you risked walking away with a string of colored blinking light bulbs sticking out your ass. Even the decorations needed decorating.

I can remember having to hump down millions of marked boxes from my bedroom closet/attic. Being the smallest, I had to crawl on hands and knees and pull the boxes from the most remote regions of the attic. I would crouch into position and cautiously push my hanging clothes away like they were giant cobwebs restraining Indiana Jones. The temperature was at least twenty degrees warmer in there which made it feel like you were descending into hell. As I inched deeper, the light would flicker, the shadows would dance, and my heart would relocate to my eardrums. I methodically slid the sailboat toward the back of the closet, giving myself ample room to get to the boxes all the while careful not to unleash thousands of venomous cobras. I quickly snatched a box from the stack and dragged it out like it contained a dead body. Each coffin was magic marked with a specific room and secondary location such as DINING ROOM - WINDOW or LIVING ROOM - MANTLE.

Once the boxes were stacked in their corresponding rooms, it was time to decorate. Miles of string bulbs would have to be unwound and tested before being hung. Each ornament was individually wrapped in last year's newspaper, officially declaring it old news. I walked around the house slowly, dragging my feet to show my discomfort, throwing in the occasional whine for good measure to help get my mood across. Thoughts of flying footballs and end zone dances filled my mind as I fumbled through a box marked FRONT BATHROOM. Tears blurred my vision as I pulled a wax snowman candle from its sports page cocoon. This four-inch monster stared back at me with his wax carrot nose and button eyes. His permanent smile made me want to bite off his little wax-wick head and slam his body into the trash while I proclaimed, "Oops, did I do that?" The thought slowly cleared from my mind, and the snowman was given a stay of execution. My mother would certainly notice it missing and ask, "Where is my bathroom snowman candle?" Somehow, she knew the exact location of every piece of "joy" in the house. I placed the snowman on the cover of the toilet tank, as blinking lights mocked me from the ceiling.

Christmas morning was always joyous. Mounds of brightly wrapped packages laid about the living room floor. I enjoyed dispersing the gifts to their recipients in their designated seating arrangements. My parents each had reclining chairs while my brother and I shared the couch. Santa Claus was always very generous to us. We would take turns unwrapping a gift and share in each other's enjoyment.

But it wasn't Christmas until something specific happened when it became my mom's turn to unwrap. She would always seem to have the largest pile of gifts in the house. She would spit out guesses through her smile as she ripped the paper from the box. Then she would question my father about the necessity of the hundreds of pieces of Scotch tape that were used to close the box. She held the bare red Macy's box to her ear and shook with a huge smile, offering a last second guess as to its contents. She popped the last remaining Scotch tape deadbolt and uncovered her present in slow motion. Here it comes…its bras, ladies and gentlemen! But hold on a second…Mom checks the size…and yes, they are wrong once again. It is officially Christmas! I glance toward the ceiling half expecting a stuffed duck with black rim glasses and an oversized mustache to fall from the ceiling with a hundred-dollar bill wedged in its mouth. My stepfather did have glasses and a mustache, but he was definitely no Groucho Marx, and this was certainly not *You Bet Your Life*. After a brief question-and-answer period, we moved on to the next gift.

SIX

What Do You Want To Be When You Grow Up?

One day when I was a young teenager, I came into the house to find my mother sitting alone at the dining room table. I said hi and went to the fridge for something to drink. I had sensed something was wrong as soon as I entered the room, and my mother confirmed it when she said, "I have to talk to you." In my experience, nothing good ever follows those words. I remained in the kitchen leaning against the stove as she spoke with her back toward me. My body tensed with apprehension and fear waiting for the unknown. Fighting back tears, she informed me that Jack was not my father, which was something I already knew.

Jack came into my life when I was about three years old, and even though we never spoke about it, I knew that he wasn't my real father. My mother continued, telling me my father was a Nassau County police officer. As she went on, her tears won the fight and began to fall. She said that my father was married at the time of my birth and had four or five other children with his wife and had decided to remain with them.

My mind was screaming, *GET OUT OF THERE. RUN. RUN AWAY AS FAST AS YOU CAN!* But my legs were bogged down and seemed to be shackled to the stove. Every muscle in my body tensed up in an attempt to

38

form a shield protecting me from her words. She apologized for her actions and begged for my forgiveness. She turned to me for a hug. She was mentally exhausted, and her breathing was labored as I leaned in to her open arms. She squeezed me tightly, and I could feel her hot tears on my face as she kissed me. I told her that everything was okay and not to worry.

She handed me a newspaper article from the local paper with a picture of 'him" standing with a county executive announcing his retirement from the police department. I took the picture and retreated to the comfort of my fortress. I closed my door and stared at a black-and-white representation of my biological father. This was the first time in my life that I had laid eyes on my father's face. Even though it was only one dimensional, I traced the features of his face with my index finger hoping the faded ink would allow me inside.

It turned out my father was not Tarzan after all. The emblem on the patch of a Nassau County police officer's shirt is a lion. My infant mind's eye must have been drawn to the image of the lion on his uniformed arm as he reached into my crib.

With the picture in my left hand, I started to clench and unclench my jaw as my right hand feverishly massaged my temples. My breathing quickened as I stared at my father. The newspaper photo became blurry and slowly disappeared, rendering him faceless once again. My tears masked my vision, protecting me from his image. A volcano of emotion erupted within, forcing me to hide my face in the pillow to avoid detection and help absorb my tears. If that pillow could talk, it would reveal all my inner feelings because God only knows I didn't.

I can only imagine how hard that day was for my mother, but I'm sure at the time it was very cleansing. It must have felt like a cinder block had been lifted off of her chest. For me, however, it was the complete opposite. She had carried that block around for many years and, in an instant, passed it on to me to cart around for the rest of my life. After this day, the subject was never discussed, or even mentioned between us, only by myself.

I have often wondered if it would be easier to have known your father before he left you, or not to have known him at all. I only know half the answer to that question, and it's not good. Many questions occupied my brain. Did he ever think of me, or was I nonexistent to him? Did he wonder if I thought about him? I envisioned a faceless man standing off in the distance while I stood at the plate during one of my little league baseball games. Was it ever possible?

What troubles me the most is being aware of the fact that I have many siblings and not given the opportunity to know them. I wanted to be a brother to them and wondered where I would fit in: the middle possibly or the youngest? As I grew up, people would ask, "What do you want to be when you grow up?"

My answer was always, "A twin." As ridiculous and impossible as that answer was, it was the truth. I have searched for that unique closeness that twins have which lets them sense each other's pain and finish each other's sentences, minus the matching clothing of course.

SEVEN

Ohhhhhhhhhh!

I turned to sports more and more as I got older to occupy my time. Going to junior high school and high school, I was fortunate enough to make friends who will last a lifetime. The neighborhood friendships remained but became watered down as we all started to find our own paths in life. For me, high school remains a highlight in my life. Where else could you go and have every friend you know be there. Classes interrupted our social interaction, but hey, life's funny that way.

In high school, I hung around with the jocks that were the "cool" kids and became a member of the Omega fraternity. Under the new president of the frat, Andy, seniors only had to withstand four whacks of the paddle. Other members who had gotten in under the old regimen had suffered as many as sixty whacks.

On a cool spring night at a house party at Brother Wilbur's house, I was to be paddled into the organization with four other prospects. I was held in the prone position by two brothers, one being my good friend Mitch Litke. As a safety precaution, I was told to put my wallet in my mouth to prevent from biting off my tongue. I can tell you right now that anything that requires a wallet to be shoved in your mouth for safety should be avoided.

So, in front of an entire house party, which also consisted of three quarters of the Tri Delta sorority, I was bent at the waist with my skinny ass propped up in the air awaiting the impact of a three foot long, two-by-four piece of wood. I drew four deep breaths before inserting my Macy's trifold leather wallet, which contained six bucks, into my mouth. I wrapped my arms around the legs of both of my holders as they leaned forward to secure me. Mitch had his head near mine when he whispered in my ear, "You can do this, Stud." I began to snort like a bull as the members decided which one would have the pleasure of my displeasure.

Because I was only going to get four hits, my initiating brothers decided that one whack should equal fifteen on the pain index scale in order to average out to the sixty that they had received. While I prepared by snorting and listening to encouraging words from Mitch, the executing brothers stretched and loosened up like they were pinch hitting in the bottom of the ninth with bases loaded. Once they were good and ready, they started their thirty-foot approach. All of a sudden, they were track stars who hurled their body weight down the runaway with the hunk of wood cocked and loaded. I could hear their approaching strides become louder and louder on the grass. When the first hit was delivered, an explosion was set off in my body. My ass instantly became white hot like a horseshoe that's been sitting in a blacksmith's fire pit. My eyes opened so wide, I thought they were going to drop out of my head and fall onto the neatly trimmed grass, enabling me to capture a glimpse of my own, convulsing body. Right on cue, the crowd collectively harmonized a horrified, "OHHHHHHHHHH!"

The wallet and the crowd muffled my screams as the white hot lava began to spread throughout my body. Seconds later, another impact lifted me inches off the ground and sent my thoughts scattering about and bumping into each other as if they were The Three Stooges. My body was locked in pain as the other two shots were delivered. I was suddenly transformed into Galileo as I began to see, not only stars, but whole galaxies without needing the aid of a telescope.

When it was finally over, I heard clapping above the riot of noise in my head. I was hunched over like a caveman, and it took a while for me get back into the upright position. I looked at my locked left hand which had pieces of hair wedged between my fingertips. During the assault on my ass, I managed to rip off Mitch Litke's right sideburn. I jokingly raised my open hand with the hair in it and asked Mitch if he wanted his sideburn back. Mitch just slapped it out of my hand and hugged me. To me, Mitch was a genuine tough kid and could probably grow it back before the end of the party. Wow, what a way to be accepted into a group. But for me, it was a necessary evil. My undying need to belong became an intense motivating factor. However, next time, I won't complain about having to fill out a lengthy application.

EIGHT

I Am Not an Animal

During the summer vacations between high school years, I worked digging sewers for Billy King Sewers. We would hook the households up to the sewer systems buried under the street and fill in the old cesspools with sand. We were the only company to dig by hand instead of using heavy machinery, like backhoes. The company motto was, "Your Shit Is Our Bread and Butter."

The hole we dug would have to be pitched downward from the house to the street to let gravity play a part in the flow of discharge. Since I was the smallest crew member, I had to fit into the smallest hole, which also happened to be the deepest. I dug the curb-strip hole, which connected to the cup link of the main sewer line in the street. I would start digging with a long handle shovel until the handle hit the side wall. Then I used a short handle shovel until that struck the side wall. Last but not least, I used the metal head of the shovel, without the handle. It was sometimes difficult to throw the dirt out of the hole when it got deep, and I would miss on occasion, having it rain down back on me. It was a tough way to earn a few bucks but somebody had to do it.

As high school was coming to an end, it was time to start thinking about the future. I decided I would like to attend college. I sent out letters to a variety of schools, such as the University of Hawaii and Florida State, but ended up going to Oswego State University, located on Lake Ontario in upstate New York. I went from a Speedo and sunburn, to a winter Parker and frostbite. You could go to sleep and wake up the next morning greeted by three feet of fresh snow.

I had two roommates, Matt and Cory. Matt and I hit it off and became best of friends while Cory marched to his own beat. Cory slept naked (hello!), and I often caught him looking into the mirror where he would practice talking to girls. I did my best to get along with Cory while Matt sometimes wanted to rip his arm off and beat him with it and would have been successful had I not intervened.

Matt and I were recruited to join the Delta Kappa Kappa (DK) fraternity. I convinced my parents that it was an academic frat focused on maintaining a high GPA (grade point average). The only difference was that DK had a different understanding of what GPA meant. In the DK off campus frat house, GPA stood for girls, parties, and alcohol. Art Williams, my fraternity big brother, happened to be the president of the frat, the RA (resident assistant) of my floor in the dorm, and the DJ at Buckley's, the hottest bar in town.

I made the huge mistake of telling Art that my eighteenth birthday was coming up and asked him not to tell anyone. Matt and I headed out to Buckley's to celebrate. It had started to snow, and we had about a half mile or so walk to the bar. As the bar started to crank and the dance floor heated up, Art stopped the music and announced my birthday to the club. Matt and I were still pledges at the time and the next thing I knew; Brother Don Roberts had me in a headlock and dragged me to the bar where eighteen different shots of liquor were lined up. I had about seven frat members screaming at me to drink the shots, which I did. The last thing I remember was this very hot girl named Amy saying, "In about an hour, he is going to be one hurting puppy."

I woke up the next day in my bed with vomit and dried blood clinging to my face and hair. My body was stiff and sore, while my head throbbed like my brain was trying to escape through my eye sockets with a jackhammer. Matt filled me in on the missing hours. It seems that I started to reject the alcohol and was dragged out of the bar to get some fresh air, where I passed out. Matt had the dubious honor of having to half carry half drag me back. The tops of my shoes left drag marks in the fresh snow and lead a trail back to the dorm. Matt was exhausted by the time he reached the dorm side door.

He was able to recruit the help of one of our floor mates named Bob. Bob was a guy who loved to drink excessively on a regular basis. As Bob drank, he made a chain out of the empty beer can tabs and wore them around his neck. It wasn't unusual to see Bob wearing a chain made of beer tabs linked together. Whenever Bob would go out to party, which was often, he wore a sticker on his outer garments that said, "Hello, my name is Bob. If found, please return to Scales dormitory room #330." Bob had a habit of not making it back to the dorm and would sleep anywhere that was semi vertical.

Matt acquired Bob's help in getting me into the dorm. The only problem was that their communication was a little off. They both went to open the door at the same time and thought the other had control of my limp body. However, this was not the case, and I did a perfect face plant into sidewalk, which was covered with about two inches of fresh snow. My pointy nose cut through the virgin snow like a dart hitting a bull's eye, finding the solidness of unforgiving concrete. I was lucky not to break my nose and the immediate rush of blood gave me a red necktie. They laughed their asses off as they brought me to the third floor where I was put on display like The Elephant Man. "I am not an animal!"

I managed to survive that night after promising God that I would never drink again. This lasted about ten days. Before heading out to a party at the frat house, I had a little one-on-one with God. I said, "God, I know what I said about drinking the other day, but this is out of my control. If I don't do what the brother's tell me to do, I won't make it into the fraternity, and I'll be the laughing stock of the campus and a loser for life. Thanks for understanding. Talk to you soon."

I made it through six months of pledging and a hell night from…hell, to become a brother of Delta Kappa Kappa. I finished the school year with an impressive 2.0 GPA. After surviving numerous paddlings and intense humiliation, I was proud to call myself a brother and wear the colors of the DK fraternity.

During the summer break, I reviewed my options and decided not to return to Oswego State. I planned to work and save money while hoping to gain insight on what I wanted to do with my life.

At eighteen years old, I thought INSIGHT was going to just tap me on the shoulder and say, "Hello, I am INSIGHT, and I am here to give your life meaning and guidance. Just follow me." That never happened of course, and I walked around with this confused look on my face like most teenagers do. I put my sewer-digging days behind me and worked doing landscaping and tree removal.

For entertainment, my close friends and I played beer pong on a fairly regular basis. Beer pong joins the wonderful game of ping-pong with the art of beer drinking. It was played in my basement ninety-five percent of the time. We were so serious about it that we actually kept a record of how many times an individual sank the ball into his opponent's cup forcing them to drink. I made a chart depicting the regular player's names with different categories such as Sinks, Double Hits, Spillage, Hitting Own Cup, Barfage and one labeled simply, Ozone. The Barfage (vomiting) column usually led to the Ozone column, which was defined as a participant getting really shitfaced drunk. I also charged a fifty-cent surplus tax (similar to what the government is currently doing) to each player. The money was kept in a coffee can, and at the end of our softball league, we would have a big barbeque paid for by the beer-pong fund.

NINE

Oh, Boy, This Can't Be Good

At nineteen years old, I decided it was time for a change. Since I had no steady girlfriend, actually I had no girlfriend (there I said it) to tie me down, I decided to move to the sunshine state of Florida. I took a calendar, flipped the pages using my finger to stop the fluttering paper midstream, and landed on a specific date. This would be the big day. I am almost certain that a lot of CEOs use this technique to aid them in important corporate decision making.

My close friends were in total disbelief that I would actually go, but I was determined to make a change. I mentioned my intentions of relocating to Jerry Lenze, my longtime neighborhood friend. Without skipping a beat, Jerry said he would join me. I told Jerry, "I'm serious about this, Jerry. I'll be outside your house at 4:00 a.m., and if you are not there, I'm leaving."

He said, "No problem. I'll be ready."

With about five days to go before launch time, I picked Clearwater, Florida as my target location. My cousin, Carol, lived there so I could have at least some human contact when I arrived. As it turned out, Jerry's grandmother also lived very close to that location. I prepared myself by packing the trunk of my Dodge Coronet with clothes, a television, two cases of Schaefer beer, and an alarm clock, as these are the basic necessities for survival. The day before, I withdrew two thousand dollars from the bank and was mentally and physically prepared to embark on my journey with or without Jerry.

About 4:00 a.m., I said my good-byes to my parents and headed over to Jerry's house. I beeped the horn once and waited about two minutes, and magically, Jerry appeared in the doorway. He looked like a little boy running away from home with all his worldly possessions wrapped in a handkerchief hanging from the end of a stick. He had one hundred dollars in his pocket, a little gym bag, a tape recorder, and that was it. I said, "You do realize that we are *moving* to Florida, not just going for an overnight stay."

He stated, "Yeah, why?" I just shook my head and laughed as I pulled the car from the curb.

When I tell you we listened to the band Genesis the whole way down on that tape recorder, I mean, we listened to the band Genesis the whole way down! By the time we arrived in Florida, I wanted to grab Phil Collins by the neck and squeeze every last chorus out of his body, like a dish rag.

We stopped in Georgia to grab a bite to eat and picked a little local diner. Big mistake! There were rats walking around the diner in the daytime, and nobody cared. I was waiting for one to hop up on the counter and grab a menu, but I'm sure they already knew the specials. We ate as quickly as possible and got out the hell out of there.

Trying to find my way back onto the highway, we were stopped by a big old Georgia State Trooper. He was about fifty-five years old, six foot three inches tall, and weighed about two hundred fifty pounds with a chewed up cigar butt hanging out of the side of his mouth. He waddled over to my window and asked for my license and registration. He gave us a good eyeballing and waddled back to his car. I told Jerry, "I don't think this guy likes us."

Jerry, who never takes anything serious, said, "Hey, speak for yourself, I think him and I made a connection." I don't know who I wanted to slap more, him or Phil Collins.

The big guy returned to the car and asked in a southern drawl, "Are you Huffman?"

I corrected him, "Hoffman."

He repeated, "Huffman."

Again, I corrected him, "Hoffman."

Staying with it, he said, "Lawrence Huffman."

Giving in, I said, "Yeah, Lawrence Huffman."

Finally satisfied, he asked, "Where you all headed?"

"Florida. Could you tell me how to get back on I-95?"

He gave me directions back to the highway, and we resumed our journey. I looked in the rearview mirror, and the trooper was following our every turn. I said, "What's this guy's problem, man. He keeps following us." All of a sudden, the trooper put his lights on and pulled us over a second time. I said, "Oh, boy, this can't be good. Why don't you use your connection and talk to this guy." The trooper said something over the loud speaker that I didn't understand, so I ask Jerry if he knew.

Jerry laughed and said, "He wants Huffman to step back to the car."

Now I'm thinking that I'm going to some backwoods jail never to be seen again. I step out of the car and semi jokingly tell Jerry, "Tell my parents I love them." The trooper asks me to open up the trunk, which I do if I don't want to be shot on the spot. All I can see is the two cases of beer, and I think that I am definitely going to jail now. The trooper digs around a little then closes the trunk. He stares at me for about a minute not saying anything, and I can see Jerry peering over the front seat like Kilroy.

I felt like the losing gladiator in Rome, waiting to get the thumbs up or thumb down. I think he was totally enjoying torturing me at this moment. Finally, he breaks the silence and asks me if I ever lived in North Carolina. I told him no. He informed me that someone with the same name, "Huffman" was wanted on a warrant. I am thinking to myself, *"It's Hoffman,* **HOFFMAN!***"*

The rest of the trip was uneventful, and we arrived safely. We stayed at his grandmother's house for two weeks to get acclimated to the area. We got jobs as laborers for a construction company making about three dollars an hour. We also got a studio efficiency apartment in a small motel in Safety Harbor. Our daily routine was to work every day in one hundred ten degree weather, come home filthy dirty, and flop on our beds in time to watch *The Carol Burnett Show*. When Tim Conway made Harvey Korman burst out laughing, or when Tim played "the oldest man" who shuffled his feet and mumbled, we roared in delight.

We really didn't do much for fun. We were exhausted by the end of the week and had very little money to burn. We crossed our fingers hoping that we had enough fuel to make it to the gas station when we got paid at the end of the week. This routine lasted about five months before we finally had enough and decided to head back to New York.

TEN

You're an Ass

I moved back home and tried to pick up the pieces. My mom got me a job as an assistant janitor in the building where she worked. The janitor came in early in the morning, and I started a little later so that we could overlap and cover the whole day. My first day on the job, a pipe burst on the second floor and poured down into a bank on the first floor. This happened later in the day when the janitor was getting ready to leave. He said, "Okay, I'm out of here. See you tomorrow." I nearly passed out when he left me like that, though he was nice enough to show me where the mop and bucket were before leaving.

I fell right back in stride with my friends, and it was like I never left. We would play beer pong and then hit all the Long Island dance clubs like Zachary's, Buttle's, Fulton Street, Infinity's, Uncle Sam's, and Feathers. We all thought we were the bomb, dressed in our Jordache or Sasson jeans, button-down shirts with the big collars, Capezio shoes and Members Only jackets. These were the days of Saturday Night Fever, and we enjoyed every weekend.

During one of our Friday night excursions, we were hanging out at the Fulton Street Pub in Farmingdale, when we met up with some girls who were a year behind us in high school. One of the girls was named Jane. In high school, she had a thing for me, can you blame her, but I had no interest at the time. She was at that awkward stage in a teenager's development. When I saw her again at Fulton Street, I was completely amazed. She was this beautiful monarch butterfly who had morphed from her cocoon. I was completely drawn to her and began to sling my charm her way. At first, she was resistant to it, probably getting even with me from the high school days. However, her protective shield was no match for my charisma, and she was mine. I now had a girlfriend and was officially in a relationship. This was a great time in my life. We all had an understanding that Friday night was boy's night out, and Saturday night was date night. This was the best of both worlds.

Jane's parents, Gerry and George, are an amazing couple. They are two people who are truly meant to be together. They were very loving and accepting of me, and we hit it off immediately. As our relationship grew, I would sneak into their house at night after hanging out with the boys, going through the unlocked garage and making my way to the second floor where Jane's bedroom was located. Gerry and George had no problem with me doing this. Their only request was that we were not to sleep in the bed or close the door, which we honored by throwing a blanket and pillows on the floor. In the morning, we were awakened by George playing an out-of-tune guitar with missing strings, wearing a mop on his head, singing some corny song. We laughed uncontrollably as he serenaded us. He had this laugh that was so contagious that no matter what kind of a mood you were in, it instantly changed to happy. As George would sing, Gerry stood at his side hysterical, telling him, "You're an ass," and "take a hike." After his performance, he would announce that fresh hot buns and rolls were ready for our enjoyment. Ah, life was good.

The assistant janitor's job was getting old, and I was looking to expand my horizons. Two of my best friends, Jimmy Ahern and Victor Castagna worked at Kennedy Airport as import clerks. They informed me that a small company located on the first floor of their building was looking for help. I let them know I was very interested, and they set up an interview for me.

I drove into Queens in search of 161-15 Rockaway Boulevard. I spotted the building on my left and turned into the parking lot. I made my way up to the second floor and found the boys. They escorted me down to the first floor office of Supersonic Transport. The office dimensions were that of a men's size twelve shoebox with a tiny window for ventilation. The entire staff consisted of one person named, Susan. Sue was an attractive, thin, blond woman, and I immediately wanted the job no matter what the employment entailed. Vic and Jimmy left us alone to discuss the details. We worked out the fine print, and I agreed to start on the following Monday.

I was a fairly good typist, thanks to a typing class my stepdad made me take in high school. I had had a one-sided argument with him about taking a class because it wasn't "cool" and could possibly jeopardize my high school social status. My household was not a democracy, and the argument was not debatable, so off to typing class I went. After all, what did he know about life and being cool, he was only a dad. I have to thank my stepfather now for making me take that class because this job required that I type all day long. When I wasn't typing, I was off driving through the airport, stopping at the airlines to pick up more paperwork to be typed.

The import/export business was thriving at the time, and there was plenty of work for everyone. Business was competitive, and there was a high rate of turnover. I was no exception. I worked for four companies from 1980 to 1984 and never had to change the address on my business card. All of them were great companies. The last company I had the pleasure to work for, Alpha International, continues to hold a special place in my heart, thanks to a generous boss, John, and Ray his hysterical and hardworking right-hand man. The three of us pumped shipments out of a little office, which had no window, at an alarming rate while maintaining a sense of laughter and calmness in a very hectic environment. Of course, every customer wanted their freight yesterday.

ELEVEN

What If...?

As much as I loved working at the airport, I still had my amazing affinity to be in uniform. The idea of becoming a member of an organization where the employees wore a uniform gnawed at my subconscious like a puppy teething on a rawhide bone. Why this was is beyond me. Even though I couldn't tell you the name of the vice president at the time, I registered as a Republican in the hopes that it would enhance my chances of working for the Town of Hempstead Sanitation Department.

Vic and Jimmy had moved on from the Rockaway Boulevard building to work inside the airport for DHL. I would often visit them on one of my numerous trips into the heart of the airport and secretly admired them because of their new uniforms. I badgered them to keep an eye open for any positions in the office.

I had given some serious thought to joining the United States military but decided against it because I knew it would seriously hamper my weekend plans and beer pong games. It's amazing how we arrange our priorities as we venture through life.

Driving to work at the airport one day, an advertisement on the radio managed to filter through my adolescent brain barrier to register in my mind. It was for an upcoming New York City police officer exam. I jotted down the phone number and stuck it in my pocket.

As I drove, I envisioned myself riding in a squad car and glared at the autos next to me looking for possible criminals. I would pass a car and think to myself, *Uh-oh, this guy looks bad. I better keep an eye on him.* This little game let me feel powerful and in control. The more I thought about the idea, the more intrigued I became.

I started to look at things from a cop's point of view. I became more aware of my surroundings and watched the police in action taking mental notes. If I could, I would pull over and watch the cops handle a traffic stop. They commanded respect, standing outside the police car in their light blue shirts with dark pants and a loaded gun ready at their side. I pictured myself walking up to the stopped car and interviewing the occupants.

I presented my parents with the "What if...?" question just to get their reaction. My mom was a little hesitant about the idea of me becoming a cop, but my pop was all for it. To him, it meant a secure job and career for me, a possible empty bedroom and more privacy for him.

I decided to give it a shot. I called the number and requested an application. It arrived shortly after, and I let it sit on my desk in my room. Thinking about doing something and doing something are two completely different things. My thoughts played tug-of-war with me for a couple of days before I finally put ink to the page and mailed it out. I justified filling out the application with thoughts of, *Hey, I could always change my mind later.*

I received a follow-up letter which instructed where and when I would be taking the written exam. Okay, no problem. I can take the test and always change my mind later. I notified my boss John that I would need a day off to take the test. He jokingly broke my chops but was very supportive of my decision.

The morning of the test, I woke early to make sure I had my required paperwork, identification and number two pencils sharpened. I was filled with anticipation as I found a parking spot not too far away from the Queens public school that was hosting the test. I stopped at the check-in desk setup in the school and showed my paperwork and identification and was assigned to a classroom. I walked into the room, showed my paperwork again, and was instructed to take a seat by the window. The room quickly filled up with young men and a couple of girls, all with high hopes of becoming a police officer.

Test booklets and answer keys were handed out with specific instructions not to open the test until instructed. The few pages of printed material in front of me contained the key to open the door to becoming a member of the NYPD, if only I could color in the correct oval circle with my pencil. The first part of the test was based on memorization. We had three minutes to study a diagram, and then we would have to close the booklet and answer a series of questions based on information in the diagram. I thought three minutes was not a helluva lot of time, unless of course you're in the ring with Mohammad Ali; then it was an eternity.

The clock started, and I opened up the diagram. It was a two-page sketch of buildings and streets with drawings of people and cars positioned about the diagram. It was an extremely busy layout. There were street signs, building signs, people with hats, people without hats, and people on rooftops, fire escapes, and hanging out of windows. At first, my eyes spun in circles trying to devour the whole thing at one time. Then I tried to systematically break down the diagram into sections and scan for items that would most likely be related to a police exam. I was broken out of my trance by the test monitor announcing that time was up. I flipped to the question portion of the booklet and was amazed at how much I was able to retain.

The remainder of the test went fairly smoothly for me, and I headed back to my car feeling confident that I had scored well. A sense of relief settled in me as I drove back to my life in Long Island. I tried to just put the exam out of my mind and wait for the test results to come in the mail.

Whenever I was in the city (to Long Islanders, Queens and Brooklyn are also considered the city), my attention seemed to focus on the cops. Now, they seemed to come out of the woodwork, and I studied them whenever I could. My eyes always seemed to drop down to the weapon in the holster. I was fascinated by the potentially lethal power that was bestowed upon each and every one of them. I watched how they bladed their bodies and positioned their firearms away from whomever they were speaking with.

The shit got real a couple of weeks later when I sifted through my mail on the steps up to my room, finding an envelope addressed from the City of New York in the middle of the pile. I stopped midstep and stared at it a moment before continuing on into my room. I threw the other mail on my desk and sat down on the bed holding the NYC letter. I read the front again and flipped it over to check the back for some unknown reason and then reversed the action to see if anything had changed on the front since I last looked at it, four seconds ago. Nope, still the same. I placed the mail on the bed next to my right leg and never took my eyes off of it as I removed my shoes to be more comfortable when revealing its contents.

With my shoes off, I picked up the letter and flipped it over to pry open the sealed flap. The corner ripped up to the fold, and I slid my pointer finger inside and thrust it upward. I waited a second for dramatic music, but none emerged. I separated the creased paper from its case and reversed the folds to reveal the letters contents. To my delight, the letter notified me that I had scored in the nineties and was assigned to band number one.

I continued on with the same success, as I passed a strength and agility test, and rocked a psychological exam, which basically asked the same questions over and over again using a different sentence structure.

TWELVE

Seen One Asshole, You've Seen Them All

Another interesting hurdle to jump in this race to don the NYPD uniform is the medical exam. I was to report to the Police Academy on East 20th Street in Manhattan. There were approximately thirty gentlemen, and I use this term loosely for a number of reasons which I won't get into… or maybe I will. We were herded into a room. I looked around at the unfamiliar faces and tried to size them up, realizing they were doing the same to me. So I gave it my best tough guy face and thought to myself, *You looking at me? You looking at me? I know you ain't looking at me, if you know what's good for you. That's right, you better look away punk*! and went along with the program.

This was a very diverse group consisting of whites, blacks, Asians, Hispanics, and some of unknown origin. Fat, skinny, tall, short, long hair, bald, pimples, freckles, big noses (myself included), three chins, no chins, tits, and I'm talking men here, folks! One guy actually had nice breasts, and I'm thinking to myself that if he was a girl, I would be all over those bad boys. My surging adolescent hormones were getting the best of me when I suddenly realized I was staring at some guy's man boobs. So I did the only thing I could do; put on the tough guy face. *That's right, punk.*

I actually felt bad for the guy with no chin and wondered about lost childhood experiences. He obviously couldn't play the violin or fold bed sheets with his mom. As I looked around the room, I started to analyze people to determine if they could be a good cop. One guy was in good shape. He obviously worked out and took care of himself. Now, he would make a good partner, I thought. Then I looked at other guys, and I was like, *YEAH RIGHT. WHAT WERE YOU THINKING ABOUT? GOOD LUCK, PAL*! I'm thinking they should get back to the supermarket and handle the RAGU spillage in aisle five.

Finally, the meeting comes to order. The hush of the crowd diminishes as our leader enters the room to give us our orders. He immediately commanded respect. Our leader is a police officer wearing a dress shirt with a tie undone around his neck and slacks. I was perched on the edge of my seat totally excited to hopefully fulfill my dream. He walked in with boxes of empty plastic bottles and mountains of paperwork. He studied the room eyeballing each of the potential recruits. You could tell he has done this hundreds of times before. In his mind, he can tell right away who is going to make it and who should go home now. I could actually feel his glance cross over me as if he just conducted an infrared body scan.

Then he spoke, "Okay, Skippy, when I call your name, raise your hand." I looked around for Skippy and wondered why he was singling out this one person and wondered what kind of mom would name their son Skippy, a nickname maybe but not a given name. I couldn't wait to see who this piece of work was. Then I realized that I was Skippy. EVERYONE in the room was Skippy! "Listen, Skippy; that's right, Skippy; here you go, Skippy; come here, Skippy; Go there, Skippy." When he yelled, "Skippy!" thirty heads turned toward him. It reminded me of what it must be like to live in George Foreman's house after naming all of his sons George.

So he gets to my name, Lawrence Hoffman. Like a good soldier, I raise my hand, and he says, "Here you go, Skippy" and fires a plastic bottle to me with a dead on accuracy that the peanut vendor in section twenty-one at Yankee Stadium would be jealous of. After delivering all thirty missiles, he yelled, "Okay, Skippy, write your name, date, test, and list number on your bottle."

Suddenly, Skippy in front of me raises his hand and asks, "Do you have a pen I can borrow?"

Master Skippy glares at him thinking; this one ain't gonna make it and says, "No, Skippy, you can't borrow a pen. Do you have your notification slip that you were required to bring with you today?"

Skippy says weakly, "Yes."

"What does it say on the bottom of the paper, Skippy?"

Skippy unrolls his paper notice, which looked like he kept it in his shoe and mechanically reads the bottom of the paper like the robot from *Lost in Space*, "You must bring a pen with you to fill out required paperwork. One will not be provided for you."

Our leader replies, "That's right, Skippy, so you either borrow one from another Skippy, or you're SOL."

I can't believe what a moron this kid in the first row is. To me, this was a calling and an opportunity of a lifetime. I take this shit seriously.

After searching my person, I realized that I also was in need of a pen which I had inadvertently left in my car. I did bring one! I swear! So, indiscreetly, I nudged the Skippy next to me and borrowed his pen to fill out my own bottle.

Next, we are ordered to get in line and strip down to our underwear with plastic bottles in hand. My luck positions me behind a guy with a racing stripe in his underpants. Doesn't this guy realize he was going for a physical, and that there could be a possible, slight chance, that at some point, he may have to expose himself to someone in the medical field? I mean, what are you thinking about? I guess his mom never gave him the speech, "Always wear clean underwear because you never know if you are going to get into an accident." Unless of course he has trouble determining which way they go. For him, it's yellow in the front, brown in the back. I would have been mortified to wear those, but that's just me.

We move along this conveyor belt to different stations. First stop is a blood pressure check and blood draw. As I move up to the station, I realize that there are female nurses checking BP and drawing blood. I was mentally unprepared for this. I should have realized this fact, but I guess I was more concerned about keeping a safe distance from Jeff Gordon in front of me.

I suddenly realized I was virtually naked. My face became flushed, and my body was getting hot. I casually looked down to check my package and rearranged "things" to make sure it looked like somebody was home, if you know what I mean. This act of "rearranging" MUST be done discreetly so as not to draw unwanted attention to one's self. The last thing I needed was to be thrown out of the exam for fondling myself. How could I ever explain that to my mother?

I gracefully made it through blood draw confident that the nurse realized the man of the house was alive and kicking and proceed to the next station, which is the doctor. Now it's gonna get personal. As we get closer to the doc, I can see he is sitting on small metal stool, checking the three Hs: hearts, hernias, and the old house special, hemorrhoids. I think to myself, holy shit, I hope that stripe in Jeff Gordon's shorts is from an old race, or the poor doc is in for a hell of a surprise! I hope this guy is changing gloves every person, or else doc's gonna have a problem removing my elbow from his neck. That's right, tough guy is back in town. So Jeff Gordon steps up to the plate, and I'm on deck. Of course, I do the right thing and blade my eyes toward the ground. It's an unwritten law, like using a public restroom: handle your business and keep your eyes to yourself. You usually end up looking at the ceiling or straight ahead, which most of the time is decorated with disgusting nose hair art left by some animal for your viewing pleasure.

"Next." I step into the gate.

Knowing that he is going to get to know me pretty well in the next minute or two, I shoot for some small talk, "How ya doing, Doc."

"Fine," he responds in a monotone voice, as he puts the stethoscope to my chest and listens.

Still working on the small talk, I say, "How does it sound?"

Doc says, "Pretty good. Your heart is going to last you the rest of your life." I smile and nod my head, thinking I'm sitting pretty and then I realize…hey, wait a minute. "Drop your shorts, turn your head to the right, and cough." He grabs me by the balls like he's shooting craps in Atlantic City and then says, "Turn around, bend over, and spread your cheeks." I do as instructed.

As I look upside down between my legs, with my hands parting the forbidden zone, I can only see his face from the mustache down. It seemed to me that he was taking an unusually long time looking in my ass. Does he think he's searching for a clue like in *The Da Vinci Code?*

To speed things up a bit and to get even with him for the heart comment, I ask boldly, "How's it look, Doc?"

He must be thinking, *Seen one asshole, you've seen them all.* I guess if anybody would know, it would be him. He gives me the thumbs up as he snaps off his glove and says, "Next." I felt that he should have at least given me a friendship ring after all we'd been through together.

With all that behind me, ha-ha, it comes time to put Master Skippy's missile into use. I'm brought into the bathroom by another police officer who ushers me to a urinal. The stall has more mirrors around it than the Jungle Room at the Kew Motor Inn, or so I've heard. I am expected to urinate into the plastic container with the pee police standing just inches away. I don't do so well with an audience standing right next to me. Plus, I'm seeing my member at angles I never dreamed possible, and I'm thinking to myself, *You go, boy.* After a few moments of intense concentration, I complete the mission, cover the container, and hand it to Officer Pee Body. Case closed.

I became friendly with a guy named Tommy, and we stuck together during the exam. The medical would prove to be a long day, and we were given an hour for meal. About six of us, including Tommy, went to the diner on the corner. We all seemed to be getting along great, stuffing our faces with food and discussing where we were from and the jobs, if any, we had now. Sitting next to Tommy and I was this olive-skinned, chubby kid who said he worked for the post office. The table had broken up into smaller conversations as people began to get to know each other.

The chubby kid leans toward Tommy and me and asks, "Can I ask you guys a question?"

Tommy replied, "Absolutely. What's up?"

The kid asks, "Do you guys know anything about the drug screening test we took today?"

I said, "Yeah, as far as I know, they are testing our urine for cocaine, heroin, and marihuana."

The kid thinks about that for a second and then comes back with, "How far do those tests go. I mean, how long do drugs stay in your system?"

Tommy says, "Well, it depends on what type of drug you used. Some stay in the system longer than others. You worried about something?"

The kid says, "Yeah, like cocaine. How long do you think cocaine stays in your system?"

Tommy and I looked at each other, and I took a guess as I said, "I'm not sure, but I think it is something like one to two months." I took a bite of my cheeseburger and in-between chews asked, "When was the last time you did some?"

Without missing a beat, he replies, "Last night."

I nearly spit out my burger as Tommy and I erupted in laughter. With the napkin hiding my mouth, I managed to get out, "Tell me you're not serious."

Tommy blurted out, "Are you fucking kidding me, dude?" The kid's chubby cheeks parted as he smiled and shook his head indicating that he was indeed serious.

The rest of the table caught up to our conversation and offered advice to him like, "Dude, you should go home now and save the rest of your day," and "don't quit your day job." I mean come on, the night before you go for a drug test and you do cocaine? It wasn't like it was a surprise or anything. How serious can this guy be about this job? Well, needless to say, I never saw him again after that day. As for Tommy, he would jump all the hurdles along with me, and we would go into the academy at the same time. He went on to become a great detective in his own right, and we remained good friends throughout the years.

I was assigned an officer from applicant investigations who would conduct my background check. Soon after, the endless and tedious request for paperwork and forms began. I think it was a ploy to cut the weak from the herd. Need this paperwork, need that paperwork, need this notarized, need that notarized. Where's this form; where's that form. Come here, go there. On the inside, I was screaming, *"UUUUUHHHHHHHHHHHH, TAKE YOUR PAPERWORK, AND GO HERE'S, AND GO THERE'S, AND SHOVE IT UP YOUR NOTARIZED ASS,"* but on the outside, I calmly replied, "Yes, sir, may I have another."

THIRTEEN

Police, Let Me See Your Hands

With all the testing and exams behind me, it became hurry-up-and-wait time. Finally, the call came from my investigator to report to the Police Academy on February 03, 1984 at 8:00 a.m. The journey begins. I was part of two hundred fifty men and women who were sworn in on that day, and we were considered the "mini class." We were called up to fill in with the much larger class of twenty-five hundred men and women already training in the academy who were sworn in on January 4, 1984. Even though we were only a month behind the January class, they looked at us like we were rookies. The academy is normally six months long, but we would be expected to complete the training in approximately five.

The police academy had proven to be a great learning experience for me, but it was like being a circus performer working on a new stunt with the benefit of a safety net. The only "dangers" that would present themselves were embarrassment from an instructor for failing to complete an assignment or a black eye from boxing in the gym. At the outdoor range, we would fire our weapons at paper targets which never shot back. One of the most important things I learned while in the academy was that a person will most likely do harm to you with their hands. Make sure their hands are clear of any objects and gain control of them. Identify yourself and demand to see their hands. *"Police, let me see your hands."* It can save your life.

After five months of physical training, role playing, problem solving, defense tactics, defensive driving, written exams, and firearms training, we are placed into the neighborhood stabilization units. I would be assigned to NSU-14 in Bedford Stuyvesant.

The night before I was to report to my training unit, I spent some time reviewing my notes from the academy. I came across my memo book insert which gave a breakdown of the radio signals used to describe jobs and the actions taken. The following are examples:

10-1 (ten-one): call the command

10-2 (ten-two): return to the command

10-4 (ten-four): acknowledgement

10-5 (ten-five): repeat the message

Jobs with a twenty designation were in the past:

10-20 robbery in the past

10-24 assault in the past

Jobs with a thirty designation were in progress:

10-30 robbery in progress

10-34 assault in progress

A signal 10-85 designates that a unit is requesting assistance. There are two versions of this:

10-85 non-emergency: unit may require administrative assistance only or let responding units know that the situation is under control.

10-85 forthwith: unit is involved in an escalating or threatening situation. Rapid response is needed.

The most sacred of radio signals is a 10-13.

10-13: This signal, especially given over the air waves by a unit in the field as opposed to a 911 call put over by central dispatch, means that the officer is involved in a life-threatening situation. It is the police department's version of an "all hands" call. This means you get to the requesting officer's location as quickly as possible and by any means necessary. If you are half dressed relaxing in the lounge on your meal break, then you show up half dressed and lend assistance. If a ten-thirteen is in close proximity to the precinct, then the whole precinct house empties out. As a requesting officer, you have faith in your fellow officer to get to your side as rapidly as possible and do whatever needs to be done to ensure your safety.

FOURTEEN

Statistically, One Person in This Class Will Be Killed in the Line of Duty

On Thursday June 28, 1984, at 10:00 a.m., I reported to the Seven-Nine (079) precinct located on Tompkins Avenue in the Bedford-Stuyvesant section of Brooklyn. All the rookies lined up for roll call in five straight evenly spaced lines. Sharply creased pants, fresh haircuts, and the smell of new leather were all reminders that the academy was only days behind us. The Seven-Nine cops would peek into the muster room, laughing as they whispered among themselves at the sight of fresh meat.

After roll call and inspection, we were broken down into squads. I was in Squad 1 E. We were issued memo books which we would use to record our daily activity and were assigned lockers to store our equipment. There weren't enough lockers so many of us had to double up with another rookie, as was the case with me.

On Friday June 29, we were introduced to our training officers and given an orientation of what to expect. We were told that we would be assigned as foot posts working throughout the four precincts, and each officer would be given a minimum of ten tours in the RMP (radio motor patrol or police auto).

We were given maps to all four precincts and signed out a book of twenty-five summonses.

I was assigned to a great group of cops as well as training officers. I would learn different things from the different training officers. Whitey Gilbert would teach us the job. Whitey loved the job, and the rookies loved Whitey. He was our field instructor when we would do car tours as a sector in the Seven-Nine or Seven-Seven precincts. He would always end each job with the question, "Are we correct here?"

Jerry would teach us to write red light summons and most importantly where to eat. Frank sold Knapp boots to every rookie that ever set foot in the Seven-Nine precinct. My boots actually lasted eighteen years.

We were no longer in the academy. We were now cops. Being a cop, we were given power, and with this power came responsibility. Our decisions would affect the lives of everyone we came in contact with. Oftentimes, you only had seconds to react. I wondered how this life I had chosen would change me and what effect my decisions would make on people's lives.

I had grown up on the south shore of Long Island, referred to as East Cupcake by other cops. I was raised in a middle-class family with loving parents and was fortunate to have a good upbringing and was well provided for. I was now twenty-four years old and wearing the uniform of a New York City police officer. Before becoming a cop, I had never actually seen a "project" (housing development). To me, a "project" was a homework assignment. Now, they would become as much a part of my life as the people who lived there.

On Monday July 2, I reported to the Seven-Nine (079) precinct to perform a 0635 x 1505 (7:00 a.m. x 3:00 p.m.) tour of duty. Sergeant Geraghty called the roll, gave out post assignments, and inspected his rookies. The Seven-Nine and Seven-Seven precincts were considered the *hot* precincts to work. I was instructed to report to the Eight-Eight precinct desk officer in Fort Greene for my first assignment.

After roll call, I gathered my equipment, stepped through the first set of double doors of the Seven-Nine precinct, and looked out onto Tompkins Avenue. This would be my first day of patrol.

As I stood there, I recalled a day in the academy that I will never forget. The gym class usually included about four other companies including our own. In between exercises, as we sat on the gym floor, one of the instructors stood atop a little wooden platform and stated, "Statistically, one person in this class will be killed in the line of duty. Take a good look around you and remember the faces. What we chose to do for a living is not a joke. How you perform in the academy and in this gym could save your life. Make no mistake; the bad guys are training every day. They may not go to a fancy gym and wear cute little outfits like you, ladies. But whether it is in jail or on the streets, they're training. When you get out, there you will see them. They are doing pull-ups on the "Walk/Don't Walk" lights. They'll do pushups and sit-ups anywhere they can, and their firing range is the rooftop doors of the projects. So, please, do not take what we do here lightly. And although I look damn good in my dress blue uniform, I don't want to wear it at your funeral."

Those were some very powerful words, and I wondered how true those statistics were or whether they were just a scare tactic. However they were meant, it left a vivid impression in my mind. I pushed through the second set of double doors and left the safety of the Seven-Nine precinct. I looked up and saw the green lights along the precinct's entrance which symbolized that the watch is present and vigil. I realized that I was now a member of the modern-day watchmen.

I took a deep breath, made the sign of the cross across my bulletproof vest and headed out to get my assignment for the very first time. I made a right on Tompkins Avenue and headed to Dekalb Avenue where I would take the bus to Classon Avenue. I stepped onto the bus and gave a nod to the driver. I surveyed the faces as I made my way to the rear. I remained standing, leaving the open seats for paying customers. Everyone on the bus was in their own world, and no one said a word. My eyes drifted across the expressionless faces that seemed to be staring into space when I noticed a young boy focused on my waist. I trailed his gaze down toward my hip and realized he was transfixed on my firearm. Although my weapon was safely locked in my leather holster, it still commanded respect and invoked intrigue.

I thought back to the days when I first started taking mental notes about the cops, and I was no different from this boy. I realized that although nobody was making eye contact with me, everybody around me felt my presence. How I carried myself in this uniform would make a lasting impression on people. Maybe this little boy was taking notes as well to become a cop when he got older. I hope I was able to leave a positive lasting impression on his mind.

As the bus whined its way up Dekalb Avenue, people shuttled on and off. The bus seemed to replenish itself; in the front door with the new, out the back door with the old. On one stop, the rear doors opened, and three boys entered in an attempt to skip the fare. They were taken by surprise when I gleefully said, "Good morning," with a big smile on my face.

The first kid on the bus let, "Oh, shit" slip out as he reversed his footing down the rear steps. They hustled around to the front and entered the bus properly. They were cackling like hens as they paid their fare and remained in the front of the bus.

As my stop approached, I positioned myself at the back steps. The bus dovetailed to the curb and stopped. I glanced to the front of the bus and waved to the driver as he peered through his rearview mirror. I stepped off the bus onto the curb as more people were lined up waiting to enter.

The bus rolled out of my view with its new occupants, like a large curtain being drawn, revealing the Eight-Eight precinct. I crossed the street and pushed my way through the heavy wooden doors of the precinct. I stood in front of the Eight-Eight desk where the desk officer was writing in the precinct command log. I waited patiently as he completely ignored me. Hours seemed to go by before he finally looked down at me from his throne, rustled some papers, and assigned me to my first foot post known as Robbery Post #2, covering Fulton Street from Washington Avenue to Downing Street.

I took radio number U5374 and headed out of the precinct. As I descended the steps, I removed my memo book from my rear pocket and pulled out the map of the Eight-Eight precinct. I located my post and walked in silence, while anticipation and apprehension roared throughout my uniform-clad body. I felt relatively normal as I walked to my post, but when I arrived at the corner of

Fulton St. and Washington Ave., everything felt different. The ground felt different. The air smelled different. This section of Brooklyn, this microcosmic four-block speck was my watch. Anything and everything that will happen here in the next eight hours was my responsibility. My decisions and nondecisions could affect people's lives in many different ways. All types of scenarios rifled through my brain as I stood motionless on my corner. My conscious mind finally was able to push through the waves of thoughts bouncing around my head and brought me back to the present. Then I wondered how long I had been standing there in one spot, frozen in concentration.

I started walking and focused on organizing my thoughts. I ask myself, *Okay, I'm here, now what?* I took a moment to clear my head and settle the butterflies. Now the training kicks in: get to know which way the addresses run, up or down, cross streets, walk the post, and identify hazardous conditions and potential problem areas. See where the alleyways are. Just start thinking like a cop. Look in a store window before entering. I mean, if you look in a bodega and you see everyone is lying on the floor, there is a good chance that they are not looking for a lost contact lens. I have to really start to focus. There are no do-overs. Start to look at things differently. Read body language. Watch the way people walk. Do they swing both of their arms or just one? When people go into a store, are they coming out with something or empty-handed. Start picking up clues and tip offs that might just make all the difference in the world.

Each person that passed me had a story to tell. Each has their own reality of hardships and struggles along with their accomplishments and goals. But most people pass each other without as much as a thought or gesture. The public has their own opinion and varying degrees of approval or disapproval of my presences as they pass by me. These opinions are directed toward the uniform and not at the person inside. To some people, I represent a guardian angel allowing them to get to their destination a little safer, a welcomed sight along their way. They pass by offering a smile or a simple nod, rarely communicating verbally. Others perceive me as an enemy, a wall or obstacle to hurdle each day. The uniform represents an opponent or threat to their way of life. I try to put a face and a personality to the uniform in an effort to ease tension and build the public's confidence in their police department. A community and police department working together is the most effective crime fighting strategy that a city could have.

I try to make myself as visible as possible. I introduce myself to the store owners when they open up, letting them know I'm out here for the next eight hours. These people have been here for a long time and are potentially a great source of information. I ask if they have any problems or issues that I should be aware of. As I leave each establishment, I wonder if my tactic was effective, or did it dissolve before the door closed behind me.

At 10:12 a.m., the Eight-Eight patrol sergeant stopped by my post to give me a scratch (write) in my memo book and make sure everything was okay. I assured him it was, gave him a salute and off he went. For me, this was a very quiet day, and I did not encounter any problems other than a signal ten fifty-two (10-52 / dispute) between a store owner and can collector who was trying to return the cans for the five-cent refund. I told the store owner to post a sign stating the hours that the cans could be returned to avoid any further disputes. Both parties were happy with my decision, and we all walked away content.

On July 3, I had the opportunity to write my first summons. I was again assigned a robbery post in the confines of the Eight-Eight precinct. I found a blue Buick parked right under a No Standing Anytime sign. I pulled out my memo book holder and flipped to the summonses in the back of the holder. We had written simulated summonses in the academy, but now, this was for real. There was no instructor to correct me. I was on my own. It took me probably fifteen minutes to issue the car the summons. I checked and rechecked and re-rechecked the finished product to make sure every line was filled in and that I had the right codes. I read the sign fifteen times to make sure I was justified to write the summons.

FIFTEEN

Size Does Matter

During one of my car tours assigned as a sector in the Seven-Nine precinct, we were given a signal ten thirty-four (10-34 - assault in progress), male shot at the corner of Atlantic Avenue and Nostrand Avenue. As I drove toward the intersection, I said, "Okay, here we go," flipped on the turret lights and hit the siren.

This was my moment in the sun. Once those lights and siren were in operation, people stopped in their tracks and turned their heads. As my pop used to say, "Here comes Johnny Law."

As we approached the corner, everything seemed to be in order. This was a very busy intersection, both with vehicular and pedestrian traffic. Car flow was normal, and people seemed to be going about their business. If it was a confirmed shooting, there would be a large crowd gathering, cars stopping, and a person down on the ground. Whitey got on the radio and advised Central to tell the other units responding to slow down. I stopped on the corner, we looked around, and nobody approached our auto. "You got a call back, Central?" Whitey asked into the radio.

Central responded back, "Negative on the call back."

Unfortunately, people call nine-one-one a lot and phone in bogus jobs. I wondered what their motivation was. Whitey informed me that some people have nothing better to do, and other people just like to see the police show

75

up. In other times when drug dealers are conducting business and they want the police nowhere near them, they call in a heavy job at the other end of the precinct. I asked people in the street if they saw or heard anything unusual. The response was the same: nothing.

Just as we are getting ready to leave, this guy shows up eating a sausage and peppers hero. As he is chewing, he tells me that he called the police. I said, "Unless you are going to give me half of that hero, you better have a good reason why you called us."

As he chewed, he responded matter-of-factly, "I'm shot."

I looked at him oddly and said, "Where?" He took another bite out of the hero and then turned around. Sure as shit, he had shotgun pellets lodged in the base of his head and neck. It turns out he was shot in the projects earlier, and he thought it didn't seem that bad, so he figured he'd get something to eat if he was going to be at the hospital a long time. It made perfect sense to me.

In my NSU was a guy we called Duke. He was a big hulking, no-nonsense kind of guy. He had this funny laugh, rough hands, and was always chewing tobacco. You could tell where Duke was going by the brown spittle that marked his path. When we would go out to unwind after a tour, there was Duke with a cold beer in one hand and an empty plastic cup in the other. You could gauge how long we were hanging out by the level of nasty spit in the cup. And when Duke reached a certain octane level, he would lose his manners, and the cup, and you had to be careful where you walked.

Duke was never short on stories or jokes. I'm only glad he was on our side. In the street, you could count on Duke when things went bad. And believe me, things could go bad in a hurry. If someone needed help or assistance, you knew Duke had your back. He was willing to lend a hand…or fist…or night stick. Did I mention that he was a no-nonsense kind of guy? Just the sight of him could make enemies friends on the spot. Suddenly, beefs between two people didn't seem as important anymore. Either you worked out your problems or Duke could work them out for you. More often than not people worked it out for themselves.

Duke was a sort of street therapist. His office didn't have fancy wood-work or fine art, but I can guarantee you his success rate was higher than any Park Avenue doctor. One day, I picked up a dispute in a liquor store between the owner and a customer. The customer claimed he gave the owner a twenty-dollar bill for the purchase of some top-shelf Thunderbird and demanded the correct amount of change. The owner showed me a ten-dollar bill that *he* said the customer had given him. I was brand-new, just a kid weighing one hundred fifty pounds, and I was trying to handle this like Dr. Phil would while the customer was becoming irate and loud with me. My police science studies were not getting the job done. He started getting in my face, threatening me and calling me horrible names. I felt that I am a relatively smart guy and could sense that this was going bad, so I got on the radio and called for backup. Thirty seconds later, I saw Duke getting out of a livery cab, which he commandeered in the name of justice, and he comes to my aid. My hero.

Duke says, "What's the problem here?" as he removes his night stick from the holder just inches away from the man's face, letting him get a good whiff of chewing tobacco.

The customer, who had just finished calling me pig motherfucker among other things, suddenly is speaking in the Queen's English and says, "Nothing, Officer, I thought I gave the man a twenty, but it was my mistake, and I apologize."

WHAT! So ladies, in this case, I have to agree with you. Size *does* matter.

Along with a big chest and shoulders, Duke had a big heart. One day, six of us were headed to downtown Brooklyn for a demonstration. We didn't have a ride, so we had to walk to the bus. I remember it was very chilly and raining like nobody's business. We were all wearing our three-quarter length raincoats and walking with our heads down to keep the rain out of our faces. All of a sudden, Duke yells out, "Hold up."

I see him kneeling next to a broken stoop. We walked back to him, and there was a cat that was severely injured and bleeding profusely but still alive. It was a sad sight, but there was nothing that we could do for it. Somebody said, "Come on, we gotta get downtown. It's almost dead anyway. Let's go."

We turned to continue on walking, and Duke says, "I'm staying with him."

"Come on, we're gonna be late."

"I don't give a fuck. I'm not leaving him here like this." We started walking toward the bus stop. Before we turned the corner, I looked back and saw that Duke had taken his raincoat off and placed it over the cat to protect him and was kneeling on the soaked ground petting and talking to the cat.

Duke showed up at the detail about an hour late. He took some shit from the boss about getting there late and then walked over to me. He looked devastated. I asked him what happened, and he told me he stayed with the cat until it died…buried it under some rocks… and said a prayer. That was Duke.

SIXTEEN

Who, Me?

At the end of July, I made my first arrest. I was working a four-by-twelve tour (4:00 p.m. x 12 a.m.) on Nostrand Avenue. It was a fairly busy night for me. I had handled a couple of disputes, found some lost property, and knocked out an accident report before I went to meal. I ate at a local place on my post, relaxed, and caught up on my paperwork.

At about 9:25 p.m., I see a male driving a pickup truck traveling southbound on Franklin Avenue without his headlights on. I step into the street to get his attention and motion to him to put on his headlights. He ignores me and flies right by. He pulls up to the traffic light at Bergen Street and makes a right turn through a steady red light. Now I'm thinking to myself, *This guy has got some set of balls on him to do this right in front of me. Especially after I tried to help him by motioning to him that his headlights were off.*

I hustled around the corner in time to see him parking his truck on Bergen Street. I caught up as he stumbled across the street. He stood in front of me swaying back and forth like a palm tree blowing in a hurricane. I asked him if he was driving the truck even though I already knew the answer. He says, "Who, me?"

I said, "Yes, you."

He answered, "I don't know."

I stared at him and asked, "You don't know if you were driving that truck?"

He again said, "Who, me?"

"Who am I talking to?" I said, losing my patience.

Guess what he said? Yep, "I don't know."

I had to ask again, "You don't know who I'm talking to?"

He replied, "Who, me?" That was his first correct answer.

I checked my patience pouch on my gun belt, and it was empty. "You're under arrest. Let me see your hands."

Right again, "Who, me?"

Exhausted, I said, "You're killing me. Put your hands behind your back." His eyes were bloodshot and glassy, and he had a strong odor of alcohol on his breath. It was a good thing he was driving because he could barely walk.

I put over the radio that I was holding one and needed transportation to the Seven-Seven precinct house. A unit stopped by and dropped us off at the precinct where I walked my prisoner in front of the desk officer (DO). The DO asked, "What do you got, kid?"

"I got one under for DWI, boss."

He slid a form to me and said, "Okay, fill out this pedigree form and get it back to me ASAP. Call IDTU (Intox Driver Testing Unit) and let them know you got one under."

"Yes, sir. I gotta call IDT who?"

He looked up from the command log he was writing in and said slowly, "I- D-T-U. You gotta get him down to the Seven-Eight within two hours of the arrest to be tested."

I could only imagine the look on my face because he said, "You have no idea what I'm talking about, do you?"

I mumbled, "No, sir, it's my first collar."

He asked, "You couldn't get something easier?" I just stared.

He called out, "Okay, uh…Gallagher, give this kid a hand. It's his first collar, and it's a DWI. He's gotta get this guy down to the Seven-Eight precinct for testing by highway."

My right hand man chimed in, "Who, me?" The desk officer and I stared at him. Finally, the DO told me to put him in the pen.

Police Officer William "Billy" Gallagher was a large man with a huge rack of medals above his shield on the left side of his chest. He was also the union delegate for the cops in the precinct. He emerged from behind the desk and met me in the arrest processing room. I filled him in on what had taken place in the street. "Where is the car?" he asked. I replied that it was still out on the Bergen Street where I had arrested him. He asked if I had the plate written down. My face said no.

He said, "Okay, leave him in the cell and lets go get what we need." We jumped in an RMP (police car) and headed out. First, he drove by Lincoln Terrace Park located on Eastern Parkway. The park was filled with scantily dressed women or what appeared to be women. Billy slowed the police car down, and one of the "women" who was more or less dressed in a napkin approached the car.

She floated over, grabbed Billy by the arm, and gleefully asked, "How you doing, baby?" Billy returned the smile and answered, "I'm good. You're looking beautiful tonight. Anything happening?"

She glowed back, "No, baby, everything is quiet."

We pulled away slowly, and Billy informed me that the prostitutes know everything that's going on around here. They have their fingers on the pulse of the streets, as well as on other things. He stated, "You can't imagine what men tell these women when their pants are around their ankles."

We located the pickup truck on Bergen Street, and I wrote down the license plate and other pertinent information I would need to fill out the arrest paperwork properly. We headed back into the Seven-Seven precinct, PO Gallagher ran a print out of the vehicle and helped me finish up my online booking sheet. I thanked PO Gallagher for his help and was transported down to the Seven-Eight (078) stationhouse where highway officers would give my defendant a physical coordination and a breathalyzer test. My arrestee did not fare well on the coordination test and blew more than double the legal limit for a DWI. At that time, .10 (point one-zero) was considered legally intoxicated and .08 (point oh-eight) impaired. After the tests were completed, they gave me copies of the results that I would need to take with me downtown when I met with an assistant district attorney to draft a complaint.

Arriving back at the precinct, I conducted a warrant check to make sure my collar was not wanted. I issued him a DAT (desk appearance ticket) with a date he would later have to appear in court along with five traffic summons. He thanked me and staggered out of the precinct a free man. This procedure would change in years to come because defendants who were arrested for DWI would walk back to their cars and get on the road again. Sometimes, these people would get arrested a second time with the earlier arrest paperwork in their pockets or, even worst, get into an accident.

On November 6, 1986, Police Officer William Gallagher was arrested along with several other officers in the Seven-Seven precinct in a scandal known as Buddy Boys. Another cop by the name of Henry Winter was flipped by Internal Affairs and agreed to wear a wire and obtain tape recorded evidence against other members of the Buddy Boys gang. They each had their own call signs over the radio. Henry Winter was known as Buddy Boy, William Gallagher was known as Buddy Bee, and Brian O'Regan was known as Space Man. When the code words Buddy Bob were uttered over the division radio, the Buddy Boys knew that they had a target to rob. The gang stole money and drugs and sold them through a drug dealer known as Roy. William Gallagher had an eighty-seven count indictment against him which included burglary, drug sales, and grand larceny. He pled guilty to one count of selling cocaine and agreed to testify in department trials against other cops who were suspended in the ring of rogue cops. He was given a three and a half to ten and a half-year prison term. Sadly, Brian O'Regan took his own life while alone in a hotel room.

Mike McAlary, a reporter for *Newsday*, captured this story in a book titled *Buddy Boys: When Good Cops Turn Bad*. It was a tremendous blow to me because I had looked up to him as a rookie. It was a blow to all New York City police officers because it undermined the public's trust and created a barrier with the community that we were so proud to serve.

SEVENTEEN

If You Find One Gun, Look for Two

Less than three months after my first arrest, I learned an extremely valuable lesson, one that I will not soon forget, and that I tried to pass on to rookies as I seasoned into a veteran. I was walking a foot post in Bed Sty during a four-by-twelve tour in early November when I was approached by a male bleeding from the head and arm. He told me that he got into an argument with this guy and girl, and the guy hit him over the head with a bottle. He had a nice gash on his head but nothing too serious, and he refused medical aid. I asked him for a description of the duo and put it over division radio for other units in the area. We started to walk around and conduct a search. We checked alley ways, lobbies, and bodegas but were unable to find his two assailants.

I took another look at his head and told him he should really clean that wound up a little bit. He agreed with me, and we headed toward the subway entrance, where I knew there was a bathroom where he could wash up in. He splashed water on his head and arm and washed away the drying blood. It looked like he could use a stitch or two, but he said he was okay. As we were walking up out of the subway entrance, a girl and guy were walking down. The man grabbed me by the arm and said, "That's them. He's the guy that hit me!" I drew my .38 from my hip and identified myself, "Police, let me see your hands. Now get against the wall."

They were totally caught off guard and seemed in a daze. Again, I ordered the guy to get against the wall, and this time he complied. I put the handcuffs on him and notified central dispatch that I was holding one for assault and requested a sector car for transportation. The kid was asking me what this was all about, and his girlfriend was being a real pain in my ass. She was yelling at me, "He didn't do nothing. Why are you doing this to him?" I kept telling her to back up away from us.

A sector car shows up to offer their assistance. It was a male and female unit. The female officer sees the girl giving me a hard time and tries to talk to her and get her away from her boyfriend who is now handcuffed. The female officer grabs the girl by the arm to direct her away when the girl turns around and shoves the officer and breaks into a repertoire of foul language. Next thing she knows, her face is squashed against the wall and adorned with bracelets that match her boyfriend's. Now it is the boyfriend's chance to give us his opinion about the current events. I make sure he stays put as he watches his girlfriend get frisked. We escort my two new best friends into their waiting chariot where they will be driven to the Seven-Nine precinct. The kid sits in the middle in the backseat, and his darling girlfriend sits alongside him behind the front passenger seat. I slide in the backseat behind the driver.

Have you ever been at a party where two people consistently talk at the same time? Annoying, isn't it? Well, magnify that by twenty and add a touch of hatred; and well, you get the picture. This kid would not sit still, and I wanted to ram my foot down his girl's throat to shut her up, but by law, I can't do that. So instead, I keep telling him to sit still and try my best to ignore her.

We finally reach the Seven-Nine precinct and file out of the car in the rear parking lot. I bring them in front of the desk officer who seemed to be in a bad mood. I inform the sergeant of the circumstances, and he puts two arrest information sheets on the desk for me to fill out. He orders the female officer to get the girl out of his face, and the officer secures the girl to a railing using her handcuffs.

The sergeant asks me if I tossed the male, and I said yes, not really sure if I did or not due to the commotion. He says toss him again. I tell him, "Yes, sir." I start by spreading the suspect's legs and running up each leg on the inside and outside of his pants. His hands were cuffed behind him, so I grab his hands and pull them up away from his waistband. As I'm running my hand along his waistband, I feel something hard. I reach in and pull out a loaded .22 caliber revolver. I realized why this kid would not sit still in the auto. He was either looking to dump the gun in the car, or was trying to get the gun out to shoot us!

Embarrassed at not finding the gun in the street the first time, I accidently placed the gun on top of the desk with the barrel facing the desk sergeant. If I wasn't sure he was in a bad mood before, this certainly confirmed it. He leaned into me with both sails, and he had every right to do so. I locked the prisoner in the cell and started my paperwork. Even though I was about fifty feet from the sergeant, I could still hear him cursing me out. I was mortified thinking about what could have happened. Amazingly, the girl had nothing to say. Looking back, I realized she was trying to create a distraction so that her boyfriend could dispose or *use* the handgun against us.

A veteran cop, whose name I never got, approached me in the arrest processing area. I guess he could feel my pain and embarrassment. He said, "Don't worry about the sergeant. He's a grumpy old fuck anyway. He's never happy. Listen, you got a good collar here. You got a loaded gun off the streets. Just learn from this. Always pat people down before you put them in the car. If you find one gun, look for two. If you find two guns, look for three. You got me." I nodded my head appreciating the words of advice and compassion. He ended with, "Okay, good work tonight. Be careful out there." He patted me on the back and walked away. Right then and there, I decided what type of cop I was gonna be. This guy lifted the world off my shoulders, and his advice has not left me since that day. It is amazing how the right words at the right time can make all the difference in the world. I didn't get to say it that night but would like to say it now, thank you.

A few years later, two cops assigned to the Seven-Seven precinct arrested a man for gun possession. They placed the suspect in the backseat and headed to the precinct. Unfortunately, this suspect had a second gun secreted on his person. He was able to draw the gun even though his hands were cuffed behind his back. Twisting his body, he was able to shoot both officers in the back through the front seat. Attempting to escape on foot, he was gunned down and killed by responding officers.

EIGHTEEN

You Know We're Gonna Take Shit for That One

As I walked my foot posts during my time in NSU-14, I would often see police cars with the markings BNTF patrolling the area. I asked a couple of the other rookies if they knew what unit that was. They told me BNTF stood for Brooklyn North Task Force. This unit was designed to be a rapid mobilization unit. If a large demonstration or riot was taking place and you needed people right away, you called the task force. Each borough had its own task force. At the time, it was comprised of about sixty men and woman. The unit would later grow to well over one hundred cops. The task force was designed as a mobile unit and was "affectionately" known by other commands as gas burners. It covered ten precincts in Brooklyn North: 73rd, 75th, 77th, 79th, 81st, 83rd, 84th, 88th, 90th, and the 94th. On any given night, they could be working in one or more of those precincts depending on that day's events.

The Brooklyn North Task Force had a "get the job done" reputation, as it pertained to crowd control and riots. When the shit would hit the fan, BNTF was center stage; but when it was a soft detail, they were nowhere in sight. Things tended to be handled a little different in Brooklyn North, and they were deemed a little rough around the edges. As a result, they were often hidden from sight on the nicer events that took place in the city.

One hot afternoon, a couple of weeks later, a BNTF unit pulled up to me on my foot post and asked if I wanted to sit and enjoy some air conditioning. I scooted into the backseat. The driver turned up the A/C and pointed the vents in my direction. As my body temperature started to cool, I asked the guys how they liked working in the task force. They told me they loved it. They never walked a foot post and always rode in RMPs because it was a rapid mobilization unit.

Within the command, there were specialized units. There was a DWI unit, auto larceny unit, truancy unit, and then just regular patrol squads. The guys told me that they were looking to expand the unit and recommended that I fill out an application. I thanked the guys as I got out of the RMP and got back to my foot post. I decided that I much preferred to pass my eight-hour and thirty-five-minute tour on my ass in a cool RMP then on my hot aching feet. And since I now deemed myself an expert in DWI collars after my first arrest, I decided to request a transfer to BNTF.

A month or so after submitting an application for the task force, I received a note at roll call to report to the Borough Headquarters located on the second floor of the Nine-Oh precinct for an interview. I walked into the chief's office with my fresh haircut, shiny shoes, pressed uniform, and eight-point hat tucked neatly under my arm. Behind the desk with the chief was the lieutenant who was the commanding officer of the task force. They were impressed with my arrest and summons activity. They explained what the unit was about and the details of what each squad was responsible for, and then asked if I would be interested in joining the task force. I said that I would, and the lieutenant said, "Okay, we'll see you soon."

After completing six months in NSU, we were split up and assigned to precincts. I went to the Nine-Four precinct, which covered Greenpoint, Brooklyn. The stationhouse was a three-story brick building with blue accents located on the corner of Humboldt and Herbert Street. It was the old Eight-Seven precinct, which no longer existed. The building was rundown. The bathroom stalls had no doors on them for privacy. The precinct gym was the size of a walk-in closet with brown rusted weights. The lights were dim, and the air was musty. The tired soul of the building was draining and seemed to influence or reflect the attitude of its occupants. Or both, I'm not sure.

At that time, the precinct was considered a dumping ground. The Nine-Four was like America; send us your sick, your lazy, your misfits, your drunks, your fuckups. There were also a handful of good cops. I remember I was told that I had made the first arrest of the year in the precinct in 1985. It was on January 3, for larceny of a welfare check. I was told to slow down. Other precincts in Brooklyn North usually made gun collars at 12:01 a.m., New Year's Day, when people decided that banging pots to ring in the New Year wasn't as much fun as letting loose a half a dozen or more 9-mm gunshots. So I knew I wasn't a good fit here and had to try to move on.

Being a rookie in the precinct meant not riding in the RMP too often and having to walk a foot post most of the time. When it was really cold out, I would search for an abandoned stolen auto to recover, which would get me off the cold street and into the warm precinct for a few hours. The rookies always got stuck sitting on a DOA (dead on arrival). There was a high elderly population in the precinct, and DOAs was a common job. As a rookie, we would get called to sit with a DOA for hours waiting for the ME's office (medical examiner) to show up. There is nothing like sitting alone in a room with a dead person for hours. Your mind begins to play tricks on you. You start to hear noises and see things. At times, you could swear they moved. You sit there, and you're just waiting for them to get up and say they feel better! I was sitting in a chair watching television with an elderly DOA who passed in her bed. I kept hearing noises. I would look over periodically to make sure she was still dead. I could swear she was going to ask me to change the channel and put on her story! Sometimes, the body would get ripe, and that smell would just engulf you and stay on you for days.

Most of the guys who had time on the job didn't like to work with "new jacks." First of all, they didn't trust them; and second of all, they felt the new jacks only knew the job on paper, meaning they knew the patrol guide procedure on how to handle a job. The term "hair bag" originally referred to an old crotchety veteran in the station house. In my day, the term was used for guys who had a little time on the job but acted like they had thirty years. The hair bags would tell the rookies to forget about everything you learned in the academy because things are handled differently in the streets. I have heard of these guys taking the battery off of the rookies' radio so that they couldn't use it. You had to earn your battery.

One night, I was doing a four-by-twelve tour (4:00 p.m. x 12:00 a.m.) walking my foot post when I got a call from the DO (desk officer) to ten-two the command (go back to the precinct). I returned back to the precinct, and the desk sergeant told me that Sector-Boy was granted lost time (going home); and myself and another rookie by the name of Frank T were now going to take over Sector-Boy in the RMP. This seemed like good news because it was January and very cold out to walk a foot post. We decided that Frank would be the operator and drive the RMP, and I would be the recorder and be responsible for all the paperwork.

One problem with being a rookie in the precinct is that you very seldom ride in the RMP. I was usually assigned a robbery foot post on Manhattan Avenue, which covered about five blocks. Being a rookie, Frank also had a foot post on Manhattan Avenue covering five or six blocks. When we got into the RMP, I asked Frank, "So, how well do you know the precinct?"

He replied, "I don't have a clue. I was hoping you did." We had a good laugh and wished each other good luck. I opened the glove compartment and dug through the four thousand McDonald's napkins and three hundred ketchup packets to find a wrinkled-up map of the precinct that was broken down by sectors. Using my hand as an iron and my leg as an ironing board, I smoothed the map as best I could and make it almost legible. Like Christopher Columbus, I got my bearings, and we set sail for the New World known as Sector-Boy.

It wasn't long before Central called Nine-Four Boy on the radio, and we had our first job of the night. It was a simple-aided case (sick elderly), and the person was removed to the hospital by ambulance. I filled out an aided card, and we were back to patrol.

The radio beeped with the alert for an upcoming heavy job as Central said, "Signal ten-thirty four, male shot, Provost Street and Paidge Avenue." Frank looked at me. I looked at him. He asked me if I knew where it was. I told him I never heard of it. I snapped on the overhead light, which shown with all the power of a single-watt bulb. I tried to iron out the map some more and told Frank to start driving.

The street ended, and he asked, "Which way?"

I looked left, looked right, and picked left. "Go that way." I had a fifty-fifty chance of being right. With the lights and sirens on, we sped away in search of Provost or Paidge, whichever came first.

Frank yelled, "Tell me where to turn."

Fumbling with the map, I said," Okay, just keep going!" We were going at a good clip when one of the other units rounded the turn on two wheels and sped by us in the opposite direction. Frank looked at me, and I yelled, "Turn around, follow the car!" I had the map upside down. Before we were able to get near the intersection, another unit advised Central that the job was an "X-ray," indicating that the job was bogus, and there was no one shot at that location. Frank slowed down and turned off the turret lights. We drove in silence for a little while. After a minute or two, I said, "You know we're gonna take shit for that one."

Frank nodded his head and said, "Oh, yeah, big time." And of course, we weren't disappointed.

NINETEEN

Just Licked a Cow's Ass

After spending only three weeks in the Nine-Four precinct, I was transferred to the Brooklyn North Task Force (BNTF). The task force occupied a small office on the second floor of the Eight-Three precinct located at 480 Knickerbocker Avenue in the Bushwick section of Brooklyn.

The infamous Blackout of 1977 ravaged the city for two days in July. Three days later, Schwaben Hall, an abandoned knitting factory, was set on fire by three kids playing in the building. An "All-Hands" fire was called, and it took fifty-five units of firefighters from Manhattan, Queens, and Brooklyn to extinguish the fire. In the aftermath, twenty-three buildings were destroyed across seven blocks. The area was a desolate wasteland until members of the community board decided it would be a great home for the already overcrowded precinct located on Wilson and Dekalb Avenue. The new precinct opened in 1983.

Assigned to the task force meant not being a slave to the division radio, and we weren't required to be assigned jobs (nine-one-one calls) from central dispatch. This gave us freedom to roam about the precinct under the radar and allowed us to target the high crime areas while sector cars got stuck with aided cases, accidents, and family disputes. We could pick and choose what jobs we wanted to respond to. We would always provide backup for the precinct sector cars on "heavy" jobs such as robberies and shootings.

I was assigned to the DWI unit for approximately eight months. I would stand for hours, sometimes in the freezing cold, on DWI checkpoints at designated areas in Brooklyn. We conducted random stops and interviewed the operator. We would look into the eyes of the driver and either wave them through or stop to talk to them. We would take turns on the line questioning drivers. If we suspected someone of drinking, we would call over another officer who would ask them to blow into an Alco-Sensor. The Alco-Sensor was a device that would give us a preliminary reading of a person's blood-alcohol content. Based on our observations and the results of this test, we could then place a driver under arrest for suspicion of driving while under the influence of alcohol. The driver would be taken to the local precinct for processing, then brought down to the Seven-Eight (078) precinct where a Highway Unit working the IDTU detail would administer a more accurate test for blood-alcohol results. Based on the results of this test, a complaint would later be drawn up by the district attorney's office charging the driver with DWI.

When I worked the line, I would have the car slowly roll up to me as I tried to make eye contact with the operator. If his eyes looked glassy and sleepy, I would have them stop and ask them to roll down the window if it wasn't already. I would stick my head in the window and engage them in conversation in an attempt to assess their condition.

Not all people put grooming and self-hygiene at the top of their to-do list. I have had the opportunity to subject my olfactory sense to some of the nastiest smells on this earth. New York City is considered a melting pot of cultures, and I can tell you right now that some things in the pot are rotten. The breath and general smell of some people can only be described as "wrong." You cannot still be alive and have a smell like that escaping your body. I can't tell you how many times I have stuck my head in someone's window, and their breath literally smelled like they just licked a cow's ass, and the cow was in the backseat with them. That smell just slaps you in the face. It is wrong!

When I suspect someone of being drunk, I will attempt to engage them in conversation and see how coherent they are. People will do the craziest things to convince you they are not drunk, but this accomplished the exact opposite and would give me tons of probable cause to arrest them. One guy stepped out of his auto and dropped to the ground and started doing pushups without saying a word. He could only do ten, and they weren't even pushups. He kept his arms straight and bobbed his head up and down. Another guy initiated his own field sobriety test. He started touching the end of his nose while marching in place. He ended up poking himself in the eye and banging his head of the car door. One gentleman said to me, "I'm not drunk. Watch this," and proceeded to tried to walk a straight line. He veered off to the left and just kept walking. I had to run and grab him before he walked into oncoming traffic.

One night, we had a checkpoint setup on Atlantic Avenue at St. Andrews Place in the confines of the Seven-Nine precinct. Westbound traffic on Atlantic Avenue was narrowed down from three lanes to one. I was standing off to the side with other officers making sure that everything was running smoothly when we heard screams coming from the other side of Atlantic Avenue. A female was screaming for help. The sergeant, Herbie, grabbed Miles and we headed over to see what was happening.

There was a male standing on top of the railing on the third floor balcony threatening to jump. One officer stayed below trying to talk to the man while the rest of us flew up the stairs to the third floor. When we arrived on the balcony, the man seemed unresponsive. He had no shirt on and was sweating profusely. The screaming woman was his mother. She told us that her son was mentally ill and had not been taking his medication. He did not respond to our pleas to get down. He turned and looked at us a second and then faced away. He was going to jump.

We rushed him just as his feet left the railing. The three of us grabbed for any available part of his body. I got a hold of his right arm near his shoulder. I'm not sure where the other officers had him because I closed my eyes and held on as tight as I could. I had a pretty good grip at first, but it started to slip because of his sweat. My hold moved down to his elbow as I heard grunts from the other officers attempting to pull up his legs.

He was not cooperating at all, and his mother's screams had become desperate. At this height, he might not be killed, but he would certainly be seriously injured. My body hung over the railing as my grip slid to his wrist. I told myself there is no way that I am letting go. The three officers were able to get the man by the pants and roll his body back over the railing. My grip had gone down his arm, and my hands only had him by his fingers.

Once back on the balcony, we were able to handcuff and control him so that he was not a danger to himself or us. An ambulance had been dispatched, and he was removed to the hospital. The whole incident had taken about twenty minutes from the first screams we heard to the final scream of the ambulance as it took him away.

We walked back over to the DWI checkpoint laughing among ourselves at what had just happened. The cops who remained at the checkpoint had a hundred questions for us as we badgered each other over who saved his life, who did all the work, and who was just getting in the way. It was all in good fun because we all knew we had just prevented someone from killing himself, or at the very least saved him from serious injury. Fifteen minutes later, I had my nose back in the melting pot.

As the task force expanded, I rolled over into a regular squad, and the newly transferred cops took their turn on the DWI checkpoints. The DWI unit was not considered a good squad at the time because there was little or no overtime to be made. Intoxicated drivers were issued DATs (desk appearance ticket) and released from the precinct with a date to show up at court in the near future. Cops referred to DATs as desk *disappearance* tickets because defendants often didn't show up at court on their given dates and vanished once released from the station house. A warrant would be issued for their arrest to answer criminal charges.

When it was determined that DWI collars would not be given DATs anymore, the defendants were considered "keepers," and the unit became much sought after. The defendants had to go through the system and be lodged overnight at central booking to be arraigned by a judge in the morning, which meant a lot of overtime for the arresting officer.

TWENTY

My Mom Did Not Raise a Fool

One Halloween night, I was assigned to a transit overtime tour working 2:00 p.m. to 11:35 p.m. It was a solo post known as 3316A, covering the station for the Double L line located on Sutter Avenue and Van Sinderen Street. This post was situated in the confines of the Seven-Five precinct in East New York, Brooklyn. It was one block from the border of the Seven-Three precinct, which covered Brownsville.

Historically, Halloween is a very busy night anywhere in this country. It is a night of mischief and fun. At that time in Brooklyn, however, mischief had a different meaning. My duties were restricted to the train station. The token booth clerk was delighted to see me when I checked in. I introduced myself and asked her how her day was going.

She said with a big smile, "Very well so far." I greeted the commuters as they passed through the turnstiles and made their way to and from the train. The police radio in this area was never quiet, and the dispatcher assigned jobs to sector cars nonstop. Police and ambulance sirens were a constant sound in the air. The sun began to hide and nighttime approached like a heavy quilt being pulled across the sky. My day had been uneventful, and my feet began to ache to let me know that the end of my tour was approaching. The transit supervisor made his rounds on the train and gave me a scratch (signed my memo book) to make sure I was on my post.

When night fully engulfed the sky, there seemed to be a change in the air. I would occasionally walk out of the station to get a different view, to stretch my legs, and catch some fresh air. About 9:00 p.m., I stepped out and shuttered, noticing it had gotten a lot chillier. A sector car announced over the radio that a large roving band had assembled and was moving through the streets of Brownsville. All of them were dressed in masks and hoods to hide their faces, keeping in the spirit of Halloween. In their case, I think Halloween may have been only an excuse.

After a few minutes, I went back inside and resumed my station watch, keeping an alert ear to the radio. The Seven-Three sector car updated central dispatch that the roving band had grown in size to about two hundred kids. They were like a swarm of angry bees buzzing around the streets of Brooklyn, leaving a wake of shaving cream and broken eggs behind them.

The swarm hit Sutter Avenue and turned east, heading in my direction. I knocked on the token booth door and let the clerk listen to the radio about the group. She looked at me with wide-open eyes and shook her head. I tried to imagine what I would do if this tornado decided to seize the train station. I wanted to board up the windows, go for batteries and water, and wait this thing out. To be honest, I don't think there was much I could do. I decided to make myself visible to the crowd and hope that that would be enough of a deterrent.

The train station was set back from the street, so visibility up Sutter Avenue was limited. I could now hear a low roar, as this mass of destruction headed my way. People began to run toward the train station for safety. I could not yet see them coming but could feel the rumble through the concrete floor. They felt like an approaching locomotive. I stood on the steps of the train station with my legs spread shoulder length apart. I puffed out my chest like a rooster defending the hen house with the radio in my left hand, and my right hand poised on my gun. I felt like there should have been a cape waving off my shoulders.

The front of the roving band came into my view. I saw them pointing in my direction, yelling back to the middle of the group. They stopped, looking up at the entrance, and seemed to confer. I stood my ground and dramatically raised the radio to my lips never taking my eyes off the group. The leaders of the group seemed to come to a decision, and the mob proceeded to bypass the entrance to the train and continued on Sutter Avenue. The group had grown in size to what seemed like three hundred.

Still poised in my super hero stance, I let the other units in the field know the location and size of the group. Suddenly, I hear a loud bang to my right and then another to my left. I look down to my right and see an Idaho potato awkwardly rolling on the floor with the business end of about six heavy-duty four-inch nails sticking out of it. To my left, I see its twin brother. My mom did not raise a fool, so giving up the super hero stance, I did a quick about face and ducked for cover inside the station. I peered out of the window to keep an eye on the group. As I updated central dispatch to the recent events, my view out the window became distorted from eggs bursting against it. Every few seconds, I would hear that familiar bang of a loaded potato hitting the wall.

As the rear of the group passed, the assault seemed to diminish. When the group was completely clear of the station, I ventured out to see the aftermath. It was as if the front of the station had been riddled with a paintball machine gun spitting dripping, oozing ammo. I don't know if my super hero performance was a deterrence or not, but I was grateful that my fort had withstood the attack with no casualties, myself included.

The look on the token booth clerk's face was priceless. She was extremely thankful and appreciative of my effort. Doing my best John Wayne impression, I said, "Well, that's what I'm here for, ma'am;" and as 11:00 p.m. approached, I rode off into the night. Well, not exactly, but I did feel good knowing the people in the station were safe.

I got picked up about 11:00 p.m. and headed back to the Eight-Three precinct where my office was and signed out. I went home, cracked open a cold brew, sat on the couch, and started to laugh out loud replaying what I must have looked like standing there like Superman or Batman wearing my tough guy face. The whole scenario seemed ridiculous, and I was grateful for the ability to laugh about it now. God only knows what would have happened had the group decided to make a stand and fight. Would I have had to draw my weapon and use deadly physical force? The thought gave me a sudden chill. Pulling the trigger on my gun is the absolute, last thing I wanted to do. I hoped I would never have to make that decision. I put my feet up on my coffee table, took a swig of beer, and thanked my guardian angel once again.

TWENTY-ONE

May God Rest Your Soul

On May 19, 1986, I was scheduled to attend Auto Crime School. It was a four-day training course held in Queens. Many stolen cars are "tagged," meaning the VIN (vehicle identification number) is removed and replaced with the VIN from another auto, usually damaged, and the tagged car is reregistered and sold. This course would teach us where to find the hidden confidential vehicle identification number (CVIN) on autos and learn the true identity of the auto. It would also teach us about insurance fraud and detecting fraudulent driver's license. Working in the auto larceny unit, this information was extremely valuable.

Arriving at the class in Queens, I met up with a friend I had made while in the academy. Scott Gadell worked in the One-Oh-One (101) precinct in Queens. Scott was one of those guys who could not keep still. When we were on a break, we would go outside, and he would start doing jumping jacks. He had so much energy; he had to burn it off somehow. At the end of the day, Scott and I decided to car pool to class for the three remaining days of the course. Scott lived in Wantagh, and I lived in North Bellmore at the time, so it made a lot of sense for us to drive in together. During our commute to work, we talked about the job and really got to know each other better. After the completion of the class, we wished each other luck and promised to keep in touch.

Five weeks later on June 28, Scott Gadell was shot and killed in the line of duty. He was on patrol in Sector-Boy in the One-Oh-One precinct with his partner, James Connelly, when they were flagged down by a male stating that he was being chased by a man with a gun. The officers transmitted a description of the suspect while they conducted a search with the complainant in the auto.

They spotted the suspect and gave chase but momentarily lost him among bungalows near Seagirt Boulevard. and the beach. They continued searching and spotted him a second time outside a rooming house at 30-15 Seagirt Boulevard and began pursuing him. The perpetrator opened fire on the officers using his 9-mm handgun, and he fled. The officers split up in an attempt to arrest the subject. Scott exchanged gunfire with the perpetrator, firing all six rounds from his .38 caliber revolver. While reloading his gun from the reserve ammo in his dump pouch, the perp walked right up to Scott and shot him in the head, then fled to escape capture. James Connelly rushed Scott to Peninsula Hospital Center where Scott was pronounced dead at 6:17 p.m.

The perpetrator was identified as Robert Roulston a.k.a Errol Campbell. It was reported that while using the name Errol Campbell, he was arrested and indicted in a 1985 drug-related homicide, where the victim's body had been dumped on the beach. He was out on bail awaiting his next court appearance scheduled in September.

I was home that day and had heard that a cop had been killed in Queens but wasn't aware of who it was. It wasn't until the next day when my friend Ron called my house and spoke to my mother. I had been out all day, and when I got home, my mom told me that Ron called and wanted to know if I had heard about Scott. I remember exactly where I was when my mother uttered those words. I was standing at the top of the stairs on the second floor of our house. When I realized who and what had happened, it was as if a sledge hammer hit me in my chest. I sat down in a daze and felt hot tears start to stream down my face. Those words spoken by the instructor in the gym that had haunted me came full circle. I was angry. I was angry at the person responsible. I was also angry at the instructor for reasons I couldn't explain.

We take for granted that every day, we are going to go to work, and that we will return home safely. We have to believe it. But when a cop gets killed in the line of duty, especially someone you consider a friend, you lose a piece of yourself. I tried to imagine what Scott experienced that day, and it totally crippled me for weeks. Yes, we have to believe we are going to come home, but way in the back of your mind, you wonder: is this car stop or this family dispute going to be my last?

As good as cops are at keeping those kinds of thoughts hidden on days like June 28, 1986, they manage to poke their evil heads out and make you think. It takes good friends and family, sometimes a drink or two, to press thoughts like these back into the dark recesses of our mind, where we can deal with them the best.

I taped a picture of Robert Roulston to my memo book and looked at it every day I worked. I engrained his face into my brain. His picture is still attached to my memo book to this day. It has his description, age, and what car he drove written alongside his face. Robert Roulston was captured on August 18 in Brooklyn.

After Scott's death, the police department decided to issue speed loaders and do away with the dump pouches. A speed loader contained six rounds in a circular pattern that would align with the chambers of the revolver. A twist of the device would enable the rounds to fall into each chamber in a minimal amount of time. As a memorial, the street alongside the One-Oh-One precinct was renamed Scott Gadell Place.

You are missed Scott and will never be forgotten. May God rest your soul.

TWENTY-TWO

Crappy Foot Post

Although the Eight-Three precinct was a new facility, it had its issues. The police officer's locker room was located in the building's basement, and on at least two occasions, the sewage system backed up. The open mouths of the toilets suddenly vomited up raw sewage and human waste, spilling this combination onto the bathroom floor. It was as if the toilets were exacting revenge after all the crap that had been forced down their throats.

The constant surge of waste spread across the floor like red hot lava burning up everything in its sight. My locker was near the back end of the room, so I thought I would be spared, but it just kept coming. The lockers closest to the bathroom were overrun immediately. I wish I had had more time to set up sandbags to deflect this shit storm, but I'm not sure it would have made a difference. Before long, I was overrun as well. Being the police, we couldn't just shut down shop. We still had to patrol, make our arrests, and issue our summons. If your monthly activity report was "light," having shit in your locker was not a valid excuse.

Getting to and from your locker during this tidal wave had become very interesting. Cops had different styles depending on their location and the depth of the mixture. Many cops learned to become long jumpers, while others became bull frogs, leaping from lily pad to lily pad. I used a combination of styles while adding the Olympic gymnastic approach. I would leapfrog onto a manmade lily pad, jump upon the balance beam which doubled as a bench, and then long jump from balance beam to balance beam. I took to holding my breath during this process because catching a good whiff could offset your equilibrium which would cause you to lose points.

It took at least a week each time to clean up the mess. It didn't matter how many times they went over the floor, it would still stink. The red hot lava left a line at the base of the lockers like the tide on an old wooden dock. We all took it in stride. Sorry. We did it because any cop, working anywhere, in any state, will tell you, as long as there were cops on the streets, we would overcome any shit, literal or not, to make sure we all went home safely. That was our single most important priority.

I was in the Eight-Three precinct lounge one day eating my lunch while task force cops and Eight-Three cops spilled about on couches and reclining chairs either sleeping or watching television. One of the old timers I worked with came into the lounge. Joe K was a mountain of a man and always carried a big smile. Joe loved to strike up a conversation, much to the dismay of the sleeping cops. He also had some of the worst jokes on the face of the earth, but that never stopped Joe. He would rattle them off and laugh as if he had heard it for the first time, and most of the time, his laugh was the only one. He had a resounding laugh that bounced off the lounge room walls like a super ball.

If he had an audience, he had a story. I loved these old stories. He brought a bit of nostalgia to the job. He had my attention as he recalled one story about a boss who had a hard-on for him. The sergeant had given him a crappy foot post to walk one day and would stop by frequently to try to catch Joe off guard. Fortunately for Joe, there was a firehouse on the post which Joe decided to use as his dining hall. Since firemen stay over and sleep in their stations, they tend to be well furnished and extremely comfortable. Joe got a little too comfortable and fell asleep in the firehouse lounge. The sergeant came around looking for Joe, but he was nowhere to be found. The sergeant seemed to be enjoying this scenario and felt he finally had his chance to get Joe, thinking there was only one place for Joe to be—in the firehouse.

They parked the RMP in front, and the boss sent his driver in to get Joe. The driver found Joe dead asleep in the lounge and woke him saying, "The boss is really pissed off and wants you outside right now."

Joe collected his thoughts and told the driver, "Do me a favor and tell the boss you didn't find me in here and stall him a bit."

The driver exited and gave the boss the message. A moment later, the firehouse doors rolled up, and the fire truck screamed out of the bay to handle a call.

As the sergeant sat in front of the firehouse, Joe came lumbering around the corner. He stepped up to the sergeant's window, offered him a salute, and asked, "You looking for me boss?"

The boss barked back, "Where the hell were you? I've been looking for you."

Joe said he was handling a dispute around the corner. The boss scratched Joe's memo book and left in a huff. Joe laughed and explained that he told the firemen in the station the predicament he was in. They decided to go on a phony run and gave Joe a bunker coat, helmet, and boots and let him hang on to the side of the truck until they got around the corner where Joe jumped off. Had the sergeant gotten out of the car, he would have realized that Joe was still wearing the fireman's rubber boots. I don't know if the story was true or not, but I enjoyed it just the same.

TWENTY-THREE

Vehicle Pursuit

I was assigned to BNTF for eight and one half years of my career. I spent six of those years in the Auto Larceny Unit (ALU). The ALU was made up of six to eight men who were very active in the street and one sergeant. Our patrol cars were equipped with mobile digital computers which enabled us to conduct various checks on autos, vehicle identification numbers, and operators. If the computers were functioning properly, we could determine if an auto was reported stolen in a matter of seconds.

Having been involved in hundreds of stolen car arrests, I can honestly say they are potentially one of the most dangerous arrest situations because of flight risk. If not handled properly, an arrest situation can turn deadly. A vehicle traveling recklessly at sixty or seventy miles an hour down heavily populated city streets is never good.

To help prevent this type of reckless situation from occurring, there is a certain technique which requires reliable team work and calmness. If done properly, it can avoid an exhilarating and also scary vehicle pursuit. Unfortunately, this is not always the case. Take a stolen car, then add a dab of violent felon with a case of, "I'm not going back to jail for shit," mix this up; and you have a recipe for disaster.

I recall one such recipe which I didn't have the taste for. I was on routine patrol in the Eight-Three precinct when I observed two males acting strangely in an idling, double parked auto. It's hard to explain the feeling that you get when you sense trouble. Ask any active cop with time on the job, and he can tell you what it's like. Sometimes, you can just glance at someone and sense the evil in them.

Well, my evil meter was reading high when I saw these guys sitting in the car. I said to my partner, "I like these guys." In cop talk, if you like someone, it's never for a good reason. I ran the license plate of the car through my third partner, the computer, and seconds later, he tells me that the auto is a felony vehicle, wanted in connection with thirteen robberies in Manhattan. During the commission of one robbery, the perpetrators had struck the victim in the head, and that victim was listed as "likely to die." Bingo! As soon as that screen popped up with its yellow print and advised me that my evil meter was right on target, my adrenaline level popped into overdrive. I took a deep breath, collected myself, and in a calm and professional manner advised the central dispatcher of our situation and location, and requested backup with, "No lights, no sirens."

During my transmission, the boys decided to go for a drive. We followed loosely behind giving our location at every turn, patiently waiting for backup to arrive. Then in the background, I heard a police car coming with its siren wailing. I yell into the radio, "Central, I said no lights, no sirens." It was too late; our boys were on to us and decided to up the ante. Then I uttered those two words over the radio that makes any supervisor on patrol cringe: "Vehicle pursuit."

Now the air was alive with flashing lights and screaming sirens as our technique was blown to bits. Instead of being able to be proactive, we were forced to be reactive, giving the bad guys the upper hand. The pursuit became dangerous with these idiots traveling at high speed, paying no attention to traffic regulations or people on the street. Because of sudden turns and reckless driving on their part, I was no longer the lead vehicle in pursuit. I had been joined by numerous units from different commands. We had BNTF, Eight-Three, Nine-Oh, Nine-Four, Housing, Transit, and other unknown units working in the area involved in the chase.

Due to the violent nature of the original crime the occupants were wanted for, the patrol sergeant bravely let this pursuit go on as long as he could. I'm sure he was sitting there with his ass cheeks clenched so tight he could have cracked walnuts. He attempted to terminate the pursuit in the name of safety but was unable to get a word in edgewise on the radio because he kept getting cut off by officers in the field as they communicated back and forth during the pursuit. I heard the lead car state they were heading into Queens, and that the bad guys were driving on a rim with no tire on the car's right side. The dispatcher, whose head was spinning at this point trying to keep calm and keep everyone advised as to what's going on, finally acknowledged the sergeant's transmission to terminate the pursuit. An officer identified himself on the radio and said that the bad guys had attempted to run him down in the street. The sergeant let the chase continue. Game back on!

I was the fifth car in this motorcade when the lead car stated that the felony vehicle had lost the other right side tire. The rims were cutting a line into the pavement as they drove. It was like they were dropping bird seed to find their way back.

We now had units from Queens involved in the pursuit. Talk about drawing a crowd! The perps lead the motorcade down a ramp behind the Metro Mall and drove to the rear of the parking lot where they bailed out of the car. The patrol sergeant was able to unclench his ass cheeks when the car came to a stop. No need to use the thigh master tonight.

As we approached the abandoned car, I could see the two perps running. I focused on the driver who decided to run up a steep hill of dirt toward the train tracks. I started up the hill, while my friend George closed the gap behind him. The driver got to the top and stopped in the middle of the train tracks. He turned around to look at us coming up the hill and then looked back at the tracks.

George was closing fast. The driver walked further on while looking down at a piece of wood that ran across the top of the metal tracks. I realized that this wood was covering the third rail which the train uses to draw its power. I called to George, who was only steps from the driver, to warn him about the third rail. As I yelled his name, George tackled the guy, and they fell over the wood onto the ground. My heart stopped for a second while I expected them to light up like a Christmas tree. It kicked back into gear when they hit the ground safely. We handcuffed the guy and brought him back down the hill. I said to the suspect, "Are you fucking crazy? You were almost standing on the third rail."

He looked at me calmly trying to catch his breath and said, "I know. I have AIDS and wanted to die." He was willing to take George with him.

A couple of the other five thousand officers involved in the chase brought the second perp back to the car under arrest. I searched the auto and found two pipes that were taped together which these knuckleheads used to simulate as the barrel of a shotgun when they committed their robberies.

As everything was starting to settle down, a couple of cops brought over a third guy who was filthy dirty and bleeding from the head. I said to the cops, "Who's that?" They said it was the other perp from the car chase. I said, "No, it's not; we got both our guys."

The guy in handcuffs said to the cops, "I told you I was just collecting cans." I turned away and started to laugh.

The sergeant told the guy in a deep voice, "You know you're not supposed to be up on the tracks. That's trespassing."

The guy put his head down and said, "I know, sir."

The sergeant said, "Give him a summons for trespass and let him go." It was just a simple case of being in the wrong place at the wrong time.

TWENTY-FOUR

Good Work Today, Partner

Sometimes, it seemed as if I possessed my own personal "black cloud." I was on patrol in the Eight-Three precinct with my partner, Frank Napoli. We had been enjoying a gorgeous, sun-shiny day. It was about 12:00 p.m., and we were driving down Flushing Avenue when suddenly, you know what showed up for a visit. It's funny how this cloud just appeared without any warning no matter what my plans might be.

Frank was driving, and I was riding shotgun with my feet up on the dashboard. I know that doesn't seem very professional, but if I'm going to tell the story, I might as well tell it exactly as it happened. So, as Frank was driving, I looked between my Knapp boots, and I see a male running onto Flushing Avenue and then suddenly duck down behind a car in the street. Without taking my eyes off the man, I said to Frank, "What the hell is this guy's problem?"

Frank says, "I don't know, let's check it out," because that's what we do, we're cops, we check things out.

We roll up on the gentleman, and I ask him very politely, "What the hell are you doing?"

He is shaking and says, "They got guns; they got guns!" As I look up, I see two males, each carrying large white sacks, running toward a maroon car occupied by two other males. One of the runners had a black metal object in his right hand, and it didn't look like reading glasses. Both guys entered the rear doors of the maroon car as it started to pull away from the curb. I had no idea what was going on but knew it couldn't be good.

We start to follow the car, and I'm trying to read the street signs along the way so I could give directions over the radio for backup units to assist us. There was no rear license plate visible so I could not advise Central to get the vehicle's registration. As we got closer, I noticed that the license plate was intentionally bent upward to hide the vehicles identity.

We're catching up to the car as I am giving directions over the radio. As I'm talking on the radio, I'm also telling Frank not to get too close to them because I believed that these guys were armed. It sounded something like this:

13-86 North: *Thirteen eighty-six, north to Central.* Don't pull next to them, Frank.

Central: *Go ahead, eighty-six north.*

13-86 North: *We are following a maroon auto,* don't pull next to them, *west on Flushing Ave,* don't pull next to them, *toward Wyckoff Ave., Central.*

Central: *Ten-four, eighty-six north. What's the condition?*

13-86 North: *Four males armed with guns, Central.* Don't… pull…next… to…them.

Central: *What's the vehicle plate number, eighty-six north.*

13-86 North: *Unknown Central. Plate is bent up, so I can't read it.* DON'T PULL NEXT TO

THEM!

Frank was so zoned in on the car that I think my words did not register. I didn't think Frank would pull next to them so I was totally unprepared for it. I slid across the seat toward Frank as we got closer. At one point, I think I had my arms around his head and my legs across his lap. If we were newlyweds on our honeymoon in Vegas and he was carrying me across the threshold, this would have been perfectly fine. However, I wasn't wearing a wedding dress, just ten layers of Kevlar, and we were in Brooklyn chasing four males with guns in a speeding car.

Frank then fell back in line behind the car and continued the high-speed chase. I was updating our position on the radio for the backup units when, out of nowhere, this big black sedan with heavily tinted windows pulled up next to us. I thought to myself, but I may have said it out loud, "Who the fuck is this!" I don't know if they were good guys or bad guys! The front passenger was smart enough to stick a police parking plaque out the window, and I am happy to learn they are on our side. Their auto was faster than ours, so they now took the lead. Using my side view mirror, I could see a marked BNTF van being driven by Philip with Lee in the passenger seat, following closely behind the black sedan.

The black sedan decided to pass us and pulled up next to the bad guy's passenger side. All of a sudden, the muzzle of a machine gun appeared out the front passenger window, pointed directly at the black sedan. The sedan slammed on its brakes, and Frank does a nice job of avoiding them and put us back in pole position. At that point, the radio was buzzing with activity, but I couldn't make out what they are saying.

Frank and I were totally engulfed in the moment. I don't know if we even talked to each other since the honeymoon, but we didn't have to. Up ahead was a huge tractor trailer coming straight for us. The operator saw that we were attempting to apprehend this vehicle, so he decided to lend a helping hand. He pulled his truck into the path of the fleeing car, attempting to block them. The bad guys tried to avoid the truck but had no luck. The front bumper of the truck clipped their rear tires, forcing the car into a forklift causing the car's axle to break.

With the car now crippled from the impact, the boys inside must have been planning their next move. The car limped along which limited their options. Either they could roll to a stop and sit in the car with their hands up and tails between their legs, or they could attempt to shoot it out with the police and hope for the best.

With the wheels falling off, the car rolled to a stop at the left curb. I jumped from the passenger seat and set up shop behind a thin light pole. It's surprising how skinny you can make yourself when there is a chance of you being shot. As I jockeyed for position behind the light pole, I observed the rear passenger door open. The next thing I see, the black sedan smashed into the opening rear passenger door and pinned it shut. The maroon auto lurched forward as the front passenger attempted to exit.

Philip slammed the BNTF van into the front passenger door, eliminating that as an escape route. The driver was able to exit the battered car and fled on foot. Lee jumped from the BNTF van and gave chase on foot while Frank pulled our car around the pileup, cutting off the driver, and then helped Lee subdue the runner.

As the police autos are slamming into the felony auto, I'm trying to figure out what the hell was going on. Time seemed to slow down. After the second crash, I see the rear passenger door on the driver's side open up, and one of our boys got out of the mangled car. He used the open car door for protection and pointed a gun at me! The light pole suddenly started to shrink and thoughts of being shot entered my mind.

Next thing I heard was a shot go off. Holy shit, this guy's shooting at me. Am I hit? It doesn't hurt. Maybe it doesn't hurt for a couple of seconds. But wait a second, the shot sounded like it came from my right. Unless this guy had a ventriloquist's gun, it's not him. My head snapped to the right, and I saw the driver of the black sedan, standing with a gun in his hand, pointed at the bad guy. A ring of smoke hung above his bald head and handle bar mustache like a halo, giving him the appearance of a tough angel. I think to myself, *"Pop? Is that you?"*

My head swiveled back to the car, and the gunman wasn't there anymore. He must be crouched down behind the door. With our friends distracted from the gunshot, we decided it was a good time to make our move. We charged the car while the gunman decided to drop for cover, and the other two males were tripping over each other trying to get out of the auto's two working doors.

They were met by the NYPD Welcoming Committee. We didn't bring cake; we brought handguns and handcuffs. After a brief struggle, we had four dangerous felons disarmed and handcuffed on the ground. This time, we win, you lose!

I opened the rear passenger door and couldn't believe what I saw. There was money all over the inside of the car; hundreds of bills, in all denominations, scattered about. I thought I was at the Imperial Palace Hotel in Las Vegas, and I was inside of the money machine with sixty seconds to stuff as much money into my shirt as possible. But reality kicks my ass; I'm back in Brooklyn with four "gentlemen" who just tried to kill me, looking forward to tons of paperwork.

As everyone was getting a chance to catch their breath, we had to figure out what happened. Where the hell did all this money come from? It turned out that an armored car had set up a check cashing table in one of the large corporations on Flushing Ave., so its employees could cash their checks at lunch time. Three of our new friends went into the business and fired a round into the ceiling officially declaring a holdup. The two guards were disarmed, relieved of large bags of cash and coins along with checks. The perps left the premises in a hurry to meet up with their other accomplice waiting in the get-away car, the one with the bent license plate.

I'm sure to them, it sounded like a great plan. Only they didn't anticipate meeting up with the amazing duo of Officers Hoffman and Napoli who thwarted their feeble attempt with remarkable crime-fighting skills and feats of bravery. I know you're thinking, "Come on, Larry, you were just cruising around, killing time, checking out broads with your feet up on the dashboard and got lucky for crying out loud. That's where you're wrong, my friend. That's what we want you to think. I do some of my best work with my feet up on the dashboard. So next time you see a cop who looks like he is checking out girls and killing time…be afraid, be very afraid. We are lulling you in to a net to be pounced upon like a viper.

We got lucky. The other officers in the black auto turned out to be from the Vice Squad. The driver with the handlebar mustache (Pop?) who fired the shot was a captain. The two other plainclothes officers were detectives. They were surveying the area for prostitution, which was very prevalent in the area. They observed us in pursuit of the auto and decided to lend a hand. I thank God for those officers, and their amazing efforts which helped us all go home safely that day.

The four individuals were placed under arrest and transported to the Nine-Oh precinct. The arrest location was blocked off with yellow crime scene tape. Pretty soon, this place would be crawling with police department brass. The Crime Scene Unit would show up and go over this area with a microscope. The duty captain responding to this job better have three pens handy to fill out all the reports because this was a high-profile arrest with a firearm discharged by the police and a vehicle pursuit in which two department autos were involved in intentional accidents.

Back at the Nine-Oh, we were able to go over the evidence. A count of the money revealed that we had recovered in excess of $120,000. Also recovered were four weapons: Tec Nine 9-mm machine gun, Mac Eleven 9-mm machine gun, Raven .25 caliber semiauto handgun, Smith & Wesson .38 caliber revolver, and two pairs of handcuffs.

With the money counted and the situation well under control, the press was invited to come down and witness the fruits of our labor. A table was set up displaying the four weapons, two handcuffs, cashed checks, and the over one hundred twenty thousand dollars in recovered bills. NJ Burkett from Channel Seven Eyewitness News showed up with a camera crew. We were advised not to speak with the media until we were debriefed by someone from DCPI (deputy commissioner for public information).

This was to be my fifteen minutes of fame. The camera crew had been set up for some time now, and I went to the men's room to freshen up. I made sure my hair was perfect, as it always was. I took pride in my hair and would often get my balls broken by jealous people stating things like, "Number four is out of place." How superficial were they? I emerged from the men's room looking marvelous and headed to where the evidence was on display. Frank, Philip, Lee and I posed proudly as we stood guard behind our capture, while the news camera scanned the table for the entire world to see. We were unable to tell the story because we were STILL waiting to be debriefed by DCPI. We returned to the squad room to help the detectives with the paperwork as the news stood patiently by. After some time had passed, Frank informed us that the news team had left and said that NJ Burkett told him they had to leave to cover an overturned tractor trailer on the New Jersey Turnpike. My hair and I were very disappointed.

While finishing up the necessary police department paperwork with the help of the Nine-Oh squad and robbery detectives, two members of our auto larceny squad showed up. Mickey and Jack were doing a 4:00 p.m. x 12:00 a.m. tour and came by to take our RMP for their tour of duty. Frank and I happily relived the events of the afternoon for them. After all, this was a dream collar for anyone in law enforcement. When we finished our reenactment, Frank gave Jack the keys to the RMP so they could remove our hats, memo books, and helmet bags. I was gliding around the Nine-Oh squad room still feeling lightheaded from my runners high when Jack and Mickey reappeared.

Jack called me over with this strange expression. I looked at him as he waved me over while he scanned the room. I stopped in my tracks, also scanning the room, trying to see what he was looking for. We made eye contact again, and he waved me over a second time. I was thinking to myself, *what the hell is going on?* I walked slowly toward him with a puzzled look on my face as he placed my equipment on one of the desks. He was still clutching my hat as I approached him. I asked him, "Hey, what's up?"

After darting his eyes around the room a second time, he whispered, "We found this in the RMP." He unfolded my eight-point hat in slow motion and revealed its contents. Inside were about seven or eight sticks of rolled coins totaling about ten to fifteen dollars. Apparently, some of the rolls must have fallen from the back of the car under the seats. He handed over the hat with his eyes wide open as if asking, "Okay, what are you gonna do now?"

I thanked him and took custody of the coins. I showed them to Frank and said, "What do we do now? They already counted up the money, and the Feds took it downtown." We pondered that question a second then decided to bring the money down to 26 Federal Plaza and explain what happened. So, off to see the wizard we went.

There was a long line of people, representing every nation in the world, trying to get into the building, which was also home to the Department of Immigration. We bypassed the long line, went through the revolving doors, and got directions from security. After signing in and getting clearance, we ascended the elevators to the office of the Joint Bank Robbery Task Force (JBRTF) comprised of the Federal Bureau of Investigation and an elite group of New York City detectives.

After the sound of a bell, the elevator doors opened, and we stepped out into the hallway. It was as if I had passed through the Pearly Gates of Heaven. We're not in Kansas anymore Toto, and we were definitely not in any police department facility that I knew of. The air was fresh and crisp, and the floor was spotless. I could see my reflection in the floor, and we waved to each other. Men and woman walked by us in business attire, smelling of expensive cologne and perfume. I almost felt like stopping and asking one of the suits if they could take a picture of us in the hallway, like we were on vacation at the Grand Canyon. This was not a precinct where the floors were mopped in dirty water, littered with cigarette butts, and where sweat and stale cigarette odors dominated the air. The hallways here were well lit, and I bet that even the copy machines worked. This was somewhere I would love to be employed someday.

We found the office of the JBRTF and walked in. The office was broken up cubicle style with each officer or agent having his or her individual workstation. As we rounded the corner, I could see the agents and cops were enjoying a fresh hot pizza.

I made eye contact with one of the agents handling our arrest, and he made his way over to us. He said, "Hey, guys, there's pizza and soda if you want. Help yourselves."

I said, "No, thanks, just wanted to drop something off to you." I had the coins in a bag and was sheepishly bringing the bag around as I began to apologetically stutter. "I'm … I'm really sorry about this, but the…the… the stuff must have accidentally got thrown on the…the floor and rolled under the seat, and we had no idea it was there until the guys from the next tour found it, and … and brought it up, and you guys had already left, and the count was done so we … we didn't know what to … to do, so we figured we just come down here and give it to you, and we are really sorry about this, it was an accident." I stopped and sucked in some air for the first time in about a minute and a half.

He opened the bag and examined its contents. He slowly looked up at me and said, "Are you kidding me?"

I held my breath and started up again, "I'm sorry it was an accident; we didn't know, and you guys…"

He stopped me before I could continue and said, "Don't you, guys, have kids at home with piggy banks?" Frank and I looked at each other and shook our heads to indicate. He laughed and said, "It's no problem. I will throw it in the safe with the rest of it." Realizing it was not the trouble we thought it would be, Frank and I laughed along with the agent. Feeling relieved, I suddenly got hungry. I asked if I could grab a slice of pizza. The agent said, "Of course. Help yourself." Frank, being a person who never turns down a free meal, joined me.

After throwing a slice or two down my throat, I asked where the bathroom was. I was given a key and directed out into the hallway. I opened the door and stepped in. It was empty, and I had the whole place to myself. I pushed open the stall door, and to my surprise, there was a clean toilet bowl with not just one roll of toilet paper but two! I removed my gun belt and hung it up on a hook that had not been broken off on the back of the door. I prepared myself and proceeded to take a seat. I looked to my left and my right and found the walls of the stall to be pristine and graffiti free. There were no hieroglyphics indicating who was fucking who, or who was sucking off the boss to get their details, or who was a rat. It took only one flush of the toilet to remove any evidence of my existence. I got redressed, put my gun belt on, and went to the sink. *What is this? Is this actually liquid soap? You got to be kidding me. There really are paper towels in the dispenser. Yes, this is definitely somewhere I would love to work someday!*

Later that night when everything was completed, Frank and I headed down to central booking to get arrest numbers. Even though the feds had taken the collar for federal prosecution, we still needed to assign the perps city arrest numbers so that NYPD could get credit for the collars. In the details section, it was marked FOA (for other agency).

It was almost 11:00 p.m., and we wanted to watch the eleven o'clock news. I was hoping to see me and my hair on national TV. We hustled up to ECAB (Early Case Assessment Bureau) where all the arrests made in Brooklyn were processed. We entered the police waiting room where arresting officers waited to be called by an assistant district attorney to draw up a complaint for their arrest. With no objections from the cops in the room, we switched the TV to channel seven.

We gloated that we were going to be on television with NJ Burkett regarding our armored car robbery collars. After a few moments, NJ Burkett's face appeared on television, and we quieted down the room to hear the story. After NJ Burkett's introduction, the magic table appeared showing the money and guns recovered along with the torsos of four cops standing behind the table. I start yelling at the TV, "Pan up, pan up!" gesturing for the camera to pull up and reveal our faces, and most importantly, my hair.

It never did, and NJ's description of what took place was nowhere near the facts. His story was, while the police were looking for prostitutes, they rammed and shot at an armored car that had been stolen. I was so disappointed. At that moment, I felt like Wyle E. Coyote pulling out an umbrella, just as an anvil lands on top of his head, crushing him to the pavement. It wasn't the reporter's fault this time. I blame it on DCPI who would not let us speak to the press, so the *Eyewitness* news team had to make assumptions.

We headed back to the base in silence. Our adrenaline ride had come to an end, and we were feeling exhausted. As we parked the RMP (police car) in the Eight-Three precinct lot, I said to Frank, "At least we didn't use up our fifteen minutes of fame yet."

He agreed and said, "Yeah, maybe we'll use it tomorrow." At least that got us to laugh. We emptied the car of equipment and left it for the cops on the next tour to use. I stared at our RMP with a big smile on my face. My eyes scanned its blue chaise with the police department logos on the front doors, white roof with the turret lights attached, and noticed all its little dents and scratches. Every one of those small imperfections has a story to it. I thought to myself, *Boy, if these cars could talk, they would have some tale to tell.*

I wondered about all the adventures these RMPs had been on. As we crossed through the lot heading toward the rear entrance, I pictured all the cars talking to each other discussing what had happened to them during the day, trying to outdo each other just like the cops who drove them did. "I got this dent driving through an empty lot chasing a robbery suspect." Then I pictured our car saying, "Oh yeah, that's nothing; I chased down four guys for robbing an armored car, and shots were fired and everything!" The other cars said, "Wow, dude, that's cool! Good job!" Yeah, I was tired, and my mind was turning to slush.

I slapped Frank on the back and said, "Good work today, partner."

He nodded, slapped me back, and said, "Yeah, good work, partner." We crossed the threshold of the precinct with our arms around each other, and even though the world didn't get to acknowledge our great work, at least we did. In the end, that was all we had.

TWENTY-FIVE

Disciplinary Action

The NYPD has two tiers of punitive discipline for its members. The first is a CD or command discipline for minor offenses such as wearing white socks, not having your memo book or not wearing your hat. Schedule-A command disciplines could be adjudicated by your commanding officer. For major offenses, you would be served with "charges and specifications" also known as charges and specs. These charges would be handled by the Department Advocates Office. If you disputed these charges, you could go to the trial room where the Deputy Commissioner of Trials served as judge. Losing in the trial room could lead to suspension or termination.

I was very passionate about my job and loved what I did for a living. For the most part, I walked a straight line and didn't have any run-ins with the bosses. Only one time in my twenty years did I ever get written up. I was working with my partner John at the time, and we were doing a 6:00 p.m. to 2:00 a.m. tour. We were assigned a High Holy Day post in the Nine-Oh precinct. It was a part of the Williamsburg section of Brooklyn that was heavily populated by Hasidic Jews. It was a very religious holiday for the Jewish people, and our assignment was to make sure there were no incidents. The Hasidic Jews are very prominent and influential people in this section of Brooklyn, and the precinct works very closely with the head rabbis. Usually, this was a very quiet section. During holidays, the Jewish people were not allowed to touch or operate anything using electricity and would flag down the police to shut off their lights.

We were assigned a 10:00 p.m. meal period. Knowing that there would be no place to buy food in our area of patrol at that time, we decided to grab something to eat on turnout from the command. There was a good Italian pizza place in the Nine-Oh precinct that we liked, and we agreed to stop there before taking our post. We parked across the street and walked over. It was about 6:30 p.m., and the place was fairly busy. Being regulars, we knew the owners by name. After exchanging pleasantries, we placed our orders.

Since it was crowded, we knew our orders were going to take a little longer than usual. Much to my delight, my favorite pinball game in the whole wide world was vacant. With a big smile on my face, I inserted two quarters into the slot. I hummed along with the music to *The Addams Family* as the machine came to life. The whole family lit up, Gomez, Morticia, Uncle Fester, Wednesday, Pugsley, and Cousin Itt. Even Thing and Lurch had special bumpers! *The Addams Family* was created by American cartoonist Charles Addams and originally appeared as a cartoon series in *The New Yorker*. It's been adapted into a television series, feature films, a Broadway musical, and electronic games such as pinball which I happened to be rocking at that moment. The machine was singing to me as my score started to rack up. I let out a big, "Oh yeah!" as the machine knocked letting me know I had just earned a free ball. If you have ever played pinball or watched someone playing pinball, you will notice that the player actually becomes part of the game, making rhythmic thrusts and bends as the ball dances around its arena.

As I helped bounce the ball off the flippers with my hips, John approaches me and says, "The Nine-Oh lieutenant wants to see you."

I didn't comprehend what he said, so I asked, "What did you say?"

He repeated his statement. I glanced away from the machine quickly to see a lieutenant and cop standing at the counter placing their orders. I continued playing, and the silver ball slid up a ramp prompting the sound of the Addams family doorbell as I asked John, "What does he want?"

He replied, "I don't know. He sent me over here to get you." Now, I've known John a long time, and he knows how much I love this particular game, and I wouldn't put it past him to just break my balls to ruin my game.

I glanced at the boss again, and he was still facing the other way. I said, "John, I almost have the high score; and if I let this ball go down, and you're breaking my balls, I'm gonna be pissed."

As he walked away, he said, "Okay, I already told you twice. Do what you want to do."

So I did what I wanted to do and got another free ball for doing it. Not five seconds later, a taller blue uniform is standing next to me, and I know it is not John. It was the lieutenant's driver, and he says, "Hey, the lieutenant said he wants to see you."

I glance over to the counter, and this time, the boss is looking right at me. I release my hands from the flipper buttons and watch the ball drain into the belly of the machine. The machine plays some anticlimactic music indicating that the ball's reign of terror had ended. The music was appropriate for the way I felt as I dragged my feet in the boss' direction. It took me about twenty seconds to walk the ten feet to the counter. I probably looked like a puppy who just got caught peeing on the carpet. When I finally arrived, the boss asked me, "What are you doing?"

In my mind, I said to myself, *You know what I was doing. Why are you asking me a dumb question?* Playing Captain Obvious, I said, "Playing pinball."

He asked, with a little edge to his voice, "I know you're playing pinball. Why are you playing it?"

I wanted to say, *Why didn't you ask me that the first time?* But instead, I replied, "We ordered food, and I was killing time till it was ready."

He asked me who my boss was, and I told him. He shook his head. Then he asked the dreaded questions associated with getting a command discipline, "What's your name and tax number?"

Like a good soldier, I gave it to him, and he left the establishment. This had happened in front of the owners and about ten patrons, so for me, it was a little embarrassing. It got so quiet, it was like E. F. Hutton was in the room.

When the boss was out of view, one of the owners asked me, "Oh, man, are you in trouble?"

I tried to deflect it by saying, "Nah, it's no big deal." We paid for our food and were headed to the door when I saw the lieutenant and driver sitting in their RMP waiting for us to leave. I said to John, "Oh, shit, he's still out there, and our hats are in the car."

He said, "What do you want to do?"

I answered, "Let's get paper bags and make hats out of them."

John just gave a look and said, "Come on. Let's just go." So, out the door we went. We got in the car and headed over to our assignment. He had us for unauthorized meal and no hats. The next thing we hear is the lieutenant's voice come over the radio:

"Nine-Oh lieutenant to Central."

"Go ahead, Lieutenant."

"Could you raise the task force sergeant on the air?"

John and I are glued to the radio.

"Ten-four. Task force sergeant on the air for the Nine-Oh lieutenant?"

"Task force sergeant on the air, Central. Go ahead with your message, Lieutenant."

"Meet me at the Nine-Oh precinct forthwith, Sergeant."

John and I can't believe what we're hearing.

"What's the condition, Lieutenant?"

We're waiting for the hammer to drop.

"Disciplinary action."

And there it was.

We hustled over to the nearest pay phone, spoke to the sergeant's driver, and gave him a heads up on what had happened so that our boss wouldn't have to go in there blind. The driver said he would tell the boss and meet up with us on our post after the meeting.

We ate our food and waited patiently until we got a call from the sergeant asking for our location. We advised him, and he showed up minutes later. He pulled alongside of us, and we each rolled down our windows. With a smile, he asked, "What the fuck did you, guys, do?"

We started cracking up, finally letting go some tension. I said, "We didn't do anything. We just picked up something to eat."

Talking to me, the boss said, "The lieutenant was really pissed off that you kept on playing pinball when he told you to come over."

I stated, "Not as pissed off as I was. I had two free balls and was on the verge of breaking the high score. He owes me fifty cents!" We all had a good laugh.

Two days later, the CDs came in. The lieutenant wrote in the story that I was playing pinball and left the premise without my hat on. John's stated that he had no hat on. Our captain was on his swing (his days off) and had not yet seen the CDs.

The next day, I was involved in a car accident off duty and received ten stitches in my head and injured my knee. I would be out of work for thirty days. While I was recovering, John called me to tell me how lucky I was that I had an accident and was not at work during this time. As it turned out, the captain ripped him a new asshole verbally and took one day of vacation time from him for failure to wear his hat. Lying in pain with dried blood in my hair and no car, I didn't feel all that lucky.

As I recovered from my injuries, I ran the inevitable meeting with the captain over and over through my head and tried to envision the worst-case scenario. I laughed to myself when I thought about using an excuse I had read about. A patrolman in the late 1890s had used a similar approach when facing charges that could result in his dismissal. Theodore Roosevelt was president of the Board of Commissioners at the time and often would preside over the trial room. This patrolman was afraid he would lose his job and tried to engage Commissioner Roosevelt's sympathetic side. The officer showed up at the trial room with eleven children in tow. He introduced each one individually, and with alligator tears in his eyes woefully told Roosevelt of his wife's untimely death, leaving him to care for the eleven children alone. Roosevelt gave the patrolman a lenient sentence with a stern warning. The officer left graciously and then returned the eleven children to their real parents.

I could just imagine my captain's face if I rolled in there with a minivan load of children with dirty faces and torn clothing. I was thinking that maybe it wouldn't go over as well for me as the cop in the 1890s. They say that honesty is the best policy, so I decided to go with a little "creative" honesty.

Thirty days later, I reported back to work as "light duty," meaning I would stay in the office and do clerical work. My first day back, the captain called me over after the troops had taken their posts. He sat me down and proceeded to tell me how much I embarrassed him and the unit, yada yada yada. I was prepared for it, so I was able to tune him out like Charlie Brown's teacher. Then he asked me why I was playing pinball.

I had thirty days to think about that answer, so here it went. "I was waiting for my food when I saw this young boy sitting quietly with his mom who was also waiting for food. I asked the boy's mother if I could treat her son to a game of pinball. (Pause for dramatic affect.) The lieutenant just happened to walk in when it was my turn to play."

He glared at me a long moment while contemplating the reason for my actions. He flipped over the green sheet of paper (CD) without taking his eyes off me. I stared right back at him with my best Texas Hold'em face without blinking. He lost the staring contest first, looked down, and wrote in the notes section, "Officer states he was conducting community policing."

I couldn't have said it better myself! He took four hours pay from me for no hat. It pays to have an answer. Also, the verbal ass whipping was much more diluted because of the lapse in time. But still, a half a day's pay for not wearing a hat thirty feet from the patrol car? I guess in twenty years if that is the best they can do, then I must have been doing *something* right. To this day, I still feel that Lieutenant owes me fifty cents and cost me my shot at achieving an unbeatable record score rivaling Cal Ripken Junior's 2,632 consecutive-games-played milestone.

TWENTY-SIX

I Want to Die! Shoot Me!

One afternoon, I was working with a cop named Billy. We were patrolling in the Eight-Three precinct which covered the Bushwick section of Brooklyn. A call came over division radio stating there was a ten fifty-two (10-52 - dispute) involving two males on Gates Avenue between Broadway and Bushwick Avenue. This type of job came over the air about a hundred times a day, so I paid little attention to it as Billy drove. Moments later, an update was given by dispatch, stating that they had several calls that one male had a bat and the other had a meat clever, and they were chasing each other up and down Gates Avenue.

As Billy headed the RMP in that direction, we laughed picturing the cartoon characters "Tom and Jerry" chasing each other around with assorted weapons. A third update came over, as dispatch upgraded the call to a signal ten thirty-four (10-34 - assault in progress) advising that she had had numerous calls of man down at that location. Billy and I were debating who the winner would be, either bat-man or meat clever-man. My money was on the meat clever, and Billy took the bat.

As we approached the block, we could see there were several units on the scene standing around a body lying in the street. There was construction on the block, and several RMPs were parked haphazardly, blocking any vehicles from driving through. An Eight-Three unit stated he was ten eighty-four (10-

84 / on the scene) and requested a bus (ambulance) and patrol supervisor to respond. He also asked Central to notify the squad (detectives). As we were pulling up, central dispatch put over a description of a male perpetrator with no shirt on, covered in blood walking toward Broadway. At that moment, my police science instructor, Officer Tiscione's voice spoke inside my head. He said, "Don't be one of those cops who pulls up to ooh and ah and gawk at the dead bodies. Start doing a perimeter search immediately and work your way around the crime scene." He had said those words to us in the police academy a couple of years ago, but they had stayed with me.

As Billy was stopping, I told him to keep going and head up to Broadway. Broadway was the dividing line between the Eight-Three precinct and the Eight-One precinct. These precincts were on a different frequency, so even though this incident happened one short block from Broadway, the cops in the Eight-One had no idea what had just taken place. As Billy drove, I had my head out the window like a German shepherd going for a ride in the car. If I could have jumped from the front seat to the backseat and back again I would have. My head was pivoting like an owl trying to cover as much ground as I could.

With the radio up to my ear and my eyes drying out from the wind, I caught a glimpse of an old woman sitting on the sidewalk in an old aluminum folding chairs with the nylon strips woven across each other and riveted to the top and bottom. A few of the nylon strips were tattered and hanging limp from the seat of the chair. She tried to tell me something as we rolled past. I had to tell Billy to stop and backup. We pulled over to her, and I asked her what she said. She repeated, "He went that way."

I asked, "Who went that way?"

She said, "The guy you're looking for, he went that way," and pointed a crooked finger up the block.

I asked her what he looked like, and she matched the description we had been given. I thanked her; she nodded slowly and off we went.

We were on the right track and closing in. We stopped at the intersection and glanced up and down the avenue. Something caught my eye on the left, and we turned in that direction. Two blocks up we spotted our subject entering a bodega. We stopped a block back and tried to come up with a plan to take this man into custody. Before we could formulate a plan, he reappeared and was walking toward us. He had no shirt on, and blood was smeared across his chest. He looked like he was chipped out of granite. He had a massively defined chest with cannon balls for shoulders and arms that looked like two lethal pythons. I felt that if we jumped out and confronted him, he would go ballistic, and we would have to shoot him. Billy and I asked each other, "What do you want to do?"

"I don't know, what do you want to do?" This man walked past us as if we were not there, and he was on his way home from work. I said, "Okay, just turn around and drive up to him." I tried to play dumb and see what happened.

Billy pulled slowly up to him as he walked, and I said to him, "Hey, are you alright?"

He looked at me a moment and said, "I think so."

"What happened?" I asked.

He shrugged his shoulders and shook his head with a dazed look on his face.

With my next move, I was taking a huge chance and breaking all the rules. I said to him, "Why don't you get in, and we will take you to the hospital to get checked out." I was asking a murderer to get into the backseat of my auto without handcuffs. I don't remember reading about this in the patrol guide, and I could only imagine what Officer Tiscione would have to say about this.

He seemed very dazed as he got in the backseat. There was no metal cage or plastic divider in the auto, so I bladed my body to the left to keep an eye on him and unlocked my gun from the holster. I spoke very softly and focused my attention on him under the guise of taking him to the hospital. I notified Central that we had a "possible" in the auto and returning to the scene.

As we pulled close to the scene, a huge crowd had gathered. Knowing that we had a small window of time before this man realized what was going on, I looked for one of the Eight-Three detectives who would be handling the case.

I spotted Detective Frank O'Keefe who seemed to be interviewing witnesses. I ran over to Frank and told him we got the guy in the auto, and he was going to go off once he realized that he was not at the hospital.

Frank asked the witness if he could identify the man who had committed the murder, and he said yes. When we got closer to the RMP, the man stopped dead in his tracks, turned around and said, "That's him." Frank grabbed one of the uniforms on the scene and told him to take the witness to the precinct house.

We hustled over to my RMP. On the way over, I grabbed another task force cop named Pete Palazzo. Pete's nickname was Pork Chop. He weighed two hundred eighty pounds but was as nimble as a cat. He used to scam people for ten bucks betting them that he could stand next to a desk and do a vertical leap onto the desk. It would seem impossible for a man his size to catch that much air, but somehow, he pulled it off time after time.

We got to the RMP where Billy stood outside the car and was delighted to see me return with reinforcements because our boy was not happy. We now had confirmation that this was indeed the man who had just committed a vicious murder, and we had to get him in handcuffs. As I reached for the door, the perpetrator locked it from the inside. He then locked all the doors. As fast as Billy would unlock the door, the suspect would lock it. Pork Chop said, "Throw me the keys."

As Pork Chop unlocked the other side, the suspect scooted over and locked that side too. We had this modified version of a Chinese fire drill going on, throwing the keys back and forth over the car until we won the game.

We finally had this sweaty, bloody, chiseled man out of the backseat and put the handcuffs on him. As I attempted to put him back in the car with handcuffs on, I grabbed the top of his head to push it below the roof of the car, and it didn't budget an inch. He stood straight up and looked right in my eyes with these glazed over, dead shark eyes and said, "I'll get in the car myself." I nodded as he bent over and took his position in the back on the passenger-seat side.

Since I had the keys, I got in the driver's seat as Billy slid in the back behind me. Sensing there might be a problem, Pork Chop jumped in the front seat. I advised central dispatch that we had one under arrest for murder heading to the Eight-Three precinct. As I got closer and closer to the precinct, the perpetrator became more agitated. He was sweating profusely and became more unsettled. He stared at Billy's gun in the holster next to him and yelled, "Shoot me. Go ahead and shoot me. I want to die! Shoot me!" He then proceeded to repeatedly bang his head against the rear windshield.

Pork Chop reached under the front seat, pulled out a fire hydrant wrench, and sat facing the backseat. Pete said, "Drive faster, Larry, before I have to crack this son of a bitch." I put the pedal to the metal.

Moments later, I flew into the back lot of the Eight-Three precinct scraping the undercarriage of the car on the driveway apron. Skidding to a stop at the rear doors, Billy and Pete jumped out and escorted the suspect inside. I got back into the car and found a spot in the precinct lot. I turned the car off, took a deep breath and reflected on what had happened. We had made a homicide collar on patrol, which was very unusual. We had the suspect who, only minutes before, had taken someone's life and ripped their face off, sitting in the backseat of our patrol car without handcuffs. I asked myself, "What the hell were you thinking?" Hey, I thought, it worked. I may have to retire that approach on a winning note. Good guy one, bad guy zero. We certainly had Saint Michael (the patron saint of police officers) riding shotgun with us that day.

The detectives informed me that the suspect and victim were best friends. Witnesses said they were smoking crack together all day when they got into an argument. The argument accelerated, and they decided to solve it with a meat clever and a baseball bat. They began chasing each other up and down the block taking swings at each other with their chosen weapons until the suspect caught the victim with a Barry Bonds swing and knocked him into another universe. The bat split, and he started thrusting it into the back of his head and neck leaving gaping holes. Then to top it off, he broke a bottle on the curb, lifted the victims head, and ripped his face off with the jagged glass.

Not a pretty picture. I don't know about you, but my best friend and I usually handle disagreements a little differently. As it turns out, Billy was right, batman won. To this day, I still owe Billy five bucks. As my pop used to say, "It's better to owe it to you than cheat you out of it."

The next week, I testified in a grand jury, and the suspect was indicted for murder. Approximately one year later, the case was set for trial. As I stood outside the court room waiting for the court officer to call my name to testify, the assistant district attorney Paul came out and said the suspect wanted to call and speak with his mother. As Paul reentered, I caught the door before it closed and peeked into the court room. I could see the defendant being rear handcuffed by court officers as his lawyer whispered something into his left ear. The suspect was dressed in a fine tailored dark suit and wearing glasses. His appearance had changed dramatically since the last time we met on that street in Bushwick. I gently let the door close and then continued to review my notes and testimony. About twenty minutes later, the court room started to empty. Paul found me on his way out and told me the suspect decided to plead guilty. He was later sentenced to twenty-five years.

TWENTY-SEVEN

You Gotta be a Complete Moron to Let Someone Do That to You

While on patrol one night in the Eight-Four precinct, covering downtown Brooklyn and Brooklyn Heights, one of our sergeants was involved in an RMP accident at the corner of Tillary Street and Flatbush Avenue. The sergeant notified Central that he was injured and pinned in the auto. We immediately responded to the scene to lend a hand. Pete Palazzo was already on the scene with his partner, Chucky Johnson. They had the crowbar out of their auto and were able to pry the sergeant's door open. The sergeant had taken a pretty good shot and was complaining of neck and back injuries.

EMS responded to the scene, and the sergeant was strapped down to a board to prevent any further trauma. The task force units leapfrogged each other, blocking traffic, so that the ambulance could arrive at St. Vincent's Hospital in Manhattan as quickly as possible. The sergeant was triaged and brought into the emergency room. He was taken to a designated area and enclosed by a curtain. About four of us remained at the sergeant's bedside. We secured his weapon and his equipment.

The boss asked Pork Chop to notify his wife of what had happened and to assure her that everything was okay. Pete left to call the boss's wife, and we remained making jokes about his driving skills in an attempt to keep him in good spirits. A doctor came in, asked the sergeant some questions and did some preliminary tests. The boss explained what had happened and what injuries he was experiencing. With the three of us standing at his bedside, the doctor said, "I am going to have to see if you suffered any internal bleeding. This is going to be a little uncomfortable but necessary. I am going to stick my finger in your rectum to see if there is any blood visible."

Well, being the good cops that we were, we offered our assistance to the doctor saying things like, "Here doc, use my night stick. You can get a better reading with this." Fortunately for us, the doctor had a sense of humor and didn't kick us out.

The boss tried to argue with the doctor by telling him he was okay, and he didn't need the test, but the doctor wouldn't budge. The boss pleaded, saying, "Please, Doc, let me stick my own finger in my own ass."

I have never heard one man beg another man to let him stick his own finger in his own ass before, so you could imagine our reaction. The doctor won the battle and had his way with the boss. After snapping on a glove and applying a little lubrication, the doctor gently rolled the boss on his side and slipped his hand under the sheet.

From the grimace on the boss's face and the hissing noise that escaped his clenched teeth, we determined that we had lift off. Slowly rolling the boss back to the starting position, the doctor turned around and checked his hand for the results. Everything seemed to be fine except for his manhood, which had just suffered a severe blow.

The doctor left, and all of us promised that we wouldn't say anything about what just happened. You can guess how that turned out. We continued to joke when Pork Chop returned behind the curtain with a look of astonishment on his face. We asked him, "Pete what happened?" The boss got nervous and asked if everything was alright with his wife.

Pete said, "Yeah, she's fine, but you're not gonna believe this! I was at the nurse's station using their phone, and when I finished, the head nurse informed me that there is some psycho impersonating a doctor running around the hospital."

I said, "Yeah, I hear that happens a lot."

Pete rebutted, "Yeah, but this guy's got big balls. You can't imagine what he's doing to people."

"What's he doing?" Chucky asked.

Pete continued, "First of all, you gotta be a complete moron to let someone do that to you."

Now he had us, "What are you talking about, do *what* to people?"

He took a deep breath and slowly said, "Okay… This guy's got the whole thing, right. He's wearing the lab coat and got the stethoscope, and he's going around sticking his finger up people's asses. Can you imagine that? What kind of test is that? If someone did that to me, I would fucking kill him!" We were speechless. Pete continued, "But I doubt he'd have the balls to show up on this floor with all the cops here."

With our jaws dropped wide open, we slowly turned toward the sergeant. He was looking straight up at the ceiling expressionless. Someone muttered, "Oh, shit," under their breath.

Pete couldn't contain himself anymore and broke out laughing, saying, "I'm just fucking with you. I was behind the curtain the whole time."

The boss yelled, "Get out of here. All of you!" I nearly wet my pants; I was laughing so hard.

Cop humor is rough sometimes, and it goes with the territory. Humor plays an important role in how we process the stress we are subjected to every day. We wear it as a shield, a sort of bulletproof vest for the soul. We use it to help keep that separation from job and personal life. Sometimes, it can be crude and appear inappropriate, but it is a necessary deflector.

TWENTY-EIGHT

Squeaky Shoes

Around May of 1990, I was on patrol when I got a call on the radio (ten-two) instructing me to come back to the office. When I got upstairs to the task force office, the boss informed me that I was picked to model the new uniform for the NYPD. I started laughing and told the sergeant, "Stop breaking my balls. You need us to pick you up food or something?"

He said, "No, I'm serious. Wednesday you have to report to One Police Plaza for a photo shoot."

I was in shock, "New uniform? A photo shoot? Me? For what? Let me see that." I snatched the notification slip out of his hand and read it. Sure enough, it had my name with a date and time to report to police headquarters along with a notation to bring patent leather shoes. I said, "I don't have patent leather shoes."

Sergeant said, "Well then, you better buy a pair. The department is looking to do some uniform modifications, and someone has a lot of faith in you. Also, get a fresh haircut and polish up your leather. You gotta look sharp."

I asked, "How did I get involved in this?"

He said, "I don't know, but I think you might get a chance to meet the commissioner too. You never know what can come out of something like this."

My reaction shifted from disbelief to becoming annoyed to anticipation. At first, I could not believe that out of forty thousand cops, I was the one chosen. Then I was annoyed that I now had to go and spend money to buy new shoes (typical cop). And finally, I was excited to have the opportunity to meet Commissioner Brown. I thought, who knows, maybe me and big Lee would become friends. We'd go out, have a few beers, share some laughs, slap each other on the back, and then he would ask me to pick the command of my choice. I have a wild imagination, and it gets away from me sometimes.

On my free time, I picked up a pair of shiny patent leather shoes, which set me back forty dollars, got my hair cut high and tight, and bought some black leather polish. I stripped my gun belt down, removing all of the accessories. I tapped the sponge applicator on my gun belt to give it a fresh coat of black polish. I hung it on a hanger for it to dry. Then I started to do each piece of my gun belt separately and placed them on newspaper to give them a chance to dry as well. I stopped a moment when I came to my handcuff case with the green paint on it. The little boy's face flashed in my mind along with the image of the crimson bedsheet in the RMP. I always wondered if my words to her in the car were heard. I can only hope that I was able to somehow make a difference. I took a deep breath and swabbed the sponge applicator across the paint. The paint was now gone, but that day could never be removed from my being.

On Wednesday, I showed up at work with my freshly dry cleaned uniform, freshly polished gun belt, and forty-dollar patent leather shiny shoes in tow. I got dressed in the locker room and started walking up to the office. My shoes were so clean I could see my reflection. They were a little uncomfortable and squeaked as I walked. I guess you could say that they were squeaking clean. Sorry. I made it up to my office and got a seal of approval from the boss and off I went to The Puzzle Plaza (One Police Plaza).

Upon arriving at One PP, I was directed to an office where I met with a few women who would be in charge of the photo shoot. One woman told me that the NYPD was planning to field test a new optional windbreaker-style duty jacket. The jacket came with a zip-out "thinsulate" liner for winter. The jacket will also display NYPD patches on both shoulders whereas the current jacket had only one. As the weather turned colder, a full-length turtleneck pullover could be worn underneath the jacket. About one hundred officers would field test the jacket over the next few months.

One of the women asked what size turtleneck I wore. I told her large, and she directed one of the other girls to go to the store and buy a large dark blue turtleneck. She asked me if I wanted anything to eat or drink, and I suggested that a bagel and hot tea would do just fine. She told me to make myself comfortable and returned moments later with my request. I could get used to this treatment.

After about half an hour, the girl returned from shopping with the blue turtleneck pullover. I removed my light blue police shirt and slipped the turtleneck on. The woman had a paper with different sized police emblem stickers attached. She peeled off the smallest sticker and stuck it to the left side of the neck portion of the pullover. She handed me one of the new jackets, and I transferred my shield, nameplate backing, and collar brass to the new jacket. I zipped it up about three quarters of the way, and the girls seemed to be very happy with the look.

The woman made a phone call, and we left her office for a hallway that didn't get much use. A moment later, the photographer showed up. She was a tall girl named Virginia who happened to be in my company in the academy. I was delighted to see her. Before she became a cop, she was an emergency room photographer. While we were in the academy, she would tell us stories of some of the weirdest things she would have to photograph. All I will say is people will do the craziest things to themselves and others.

Virginia had me strike a pose near the wall and took several pictures of me in the turtleneck and duty jacket, then with the uniform shirt and duty jacket. She even took a close-up of my feet sporting those patent leather shoes. When we finished, Virginia wrote down my command and promised to forward copies of the photographs in department mail. I thanked her, and we wished each other luck in our careers.

The woman told me we had one more stop to make before I was done. We were on our way to see the big guy. The commissioner has his own elevator in One PP. The woman and I rode the private elevator up to his office.

Unfortunately, Lee Brown was not in the building. Instead, I was introduced to First Deputy Commissioner Raymond W. Kelly. Ray Kelly was the commissioner's right-hand man and was appointed "first dep" in February of 1990. Ray Kelly asked me what I thought of the proposed uniform, and I told him that I liked it a lot. I told him it was very comfortable, but I wasn't so sure about the shoes because they didn't breathe well and were squeaky. He laughed at the squeaky part, thanked me for coming up and said it was nice to meet me. I asked him when we were gonna go for beers and share some jokes and slap each other. Alright, I didn't exactly say that. I think it was more like, "Thank you, sir. The pleasure is all mine."

The police department created and published a magazine in 1930. A competition was held for the rank and file to come up with a name for the newly founded magazine. The winner of the competition suggested the name be *SPRING 3100*. This was the telephone number for the old police headquarters which was located on Centre Street at the time. This magazine is still in existence today under that name. On page fourteen of the 1990 November/ December issue of *SPRING 3100*, you can find my mug prominently displaying the newly proposed uniform, alongside a close-up shot of my squeaky shoes. The picture of my feet and the uniform shot also hung on my parent's living room wall until the house was recently sold. You gotta love mothers.

TWENTY-NINE

Tactical Narcotics Team

After a short courtship of ten years (please, I've heard it all!), Jane and I were finally married in June of 1990. However, our relationship did not stand the test of time, and we were unofficially separated in 1993. My world seemed to be in total disarray on many different levels. Getting my life back in order became a priority for me, and I started with my career.

I was fortunate to work with many great police officers in Brooklyn North Task Force, both male and female, but I felt it was time for me to move on. It was time to complete another goal; to become a New York City detective. In June of 1993 with about nine and a half years in uniform under my belt, I decided to take aim at the Organized Crime Control Bureau. After passing an interview and a number of background checks referred to as a round robin, I was transferred to a narcotics unit in Brooklyn North, known back then as TNT (Tactical Narcotics Team) working out of the Brooklyn Navy Yard.

The entrance to the Brooklyn Navy Yard was located at the corner of Flushing and Clinton Avenues. It was a huge facility with a lot of history attached. Federal authorities purchased the property in 1801 for forty thousand dollars from John Jackson. The property became an active U.S. Navy shipyard in 1806. The Fulton Steam Frigate, the first steam-powered warship was built in 1814–1815. An accidental explosion destroyed the ship in the yard killing twenty-nine people. One of the first submarines was also built here. Many warships were constructed and serviced at these docks.

In its youth, the Navy Yard was, in a word, majestic. More than five miles of paved streets weaved throughout the grounds, circulating personnel to its hospital, barracks, machine tool shops, and warehouses. Its four dry docks housed battleships such as the USS Iowa, Maine, and North Carolina. During World War II, when the shipyard was at maximum capacity, seventy thousand people recycled every twenty-four hours to man its cranes and hoists, as the welders showered sparks that lit up the night. Armed military personnel stood sentry at the mouth of the yard conducting prudent and thorough checks of anyone trying to gain access. Secretary of Defense Robert McNamara decommissioned the navy yard in 1966, and two hundred sixty acres were sold to the City of New York for twenty four million dollars.

As I drove on Flushing Avenue toward the entrance on Clinton Street, I peered through the metal fence that contained the yard. The Navy Yard looked tired and worn. Some of the handmade painted brick buildings were littered with broken windows. Overgrown bushes attempted to hide their once glamorous appearance. Once manned by armed military personnel, the gates were occupied by pseudo-security guards who never left the comfort of their booth and who thought a wave and a smile were sufficient identification.

My new place of employment also seemed to be in need of repair. The walls were damaged and badly needed a fresh coat of paint. The uneven floors cracked and moaned as people made their way around the building. In some places, the tiles were so worn they gave way to the wood underneath. In at least one place, it was worn completely through, giving a glimpse of the darkness below. In the weight room, you could do decline bench presses and give the weather report at the same time, looking clear through a hole in the roof.

Discarded brown IBM typewriters were stacked up against the wall like car wrecks in a junkyard. Each one suffered from its own cause of death: missing keys, burnt-out motors, no ribbon, broken rollers, and frayed wiring. Their carcasses sat atop abandoned broken office chairs, which were left to die along with the typewriters. The building was rumored to be haunted by the souls of days gone by. Eerie noises and unexplained happenings were not uncommon. I believe the building was later condemned by OSHA.

I made my home in one of the vacated desks. It was available either because of a recent transfer or someone upgraded to a more upscale "neighborhood," leaving the slums open for newcomers. To me, it was home even though the surface was stained and sticky from being used as a lunch table. The Formica top had separated from the metal, curling up at the edges as if the desk had something to say. The locking mechanism had been brutally ripped from the main drawer leaving jagged metal teeth behind. The top right-hand drawer was off its tracks and closed awkwardly to resemble an underbite. My chair rested on three legs against the uneven wood floor like a dog with an injured paw. I had to take Dramamine to prevent seasickness from the rocking. The chair's vinyl covering was ripped in several places exposing the orange cushion. I cleaned it up as best I could and moved in. This was similar to how you feel when you get your first car. Even though it was a clunker, you washed and cleaned it religiously because to you, it was beautiful.

This was where my eyes were opened to narcotic-related crime, which is invisible to uniform patrol. I was assigned here only for two and a half years, and it was to be the most dangerous time of my career. However, I wouldn't swap this time for the world. The men and women who worked here were truly some of the bravest people I have ever met. We worked hard, and we played even harder.

The unit's mission was to combat street level narcotics dealing. Narcotic trafficking is a billion-dollar industry, and the people who sell drugs on the street can be very organized. There is a hierarchy. There are owners, managers, dealers, steerers, enforcers, runners, money men, lookouts, bagmen, cookers, and people on standby in case someone in the organization gets pinched. This ensures that the organization can get back to business without too much interruption. Getting arrested is an occupational hazard for these people.

We would identify problem areas; determine what types of narcotics were being sold, in what quantity, by what name brand, and by whom. After we gathered this information, we put together a tactical plan and targeted several "sets" (locations where drugs were sold). We would go into the field with a group of undercover officers and a backup team who were there to support the undercover officers and make arrests. The undercover officers usually wore a wire, but not all the time. These wires were very unreliable and could be prone to shutting down without notice. A secondary undercover, known as a ghost, would follow and keep tabs on the undercover attempting to make a buy from a drug dealer. The ghost was essentially the eyes and ears for the backup team.

On a perfectly planned day, the undercover would go to the set, buy drugs, relay a description, field team moved in, arrested the dealer, placed them in the prisoner van, recover narcotics, and move on to the next set until approximately eight to ten dealers were arrested. This was a typical day of work for us, and most of the time, we were very successful at meeting our goals.

There were three teams: the Eagles, Condors, and Montana. Each team had two sergeants and about twelve to fourteen members, men and women, white, black, and Hispanic. It wasn't uncommon for members of one team to go out and work with members of another if they needed personnel. It was nothing short of a family. I knew without a doubt that these people had my back, and they knew I had theirs. Our assignments were broken down into two designations: investigator and undercover. An investigator would generate cases and make arrests, while the undercover would go into the street and purchase narcotics or guns or whatever was related to the case. My job was as an investigator.

Later in my career, I dealt with mid-to-upper-level management drug dealers, but the local street corner dealer, selling bags of cocaine, crack, and heroin was by far the most dangerous. A lot of the street pushers had extensive rap sheets and had nothing to lose. They were determined not to get arrested again and would do anything to stay out of jail. This meant fight or flight or a combination of the two. Many a day did these thugs strap on their felony fliers (sneakers) in an attempt to evade the long arm of the law. Rarely was the case when one of these runners was not run down and brought to justice. We were that good.

Teamwork was an absolute necessity. Everyone had to be mentally and physically prepared when it was time to go out into the street. At any time, anything could happen. When an undercover got the green light from the sergeant to step from the undercover auto and proceed to the set, everyone in the field team was ready to take action.

THIRTY

Thank God This Kid Has Got an Arm Like Johnny Damon

My first week in narcotics was a whirlwind. I was in awe of the people I was working with. I had so much information thrown at me at once that my head was spinning. These cops made it look so easy. On the outside, I tried to be as cool as a cucumber; but inside, my stomach was churning. I wanted to be an asset to my team and become one of the boys.

I remember coming into work at the Brooklyn Navy Yard and sitting at my desk when Sergeant Sellers Wilson approached me and said, "You're getting on today, kid." This meant that I would be the arresting officer (A/O) for all arrests we made for the night.

I felt my face flush, and my pulse quicken as I said, "No problem, boss." To me, this was like a rookie baseball player getting his first at bat at Yankee Stadium. This is what it was all about.

About two hours into our tour of duty, the sergeant called the team together for the tactical plan. We gathered in the sergeant's office and received our assignments. The room was small, and we took up every available square inch of office space. The printed tac plan was handed out to the team. It told you what sets (street corners) we were attempting to buy from, who the undercover (UC) officers were, and what equipment each two man car would be responsible for. This was a very serious meeting, but you couldn't tell from all the levity that was going on. It usually started with Donald Bradley, a.k.a. Cody, doing his impression of Lenny Sarter, our lieutenant, which always brought the room to tears. Even the lieutenant would request Don to imitate him. Then big Patty Abdul would follow up with his impressions. Big Patty had a smile and a laugh that were so contagious but off duty you never wanted to hide his bottle of Hennessy for too long, or he would rip your lungs out through your nose. He was a bear of a man with a heart of gold and an excellent cop.

I looked around this small room and saw cops of every nationality, age, and size, and I wanted to be like every one of them. To me, this was what being a cop meant. We all worked together to get our gold shield and our promotion to detective. Some had already been promoted and hung their gold shields around their necks. I would stare at the shield and envision one also dangling from my neck.

Eventually, the sergeant got the room to settle down, and we put our game faces on. Sergeant Wilson said, "Today, we are going to break Larry's cherry. He's getting on today." This was followed with comments from everyone in the room. I laughed it off but was scared to death. "Alright, settle down. Now J. C., Eddie, and Sammy, you guys are buying. Let's start with the first set on the tac plan and work our way down. Let's have a good night and load Larry up with ten bodies." Again, the comments were flung around like paper airplanes. I stood laughing with a face pumped red from embarrassment. "Okay, I'll see everyone out at the first setup location. Let's be safe out there." Sergeant Wilson barked as the room deflated back to its original size, as the team exited.

I strapped on my gun belt, velcroed my bulletproof vest to my chest and dangled my silver shield from my neck. I proceeded to the equipment room, signed out a radio, and the aid kit which receives the transmissions from the undercover wire. I searched around the parking lot and found the sergeant's auto. I opened up the aid kit and immediately became flustered. All I saw were wires, antennas, dials, and settings. I had a better chance of repairing the

Space Shuttle then getting this thing to work. As I removed my head from the backseat of the car, I saw Melanie, one of the females in my team, carrying a battering ram to her assigned auto. She must have read the distress on my face and said, "Need a hand with that?" I nodded with an embarrassed grin. She dropped her equipment down and set that baby up like she had been doing it her whole life. I thanked her, and she said, "No problem, anything you need, just ask." I knew that she meant it.

With that mess out of the way, I started the car and pulled up in front of the office to wait for my boss. The rest of the team filed out to their cars. The guys had big smiles on their faces and were slapping and joking with each other. I could not wait to become a part of this close-knit family. This was the first step, "getting on" and proving yourself in the street.

Sergeant Sellers Wilson came out of the building. He seemed to me to be six feet five inches tall, but I'm sure he was only six foot one or two. He was in his late forties and in magnificent shape. His speech was slow, and he sometimes stuttered. He had a big smile with dimples to match. I was very fortunate to have him as my boss. He was a great leader and teacher. He would review all of the detective's paperwork for accuracy and circle all the mistakes in red. He made a point of catching errors before the paperwork made it to the district attorney's office. These little mistakes could be extremely embarrassing if you testified in court, and they could lead to a case being dismissed.

He made his way to the car carrying his fruit, which was a ritual. The fruit of the day was cherries. If he didn't bring it with him, he would stop and pick it up before we started our B and B (buy-and-bust) operation.

He settled into the car and looked over the aid kit to make sure everything was in order. He called one of the undercover officers on the radio and said, "J. C., give me a check on the Kel."

J. C. said, "Ten-four, boss." After a moment, J. C.'s voice came in loud and clear from the box.

"Okay, J. C., we'll see you out at the first set." Sergeant Wilson looked over at me at said, "Ready?"

I look him dead in the face and say, "Ready!" I took my foot off the brake, hit the gas, and *VOOM!* The engine revved, but we didn't go anywhere because Inspector Jacques Clouseau forgot to put the car in drive. My head turned slowly to my right as I whimpered, "Sorry." Sergeant Wilson just laughed. My mind was yelling at me, *You idiot! What's wrong with you!* as I dropped the shift into drive.

Having worked in Brooklyn North my whole career, I knew the area pretty well and drove to the setup location without needing directions. We drove in silence as Sergeant Wilson entertained his fruit, spitting the pits out the open window along the way. I was as tense as could be and felt the sweat dripping down my back underneath my Kevlar tortoise shell. I parked the nondescript car a few blocks from the set to avoid detection from lookouts who roamed the area on bicycles and cars looking for "five-oh." This term originated from the popular television show *Hawaii Five-O* which ran from 1968 to 1980 starring Jack Lord who played Detective Steve McGarret.

Sergeant Wilson broke the silence by offering me some cherries and asking me about my prior assignments as a cop. The point-to-point radio interrupted our conversation periodically as the field teams checked in one by one, letting us know they were set and ready for action. The last unit to check in was the undercover auto or UCs. Sergeant Wilson told J. C. to give the Kel another check to make sure it was still working, and a moment later, J. C.'s voice erupted from the backseat, "Check one, two. Check one, two."

The boss replied back on the point-to-point radio, "You're five-by-five, loud and clear. You got the green light to step. Field team, be advised the UCs are stepping from the auto." I grabbed the wheel and pulled myself up in the seat in anticipation.

I hear J. C.'s footsteps emerging from the receiver in the backseat as J. C. heads to the first set. This is confirmed by the ghost, Sammy, via point-to-point radio, "UC is approaching the set." After a moment or two, Sammy's back on the radio, "He's approaching a male on the northwest corner of Myrtle and Classon. Male is about twenty years old, wearing green tee shirt, blue jeans, white sneakers, carrying a tennis ball."

I can hear the UC talking, but I am unable to make out the words. Sammy advises us that they are still in conversation. To me, it feels like twenty minutes have passed, but I'm sure it was only three or four when Sammy is on the radio stating, "UC is leaving the set. I can't tell if he got done…hold on… he just signaled me that it was a positive buy."

Now my veins are wide open, and the blood is pumping when J. C.'s voice again emerges from the backseat, "Positive buy, boss. Male about twenty, wearing green tee shirt and blue jeans. He's got the stash in the tennis ball. Repeat, positive buy. Stash is in the tennis ball."

Sergeant Wilson takes control and advises Sammy to keep an eye on the subject and tells the field team to get ready to move in. I put my hand on the shifter getting ready to drop it into drive. Sergeant Wilson spits a cherry pit out the window and tells me to hold on a minute until we know J. C. is back safely to the UC auto. My hand relaxes for the moment. I focus on the sound of J. C.'s footsteps returning to the car. I'm not sure which was louder, his footstep or my heartbeat. We hear a door open and then close followed by static, then silence. J. C.'s voice magically appears in the front seat from the point-to-point radio after he had turned the wire off, "Okay, boss, back at the car. It was a positive buy. Kid was about twenty years old, wearing green tee shirt and blue jeans. He's got the drugs inside the tennis ball. He may be raised up a little. He seemed kind of nervous."

Sammy advises that our boy is still on the corner possibly selling to another customer. The sergeant grabs the radio and says, "Okay, field team, let's move in." I'm staring at him when he turns to me and says, "Okay, now it's your turn. Let's go get him." This time, I get the mechanics right and drop it into gear smoothly. I check my mirror and pull into traffic. As I turn onto Myrtle Avenue, my eyes are trying to adjust to locate my subject who is about four blocks up the road.

On our approach, Sammy assures us that the dealer is still on the same corner looking up and down the avenue. My heartbeat quickens as the distance between us closes. Two blocks away now and I can finally see the green tee shirt. He's being very alert and walking around on the corner, checking all four directions. One block away now, and I see nothing but him. As I closed in on the corner, our eyes seemed to lock and stayed that way until he broke eye contact. I passed through the intersection and aimed the car in his direction. As my car was slowing down and coming to a halt, he was turning and accelerating on his own wheels. The car was still rocking to a stop as I started to jump from the car. The last thing I remember hearing was the other members of the field team telling Sergeant Wilson that they got stuck at the light and were lagging behind us. As my feet jumped the curb and landed on the sidewalk, I could see that the green tee shirt had a good jump on me, and I had some ground to make up. I realized that for the moment, I was on my own.

I had no radio and could only hope that Sergeant Wilson was dishing out our location as I chased our subject. On paper, this kid had a clear advantage over me. He was much younger than I was. He knew all the ins and outs of the streets. He wasn't required to wear a bulletproof vest and carry a gun belt with all the dressings. The Vegas odds clearly favored him. I'm not sure what was at stake for him, but I was crystal clear what was for me.

In college, I had studied Anthropology and had learned that in many cultures, the young boys were set out alone to complete a task, and when they returned were considered men. This was my rite of passage into the narcotics family. How poignant is it that it was mano a mano.

My task was to bring this kid down, recover evidence, and build a good case for the district attorney to prosecute in court. Shortening the distance between us, I had a lock on him like a fighter jet. He made his evasive maneuvers, but I hung with him with every turn. He turned corners and changed directions. He slipped through a small break in a fence and into a school yard. As I was squeezing through the fence and manipulating my gear, he looked back over his shoulder to see if I was still coming. I could tell he was breathing through his mouth and was getting tired, but he still had the tennis ball in his hand. This is where I closed the distance. My mouth was dry, my lungs craved oxygen, and my legs were burning as if fire was spreading through my veins, but my desire never wavered.

Thank God he started to get Gumby legs before I did. His stride faltered, as his legs gave into exhaustion. We crossed the school yard over to the next block, and he could feel me breathing fire on his neck. Like a lion chasing down a gazelle, I was ready to sink my teeth into his flesh. He was at arm's length now as we went up four or five steps to street level. He made a left turn, and sensing his impending doom finally decided to try and get rid of his prize possession, the tennis ball. As my outstretched hands started to gather his green tee shirt, he reared back his arm and launched the tennis ball while our body weight became one. Fortunately for me, he was the box spring, and I was the mattress, as we made contact with the sidewalk, his body diffusing most of the blow. Making sure he felt every ounce of my one-hundred-eighty-five-pound frame, I pressed my forearm across the back of his neck to control his head and limit his view. I needed him to know who was in charge now. This might be his streets and his turf, but I was the man behind the curtain pulling all the switches. I shifted my weight on him so that I could get the cuffs out of their pouch, then twisted his right arm behind his back and secured it in the metal bracelet.

As I readjusted to secure his left arm, movement caught my eye on the sidewalk ahead of us. The sidewalk was pitched toward the street for drainage, and about ten feet in front of us, I see the green tennis ball limping slowly as it rolled toward the street. It kept rolling ever so slowly as if exhausted from the chase and attempting to make a last ditch effort to escape. I laughed to myself and thought, thank God this kid has got an arm like Johnny Damon (former NY Yankee).

As I fitted his left hand in the cuff behind his back, I could hear the crackle of a police radio. This was music to my ears because it meant backup had arrived. Emerging from the school yard was Sergeant Wilson. Still breathing heavily, I looked over my shoulder from the ground and saw him smile as he gave over our location to the rest of the field team. Suddenly, cars skidded to a halt in front of me. The boys had arrived. I gathered myself and got to my feet. I walked over to where the tennis ball had attempted to hide and picked it up. I squeezed it open and could see little ziplock bags containing a rocklike substance which later would be determined by laboratory analysis to be crack cocaine.

With the subject under arrest and evidence recovered, once again the comments started to fly. This time, it all felt right. I took their remarks, jokes, and jabs with a big smile on my face because at that moment, I knew I had passed my test and officially had become part of my new extended family. The subject was frisked for weapons, narcotics, and money, which Sergeant Wilson would take control over until the vouchering process later in the night.

We threw this keeper (subject) into the bucket (prisoner van) and rebaited our hooks to fish some more. Sergeant Wilson made notations in his book of the time and location of arrest and evidence seized. He looked at me and said, "Nice job out there. Your ass can run, huh? Ready to do it again?"

I was still on my runner's high as I nodded. "Let's do it."

Sergeant Wilson popped a cherry into his mouth, squeezed the transmit button on his radio, and said, "Okay, Condor team, let's set up for location number two."

THIRTY-ONE

Don't Shake It Out!

We would continue conducting buy-and-bust operations until the prisoner van was filled with eight or so bodies, head into the local precinct and start processing the prisoners. Our team was like an ant colony. Everyone knew what had to be done, and we got busy. The subjects were lined up in front of the precinct desk officer, handcuffed, and then lodged in the cells.

Once all of their pedigree information was obtained, each arrestee would be escorted to the bathroom by an officer of the appropriate sex where he or she would be strip searched. This was, for all of us, the nastiest part of the job. We would each take a prisoner into the bathroom and put them in the stalls for privacy. Because narcotics can be hidden anywhere, every piece of clothing had to be thoroughly checked. A lot of these people had not showered in days and had been wearing the same clothing for weeks.

Some of them were high, sick, or couldn't speak English, so I spoke slowly and deliberately to make this part of the process go as smoothly as possible. My standard speech in the beginning went something like this: "Listen to me carefully. When I tell you to take off your clothing, I will tell you which piece I want you to take off. When you take it off, DO NOT, I repeat DO NOT shake it out and just hand it to me and wait for me to tell you to take off the next piece. Are you with me so far?" I usually got a confirmatory head nod.

Every time I did this over the next two and a half years, it didn't usually go as planned. I would start with, "Okay, take off your shirt." The shirt comes off and gets handed to me. So far, so good. As I'm checking every inch of the shirt, he starts to slip off his shoes. I stop and ask, "Did I tell you to take off your shoes yet?"

He shakes his head and says, "No."

I replied, "Then why are you taking them off? Did you understand what I told you from the start?"

"I'm sorry," he says.

I finish with the shirt, place it on the side, and ask for the right shoe. I get the right shoe, search it then get the left shoe, and search that. I ask for right sock, and he takes it off, snapping it right in front of my face to straighten it out. Now there is shit floating it the air, and it smells like ass because his feet haven't been out of those socks in days. I yell, "What is wrong with you! I just told you not to shake anything out, didn't I?" Again, the confirmatory head nod. I continue, "Then why are you shaking it out? That's gross, man! Give me the other sock and DON'T SHAKE IT OUT!" He hands it to me, and it's wet and stinky, just like the other one. As I check the sock, he starts to undo his pants and drops them. Now I'm really pissed off, "What are you doing? You're killing me here. Just stand still until I tell you to move. Do you think you can do that?" He stands at attention with his pants around his ankles. "Okay, give me the pants." He hands them to me and is standing there in his so-called underwear, which, by the way, hasn't seen the light of day in weeks. "Okay, give me the drawers," I demand.

Over the years, you could only imagine what you would see and smell in somebody's underpants, so I will spare you the details and let you draw your own conclusions. Now he is standing in front of me in his birthday suit, but the search is not complete. He has to open his mouth and lift his tongue. Lift his arms over his head. Pick up his manhood and then turn around and bend over so that I can get a look up his ass. Pick up the bottom of his feet to make sure nothing is taped there, and then he can get dressed. After he is attired again, I walk him out of the bathroom and place him in the holding cell. I proceed to grab another subject and walk him to the bathroom stall and start over with, "Listen to me carefully..."

One day after we had filled the prisoner van, we went into the Seven-Five precinct to process the day's load of prisoners. We had them lined up in the stalls and in front of the sinks conducting our strip searches, when I hear one of our detectives yelling at his prisoner, "What was that? What do you have there?"

I step out to make sure everything is okay and hear the prisoner yelling back, "What? Where? I don't have nothing!" The subject is completely naked, and the detective is yelling for the guy to squat down. The guy squats down quickly and stands up again, stating he doesn't have anything.

The detective says, "What's in your ass? What is that?"

The guy sticks to his story and says, "I got nothing in my ass. I got nothing!" The detective tells him to squat down again. As the prisoner does, the detective smacks the guy on his ass. The prisoner flinched, and two bundles of heroin fell from his asshole. A bundle contains ten "decks" or small envelopes of heroin. This guy had twenty decks of heroin in his ass. This is the reason we have to conduct these searches for narcotics arrests. Now the detective has to take custody of the newfound evidence and voucher it. People may have jobs where they have to deal with assholes on a daily basis, but this puts a totally different spin on things. There were times where the subject would try swallowing the narcotics, forcing us to pry open their jaws, and reach in their mouth to retrieve evidence. They would risk death to escape going to jail.

Once all the body searches were completed, then the colony went to work on the rest of the process. Each prisoner had to be fingerprinted and photographed. Online booking sheets had to be prepared and faxed down to central booking. The cops assigned to the prisoner van would be responsible for transporting and lodging the prisoners at central booking. The rest of the team would head back to the office and meet up with the undercover officers, where the evidence vouchers would be prepared. The undercover officers would voucher the narcotics that they purchased and prepare a Buy Report.

One day when I was the A/O, and prisoners were on their way to central booking, the rest of the field team headed back to the barn (office) to voucher evidence. With eight to ten bodies, there can be a lot of vouchers to type, so the task is divided up among members of the field team. This was the end of our day, and we were all exhausted. I could hear the tap of the keys of Bobby's typewriter as he tackled the pile of vouchers he was assigned to prepare. I pumped through my stack at a good rate. After I ripped my last finished voucher from my typewriter, I decided to see if Bobby needed a hand. He was seated at his desk with his head down and his hands on the keys, but no noise was coming from the typewriter. It was as if he was frozen in time. I started laughing because I realized that he was dead asleep. I softly singsong his name, "Bob-by", but got no response. We worked long hours, and Bob was married with a large family to support, so I figured I would let him get a little shuteye and grabbed a couple of vouchers off his desk.

His head was slumped a tiny bit to the left, and his breathing was getting deeper, but his hands somehow remained on the keys. I would classify Bob as a "trained professional" because he was technically asleep, but his posture said he was working. His ears were trained to listen for Sergeant Wilson's creaking footsteps as he rounded the corner from his office. Upon hearing this noise, Bobby's eyes would open wide, and he would push a key, any key, showing he was awake and working. As I stood behind him, I could see that the voucher rolled into his typewriter was nearly completed, and he was at the bottom of the form in the "details" section.

Upon further inspection, I couldn't believe what he had typed. It said, and I quote, "At t/p/o (time/place/occurrence) the above listed property is affectionate." My sudden laughter startled him, and his "training" kicked in, as he jumpstarted back to life, and his finger slapped an "X" onto the form. I could only imagine what he was dreaming about, but I was pretty sure that heroin wasn't involved. I prayed that this particular case did not go to trial because I would have a hell of a time trying to explain it.

After the arrest evidence was sealed and secured, it was transported to the precinct where the vouchers were acquired. The arresting officer would get their copies of the appropriate paperwork and report to the district attorney's office the next morning, where a complaint would be drawn up against each defendant, officially charging them with a crime.

Approximately three days later, the arresting officer and the undercover officers who had made the buys were notified to report to the Narcotics Grand Jury. Here, each case would be presented to a panel of jurors who would hear testimony from undercover officers who had made the buys and the arresting officer who recovered evidence on the defendant at the time of their arrest. Once jurors had heard all the evidence, they would vote to determine if the evidence had been sufficient for the case to continue. If they believed the charges were justified, they would vote for a true bill, and the case would be assigned to an assistant district attorney (ADA) for prosecution. Once the case reached an ADA, the defendant's rap sheet (prior arrest record) would be reviewed; and either a plea bargain would be offered, or the case would go on trial. This process could take several months to a year before a case was finally adjudicated.

I would testify countless times in different courts over my twenty years, but the Narcotics Grand Jury seemed to have a revolving door. I would see the same cops and undercover officers. Sometimes, the same defendants would get rearrested for selling to different undercover officers. The wheels of justice seemed to be clogged here from the sheer volume of cases. It was a never-ending process, and it was easy to get burned out. Even the jurors, who listened to case, after case, after case, would suffer from burnout. I can't tell you how many times I have entered the jury room to offer my testimony and observed jurors ready to bang their heads from falling asleep. It was basically the same testimony over and over again with different names attached. As a juror, if you are assigned to a Narcotics Grand Jury for any length of time, you should be issued a helmet in order to prevent serious head injury.

THIRTY-TWO

Ten Thirteen, Shots Fired

I was in TNT a short time when the powers that be decided to rename our unit and shift its focus. We were now known as BNSNAG (Brooklyn North Strategic Narcotics and Guns). It was business as usual for us, only we had the additional task of focusing on gun trafficking.

A very good friend of mine had joined our ranks. George Flores, a.k.a. Papo, was a very likeable guy who I had worked with in BNTF. Papo always kept himself in great shape, and his face always carried a smile. When I worked in the auto larceny unit in the task force, we had an ongoing competition. Although Papo was assigned to a regular patrol squad, he was constantly bringing in stolen auto collars. I would tell him to stop stealing our collars, and he would joke that he made more GLA (Grand Larceny Auto) collars a month than our whole team did, and sometimes, he was right. It was like he could stick his nose out of the RMP and smell a GLA. I was delighted to see him in our office. He would be a great addition to our team.

On Monday, April 25, 1994, we were preparing for another round of buy and bust. After completing his two-day orientation into SNAG, it was decided that Papo would be getting on today and catching all the collars. We grouped together in the sergeants' office for the tac plan. Sergeant Tommy Cea stated that Papo would be getting on for the first time, and the room erupted with comments. This time, I was a part of the mob slinging jokes. It was a great feeling to be on the other side of the fence. Papo took it like a man with a huge smile. He enjoyed it as much as we did.

The tactical plan ended and we spilled out of the office to gear up. It was customary for the arresting officer to drive the boss, but today, I was assigned to drive Sergeant Tommy Cea, and Papo would ride in the backseat. After suiting up, Papo followed me as I proudly showed him the ropes. We signed out our radios and gathered the Aid receiver. We walked out to the sergeant's auto, and I schooled Papo on how to set up the receiver. I pulled the car around front and waited for Sergeant Cea to exit the building.

In my opinion, Sergeant Tommy Cea was the greatest boss I have ever had the pleasure to work for. I have been very lucky in my career and worked with many good bosses, but Sergeant Cea was top shelf. He loved being a cop, and it showed. He never forgot his roots and treated everyone equal. We loved working for him. When he wanted something done, he would always politely ask and not demand. He treated all of us with respect, and it reflected in our work.

With the preliminary checks completed, we headed out to the first set to conduct business. Big Patty and J. C., acting in an undercover capacity, successfully made a positive buy, and the field team swooped in, netted the subject, and secured him in the prisoner van. Sergeant Cea gave the word, and we moved on to prepare for the next set, which was in the vicinity of Glenmore Avenue and Hinsdale Street in East New York, Brooklyn.

I parked our car at the corner of Junius Street and Glenmore Avenue, and the rest of the field team lined up behind us with the prisoner van in the rear. J. C. and Patty drove their Jeep past the set to make sure the organization was out and pumping their product. They confirmed that the corner was open for business and parked their auto. J. C. would be the undercover attempting to buy drugs, and Patty was his ghost. J. C. tested the wire from inside the UC auto, and our receiver picked it up loud and clear. Sergeant Cea gave the UCs the green light to step from the auto.

As we sat, we talked about almost everything. We talked about the job, sports, women, and working in the Eight-Three precinct. Tommy worked as a sergeant in the Eight-Three, and the task force where Papo and I worked was upstairs. Our conversation was interrupted by J. C.'s voice stating over the wire, "We're the police. What's up?"

Then Patty's voice came over the point-to-point radio saying, "Boss, this doesn't look good. Ten eighty-five, move in Glenmore and Snediker."

Tommy grabbed the radio and commanded to the field team, "Let's go, guys. Move in. Move in. Glenmore and Snediker." As soon as Patty's words rose from the radio, I threw the car into drive and punched the gas pedal. The tires spun, caught the pavement, and propelled us forward.

With the team in motion, Patty's voice boomed that sacred signal from the radio, **"TEN-THIRTEEN, TEN-THIRTEEN, SHOTS FIRED, MOVE IN, GLENMORE AND SNEDIKER, HURRY!"**

As I made a left, the car's rear end fishtailed to the right then swung back in line as I flew down Glenmore Avenue. I heard the screech of tires behind me as the rest of the team made the turn. Snediker Street was fast approaching. An elevated train ran above, crossing over Glenmore Avenue. I could see both Patty and J. C. slowly backing up toward Glenmore Avenue in a combat stance with their guns pointed down Snediker Street. A high metal fence blocked our view of the immediate threat to the UCs.

I slammed on the brakes, and the car skidded into the middle of Glenmore and Snediker. Our view was now clear, and we could see an old 1982 black Cadillac parked on an angle toward the sidewalk. The driver's side door was open, and a male stood outside the car using the car door for cover. Then I saw the muzzle of a large firearm pointed at our car from over the top of the Cadillac's door. The gun bounced off the top of the door each time the gun was discharged in our direction.

Papo opened the rear door to exit in the line of fire when I yelled, "Get back in the car!" Papo slammed the door shut, and I drove the car across the intersection and stopped beyond the corner. After witnessing the shots fired at us in the intersection, the rest of the field team halted on the opposite corner by the metal fence. They jumped from their autos and took aim at the Cadillac.

Tommy and Papo exited the car and ran to the sidewalk, where there was another metal fence. As I rounded the front of my car, I could see Patty behind the elevated train pillar. The pillar resembled a steel leg that descended from the tracks above, fitting into a concrete shoe in the street. Papo established himself on the ground at the corner of the fence. He made himself so small he looked like one of those deflated Christmas lawn balloons. Tommy took up position higher on the fence.

J. C. dropped an empty magazine to the ground and punched in a fresh ammo clip, reloading his .380 caliber Sig Sauer. As I was moving into position, J. C. stepped in front of me to get back into the gunfight. Tommy yelled to J. C., "Get back, you don't have on a vest!" (bulletproof vest). As if the sergeant was lying to him, J. C. picked up his shirt and checked. Realizing the sergeant was right, he stepped back.

I slid into a small space between Tommy and Papo like a missing jigsaw puzzle piece. I used the fence for as much cover as I could and punched out my blue finished Smith & Wesson .38 caliber handgun. I pointed the four-inch barrel in the driver's direction who was still using the car for cover. My right forefinger pulled the trigger, causing the hammer to step back from its resting place. As the hammer traveled back, the gun's cylinder rotated counterclockwise. The hammer reached its end mark then snapped forward, lead by the firing pin.

With the rotation completed, the cylinder containing the ammo aligned with the firearm's chamber. The firing pin made contact with the primer cap at the base of the bullet's cartridge. An explosion of gun powder propelled the lead projectile through the four-inch barrel. The barrel has grooves inside called rifling which cause the bullet to spin, much like a football, carving "fingerprints" into the projectile. These "fingerprints" are unique to each weapon and can be traced back to the gun it was fired from. The expanding gasses forced the spinning lead toward my target. I squeezed the trigger five more times emptying my gun, firing my remaining ammo at our enemy.

I heard no one speak. The air was dominated by gun bursts, concrete chipping, and lead striking metal. The stop sign affixed to the train pillar where Patty hid from the assault, fluttered and hummed as it was pierced with return fire. A dim haze of smoke tinted my view as burnt gunpowder hung in the air. Shell casings were catapulted from the ejection port of Tommy's 9-mm semiautomatic Glock 19 handgun. Each smoldering brass shell casing struck the sidewalk, emitting an eerie musical tone as it danced before rolling to a rest.

The Cadillac's engine suddenly roared to life as the auto went into motion. The firing stopped except for one or two final bursts. The car sped straight up Snediker Street emitting black smoke from its tailpipe. As it crossed in front of me, I could see holes in the body of the car where our rounds had pierced its skin.

I stood amazed that anyone could drive away after the barrage of fire power that was just unleashed. I wrestled the keys from my pocket and jumped into the driver's seat. With Papo and Tommy safely in, I spun the car around. The field teams were already in pursuit. Anticipating another encounter with the suspect, I handed Papo my gun with the spent shells. I unsnapped a speed loader from its pouch on my gun belt and tossed it over my right shoulder to Papo saying, "Load me up." As I wheeled the car around, Papo opened my gun's cylinder, dumped the empty silver casings on the floor of the car, and quickly reloaded my weapon.

He passed it up to me saying, "You're good."

I was trailing the pursuing cars when I heard J. C.'s voice come over the receiver. His voice was inaudible and high pitched. He seemed to be screaming. My first thoughts were that he had been hit in the firefight. I said, "Sarg, I'm going back. I think J. C. is hit." He agreed, and I spun a U-turn and headed back to the original battleground. Upon returning to the intersection, I could see that two officers had remained on the scene. Steve Brown and Kenny Lutz were helping J. C. subdue and handcuff a male near the curb.

I parked the car and ran over to them. J. C. was out of breath as he said, "Motherfucker tried to just walk away." I asked him who the male was. He said, "Motherfucker tried to kill me, man. He got out of the passenger door and stepped to me. I told him we were the police, but he didn't give a fuck." I had not realized that there was a second male in the car. When we had skidded into the intersection, all my attention was focused on the driver and the loud machine gun he was firing right at us. When I pulled out of the intersection and got in between Papo and Tommy, I had used as much of the fence to cover me as I could and had only concentrated on the driver.

The air was screaming with police sirens now as Seven-Five patrol cars headed in our direction. Cars came from all over, and I was glad to see every one of them. Tommy met up with the first arriving RMP and told them to tell everyone to slow down. The Seven-Five patrol car advised central dispatch over division radio, "Slow it down at Glenmore and Snediker, Central. Slow the units down." We didn't want responding cops to get hurt if the threat was over. But when a confirmed ten-thirteen is given over the air, there is no stopping.

Lieutenant Berkowitz from the Seven-Five precinct arrived on the scene. He was an ex-Navy SEAL officer with many years of military and police experience etched on his face. He had a rack of medals that flopped over his left shoulder like a bandoleer. Some of the field team was returning to our location. J. C. and Patty sat in one of our cars which had tinted windows in order to protect their identity from the public. Sergeant Cea was advised by Sergeant John Valdes that the shooter had crashed his car at the corner of Junius Street and Liberty Avenue. He was unconscious and had suffered several gunshot wounds. He was taken by EMS to Brookdale Hospital.

When I heard the news that the shooter was hit, I ran over to car with the UCs inside. I let them know that the driver was shot and removed to the hospital. J. C. asked me if I could pick up his empty ammo clip he dropped when he reloaded. I looked over my shoulder and saw it lying on the sidewalk where we had stood our ground during the gunfight. A large crowd was forming, and Lieutenant Berkowitz took control of the crime scene. He had the uniform officers push the crowd back and set up a perimeter with yellow tape. I jogged across the street, picked up the empty clip, and jogged back, handing it to J. C. I joined Sergeant Cea who was briefing Lieutenant Berkowitz on what had just taken place. The lieutenant nodded his head, seeming to absorb the details of the incident. With a deadpan face, the lieutenant said to Tommy, "I think you, guys, need to go to the range." His poker face never changed which made it difficult to decipher if this statement was for amusement or if it was serious.

There was no mistaking his seriousness when he barked, "There was an ammo clip on the ground over there, and now it's gone. Looks like we got a good shoot here, let's not fuck it up. I want it put back!" I quick stepped back to the car with the UCs and told J. C. I needed to return the clip back to the sidewalk. He was hesitant to hand it to me, knowing that it would be vouchered as evidence and never seen again. He was a little upset because this meant that he would have to purchase another one (typical cop). I pried it out of his sweaty hand and returned it to its original location. As I crossed the street, I saw a black object lying where the Cadillac was stopped. Moving closer, I could see that it was the driver's gun. It was an Intertec Nine 9-mm semiauto machine gun with a fifty round clip attached. The muzzle was quiet as it lay in the street motionless as if *it* was a victim.

Emergency Service showed up—along with the Crime Scene Unit—to conduct a search for evidence as detectives interviewed the crowd for witnesses. As word of the incident spread, numerous unmarked cars arrived, discharging men in suits.

As is customary, the entire field team, a total of eleven men, was ushered to Jamaica Hospital and treated for trauma. We were met there by a Patrolmen's Benevolent Association (PBA) delegate. He informed us not to make any statements to any bosses about the incident. This was the first time the eleven of us had been together since the shooting, and we started asking each other questions. Only Donald Bradley (Cody) did not discharge his weapon. This meant that Cody was considered a witness and would have to give a statement regarding the events of the shooting, as per Patrol Guide 118-9. Don joked saying, "Had I known that, I would have let one go into the ground."

We were all in good spirits and thankful to be alive. None of us were injured except for Kenny who suffered a minor laceration to his left index finger restraining the second suspect. Though not injured, Big Patty had been the most affected by the incident. He was clearly traumatized. His blood pressure remained high, and he was given Valium to help him relax. Because he was acting in an undercover capacity, neither him nor J. C. had been wearing body armor.

Patty carried a Smith & Wesson .38 caliber revolver. His eyes were damp and distant as he relived the incident, "I fired my six rounds and then just stood there with an empty gun pointed at them. I just keep pulling the trigger on an empty gun because I didn't want them to know I was out of ammo. I thought that I was going to die today, and thoughts of my family ran through my head." Hearing those words brought back memories of my friend Scott Gadell who was killed reloading his gun. I wondered if Scott had chosen to do this, would things have turned out differently.

They say that laughter is the best medicine, so we decided to prescribe some for Big Patty at his own expense, with a huge co-pay. We started in on him with, "How the hell were you able to hide that fat ass and belly of yours behind the pillar?" Someone added, "There's no way. If he tucked his fat ass in, his belly stuck out; and if kept his belly tucked in, his fat ass hung out. You must have looked like Homer Simpson doing the Hokey Pokey…You put your fat ass in. You take your fat ass out… That image played in my head, and I thought I was gonna need a diaper I was laughing so much. "D'OH!" I love these guys.

We were treated and released from Jamaica Hospital and headed over to the Seven-Five precinct. The cops in the precinct stopped and nodded their support to us, as we headed up to the second floor. One by one, Lieutenant Berkowitz inspected our weapons and made note of the rounds in the gun and any evidence of recent discharge. It was determined that the ten of us had fired a total of eighty rounds. We got news that the driver had died at the hospital after suffering four gunshot wounds.

Cody gave an official statement of the events with a PBA attorney present. His statement was recorded and retained as evidence. The detectives assigned to investigate the shooting were able to find three witnesses who, thankfully, corroborated the statements made by Cody. Firing eighty shots and having no injuries to civilians, with only minimal property damage, was a miracle and a credit to our training.

The bloodstained, bullet-holed black Cadillac was separated from the light pole and removed as evidence. At arm's reach, in the belly of the glove compartment, was another fully stocked fifty-round ammo clip. Because of all the bullet holes, the 1982 Cadillac resembled the gray Ford the outlaws Bonnie Parker and Clyde Barrow drove when a posse of six lawmen ambushed them with 167 shots near Gibsland Louisiana on May 23, 1934.

It was a long day, and I had time to reflect on the ride home. The scenario replayed over and over in my mind. I realized how blessed we all were not to have been injured. Our room for error was nonexistent, and the slightest change in our actions could have proved disastrous. I couldn't stop thinking about the second gunman who I never saw until I returned to help J. C. It scared me to death that I was not able to realize there had been another shooter. If the situation was different, and I was alone, who knows what the outcome might have been. Once again, my thoughts turned to Scott Gadell and the fear he must have experienced. I thanked my guardian angel for watching over me and realized that although I had ten years on the job, I was still evolving into a seasoned cop.

I suddenly broke out in laughter as my mind shifted to the prisoner van. It just dawned on me that we had one prisoner in the van from the previous set. I could only imagine the thoughts that must have run through his head as he lay in the back of the van with his hands cuffed behind him. Poor guy couldn't even cover his eyes. He probably rolled on the metal floor into a corner and curled up into a ball. I'm sure it wasn't so funny for him, but the image of him flopping around in the van like a fluke on a boat deck, as over one hundred rounds crisscrossed in the air around him allowed me to release some tension which made a home inside my body. Once again, humor helped me deflect and gain the separation I needed to maintain my sanity.

An article titled "Gunman Slain in Cop Shootout" appearing in the newspaper on Tuesday, April 26, 1994 quoted the dead gunman's wife as she questioned the police account of the story. She said her husband was a hard working Port Authority electrician for thirteen years. A spokesman for the Port Authority said they had no record of him. Nuff said.

When we went back to work, our team was given some downtime, and we remained in the office to catch up on paperwork. I used a lot of this time to work out in the gym. We shared the events of the incident with the Eagle and Montana teams. We were all very much in agreement that this could easily have happened to anyone of us at any time. This time, events played out in our favor. A life had been taken at the hands of the police, our hands. Although we had all physically survived the gun battle and were totally justified in taking that life, a piece of each one of our souls was left on that street like a discharged shell casing.

THIRTY-THREE

Hammer

J. C.'s time as a white shield was up, and he was to be promoted to the rank of third grade detective two days after the shooting. The whole office packed into the auditorium in police headquarters. There were promotions to all ranks, and we patiently waited for J. C.'s turn on stage. It was a kind of assembly line promotion: cops would line up along the right side of the stage and wait for their names to be called. You'd step onto the stage; stop ten feet in front of Commissioner Bratton, salute, walk up, shake his right hand as you accepted your certificate of promotion in your left hand, then exit the stage from the left side.

The assembly line was working at a quick pace, and J. C. inched along toward the stage. Our anticipation grew with every step J. C. took. Finally, the name "Johnny Celestin" was announced, and we let loose on the cheers. Commissioner Bratton halted the ceremony and quieted the audience. Commissioner Bratton acknowledged J. C.'s involvement in an armed confrontation during a buy-and-bust operation only two days prior. The audience applauded, as we let loose a second time, letting the crowd know he was one of ours. It was a proud day for me because we really were like a family. I envisioned myself inching up in the line filled with anticipation and then finally reaching the stage for my moment in the sun with my mom and dad in attendance. Just the thought of it brought me goose bumps.

After some well-deserved days off, it was back to business as usual. We each took turns as the A/O (arresting officer), as we continued pounding the street corners of Brooklyn, where narcotics were sold. Even with all the arrests we made, the spots were able to remain open for business. As we picked off dealers, the organization had a steady supply of others to take their place. We needed to get inside information to do some real damage to the core of the organization.

One day after hitting sets in the Seven-Three and Seven-Five precincts, we headed to the Seven-Five station house to start processing that day's collars. The suspects were presented in front of the Seven-Five desk officer, and we were given pedigree information sheets to fill out for each of our guests. They were put into the holding cell rear cuffed and were pending a strip search.

One of the locations we hit regularly was a heroin spot at the corner of Livonia Avenue and Williams Avenue. Drug dealers sold ten-dollar decks (glassine envelopes) of heroin from inside a bodega. The bodega operated on street level with three floors of residential apartments above it. We believed that there were one or more apartments being used as a stash house. When supply in the bodega ran low either a call or a visit was made to the apartment and the bodega would re-up (restock) its supply. This allowed the bodega to operate while keeping only a minimal supply on hand at any given time. This form of risk management was done to prevent severe loss of product due to police raids. Many locations worked this way, and if a spot was busy, many calls or visits were made to the stash house to keep the spot running. This bodega had been working steadily for a long time and had become a thorn in our side and an eyesore for the community. On this day, this spot produced a two-piece set, meaning two arrests were made. One dealer had conducted a hand-to-hand transaction with the undercover while the other piece had taken control of the buy money.

A couple of us grabbed a subject and walked them to the bathroom at the Seven-Five precinct to be strip searched. My dance partner was a male Hispanic about twenty-four years old. I was the first one in the bathroom and had my prisoner occupy the stall closest to the wall as the others followed suit behind me. He walked into the stall with his back to me so that I could remove the handcuffs. He turned around and faced me, standing in front of the toilet while rubbing his wrists to get the blood to return to them. I stood at the mouth of the open door.

As I broke into my patented "Listen to me carefully" speech, my guy starts this animated, modified mime act. His eyes opened wide as he mouthed words and gestured to the stall next to us. I took a peek in the next stall and realized it contained the other male Hispanic arrested with him. He was trying to relay information regarding his buddy, but his enthusiasm was getting the better of him. I gestured for him to slow down and breathe as I requested a clothing item so as not to bring attention to us. He lip-synced, "He's the boss" as he motioned again to the stall next to us. I assured him that I understood, but that this was not the best time and place to talk about this.

I pointed to my watch and put up five fingers conveying that we would talk again in a little while. He nodded in acknowledgement as we brought the search to an end. He spread his cheeks and took a squat, and then I told him to get dressed. Even when he was getting dressed, he motioned and gestured to the stall next door. Using my body language, I told him to take it easy, and that we would talk in a little while.

After he redressed, I rear handcuffed him and headed out of the bathroom. My teammate completed his search of the prisoner next to us and left. We followed out behind them, and my guy started gesturing with his head. Now I felt like slapping him. With my eyes I said, "I get it! He's the boss, and you want to flip on him. I get it!" I removed the restraints and pushed him into the cell and said, "I'll let you use the bathroom later after we get settled."

After placing him back in the bullpen, I approached Tommy Cea and said, "Boss, one of the guys from Livonia and Williams wants to talk. If Donald (A/O) doesn't want him, I'll work with him. He's a bit of a nut, but I'll see what he's got."

He nodded and said, "Check with Don." As the arresting officer you had first crack at any prisoners who had been arrested and wanted to talk. Don had no interest in him and gave me the go ahead.

Once arrest processing was underway and near completion, I walked to the cell. My guy was like a puppy at the pound that needed a home and came to the gate wagging his tail. I asked, "Do you still need to use the bathroom?" I unlocked the cell door and told him to place his hands behind his back as I walked him out of view of the other prisoners. I sat him down in a quiet spot, and Tommy joined us. I said, "Okay, what do ya got?" It was like I had just popped the cork on a champagne bottle. This guy couldn't speak fast enough and was all over the place. I could see he needed to be slowed down and given some guidance. I asked pertinent, systematic questions and was able to get some valuable information regarding the heroin spot. We learned that the other guy arrested with him was the manager of that spot.

As we suspected, they had a stash apartment in the building on the third floor, but he didn't know the apartment number. There was a guy from San Salvador who worked in the apartment, cutting and bagging the heroin into the decks (glassine envelopes). When the dealer in the bodega ran low, he would place a call to the apartment, a runner would pick up a fresh supply and deliver it to the bodega. They also had a buzzer that was hooked from the bodega directly to the stash apartment which acted as a security system in case of a raid. This would alert the worker in the apartment to either destroy the evidence or get out before police arrived. He stated that they had about three lookouts working at a time. I asked him what his motivation was to talk to the police. He said that this was his third drug sale case, and he had a wife and son. If convicted, he would be sent away for many years and risked losing his family.

We didn't want to keep him out of the holding cell too long because that might raise suspicion of his codefendant. If the manager suspected even the slightest that he was cooperating with us, it could put his life in jeopardy. I wrote my first name and telephone number down on a little piece of ripped paper and told him to call me when he got out of jail. This way, we could have sufficient time to debrief him and determine if we wanted to sign him up as a confidential informant. He thanked us and agreed to call after his release, and I returned him to the pen in a timely fashion.

Although these arrests were made in Brooklyn, occasionally we brought cases to Manhattan to be prosecuted by district attorneys in the Special Narcotics Bureau. Attorneys working in the Office of the Special Narcotics Bureau could prosecute cases anywhere in the city, which was the case this day. I asked Don to tell the ADA (assistant district attorney) that was handling the arrests of the two-piece set at Williams and Livonia that one of the defendants may be cooperating. He passed along the information, and the ADA asked to be kept informed.

About three days later, I received a call from the defendant who said he still wanted to work with us. We set up a time and place to meet. All informants working with the police must be registered with the department, so I took a Polaroid camera and a CI (confidential informant) registration form with me in case we were going to use him. I grabbed the keys to a nondescript auto with tinted windows and headed out with Sergeant Tommy Cea and Stephen Brown.

Once we had him in the car, I explained the rules he had to abide by. I let him know that I could not promise him anything, but the more reliable information he provided, the better it would be for him. I made it clear that he was not to feed me bullshit, and if he didn't know something, he was to say so. He would also have to stay in touch with me on a daily basis. He agreed with all our demands and was willing to cooperate. CIs can either work for money or time (court consideration). Since he had three cases pending, he would be working for time.

I took two photographs of him and filled out the registration form. We needed to come up with a code name that would be used whenever we made contact. Tommy said he wanted to hammer the heroin spot on Livonia and Williams, so it was decided that this guy's CI name would be "Hammer." He would be our tool to get inside. He said that he could get access to the bodega and the stash apartment. I explained that we need "looks" inside the apartment to get a search warrant. He needed to pay close attention to details in the apartment and keep a log of when he was there, who was there, and what was there.

When Hammer got out of the car, we headed back to the barn. The three of us discussed whether this guy was telling us the truth and whether he could be of use to us. We all agreed to give him a shot pending his performance regarding gathering information and his ability to follow the rules.

His first assignment was to get the apartment number and an accurate layout of the rooms. Once I had the apartment number, I could enter it into the UDECS (Unified Drug Enforcement Coordination System). This system referred to as DECS would alert me to any other law enforcement investigation that involved this location. Usually, if I got a hit on a DECS, it meant that another team or agency had interest in the spot. I would contact the case officer and see if they were actively investigating the place. If the DECS came back clean, that meant that the spot was mine, and other agencies or teams would have to contact me before they could pursue it.

THIRTY-FOUR

The Arena, Where Muted Business Suits Waged War

Hammer was diligent in gathering information and kept in regular contact as instructed. Once he had gotten his looks inside the apartment and the information seemed to be consistent, I contacted ADA Aida Vernon to advise her of Hammer's observations. She invited me down to her office, located at 80 Centre Street in Manhattan, to go over the details and to draw up a draft affidavit applying for a search warrant for the location.

Having worked in Brooklyn my whole career, this was my first trip to the Manhattan court buildings. After I exited the elevator, I stopped to get my bearings. Without asking for directions, I started circling around the floor. My head pivoted left to right as I walked peering into each open door like I was attending a tennis match on wheels. The floor was inhabited by muted business suits that blended into the dull surroundings. Carrying folders and documents seemed to be a requirement. Occasionally, I would see the glimmer of a shiny silver or gold shield which made me feel safe. After completing a half circle, I finally had located my destination.

ADA Vernon was an attractive slender woman with an easygoing attitude, and we seemed to click immediately. Case folders tagged with sticky notes littered her desk, giving her office a sense of urgency while her demeanor remained relaxed. As we talked, her phone rang. She excused herself to answer the call. The phone call pertained to one of the other hundred cases that were assigned to her, and she was able to locate the folder without hesitation from the rubble.

Even though there were case folders and law books piled about the office, she had everything under control. Needlessly, she apologized for the interruption, and we picked up where we left off. She plucked Hammer's case folder from a stack and reviewed it while I spoke about the information he had gathered. She made a notation on the folder jacket and placed it back on the pile. She listened intently while I read from notes I had taken regarding the heroin spot. She seemed to let the information process in her head then slowly turned toward her computer and let her fingers transfer the new information onto the screen.

She had done this hundreds of time before and asked me only relevant questions without taking her eyes off the screen. Then she sat and stared at the screen while muttering to herself. With one click of the mouse, the printer next to me sprang to life as it started spitting out pages from its belly. Once the machine finished its job, I passed the pages across the desk to her. She sat quietly while her eyes darted across the paper. She made corrections, printed out another copy, and told me to give it a read through to make sure the facts were correct. The affidavit spelled out the days and times that Hammer was in the target location and his observations of product and personnel working at those times. I checked the details against my notes and found everything to be in order.

Because this was Hammer's first time working with us, he would have to appear in person in front of the judge and swear to the information in the affidavit. Once we executed the search warrant and obtained positive results, which consisted of arrests or product recovered, he would be deemed a credible confidential informant and would not need to be present for future search warrant affidavits. ADA Vernon told me, "We need to get him in front of a judge before this information gets stale. Otherwise, he is going to have to get another look, and then we have to amend the affidavit."

Two days later, I made arrangements for Hammer to meet with ADA Vernon. Steve Brown and I picked up the CI and transported him down to Centre Street. ADA Vernon went over the details of the affidavit with him again to make sure there were no discrepancies. She explained what would take place. She told him that we were going to meet in the judge's chambers where the judge would read the affidavit and determine whether there was probable cause to issue a warrant. Depending on the judge, he may or may not be asked questions. Each judge was different.

I told Hammer to leave and head over to the courtroom where we would meet him later. I advised him not to acknowledge us and to just sit tight until we exited the court. About two minutes after we left, he should meet us in the hall so as not to raise suspicion.

After ADA Vernon got the affidavit and search warrant in order, we proceeded across the street to the court. I held open the heavy wooden doors that guarded the courtroom, and Aida and Steve crossed the threshold. Out of the corner of my eye, I spotted Hammer sitting comfortably in the third row of wooden pews where defendants and family were scattered about. Steve and I sat in the first row, which was reserved for law enforcement and lawyers, while Aida ventured through the spring-loaded, wooden gate into the area I call the arena where the muted business suits waged war.

In this arena, an assistant district attorney occupied the table to the right and defense lawyers occupied the table to the left. We sat on the right showing our loyalty with our shields prominently displayed on the outside of our garments. The two opposing sides gave their demands and made their arguments without making eye contact. They stood facing the judge like an estranged couple going through marriage counseling. The defendant stood motionless wearing a blank face next to his mouthpiece (defense attorney), while bored court officers were strategically placed around the room.

Careful not to interrupt the therapy session, Aida approached the court clerk and handed her our search warrant application and stepped back out of the arena to join us in the first row. When a decision was finally reached, the judge slammed down her gavel which sent people into motion. The ADA jotted down notes on the case file jacket then slipped it back into the pile of folders, which were spread out like a magician's playing cards. Pick a case, any case. The defense attorney leaned over and whispered into his client's ear, which caused the defendant to get a pained look on his face like he had gas. While the defense attorney gathered his folders, the court officer rear cuffed the defendant who was blowing kisses to his mommy and girlfriend who had started crying. A court officer announced the next case, and the ADA picked the queen of hearts from her deck, while another muted suit defense attorney entered the arena. The ADA reviewed the case folder in preparation for therapy with her second husband.

The court clerk spoke softly with the judge as she pointed in our direction. The judge turned and spoke with the court officer who announced that the court will take a fifteen-minute recess. The judge nodded to Aida as she rose from the bench. That was our cue, and we stood and walked out the back of the court room. Aida showed me a door where we were to enter when we had Hammer. Hammer nonchalantly moseyed out of the court room as instructed, and when the coast was clear, we whisked him away into the unknown.

We stood in the judge's chamber awaiting her arrival. I found the room to be very daunting with hundreds of law books and prior case-law decisions lining the walls. I was one of the good guys with nothing to worry about and could only imagine what Hammer must be feeling. He was definitely out of his element. The judge entered the room with her black robe flowing behind her. The court stenographer scurried in after her, quickly setting up her miniature magical typewriter and stool. We exchanged pleasantries as the judge affixed her glasses and reviewed the affidavit.

The judge began to speak for the record, and the stenographer's fingers captured the judge's words on paper in a foreign language. She stated the purpose of our visit and the location in question. She asked which one of us was the informant. I gave my own puzzled look thinking, *He would be the one without the New York City Police Department shield hanging around his neck.* As requested, Hammer identified himself for the record. The judge swore him in and asked Hammer if the information presented in the affidavit was true, and he stated that it was. Then I was sworn in as the case officer and asked if the information provided by the informant was reasonable and accurate according to my investigation. I also stated it was, and the judge determined that probable cause did exist to grant us the search warrant.

The judge signed the document in her designated area, and we thanked her for her time. She instructed us to be safe and wished us happy hunting. The judge exited through her door with the court reporter scurrying behind her. We exited through the same door we came in and returned to the courtroom to get the signed warrant stamped by the court clerk.

The courtroom seemed to be in standby mode as Steve and I reentered. I passed through the arena gate as Steve waited just outside. It felt different when you crossed over that threshold. The air seemed cold and thick, making my approach to the bench difficult. I was greeted with a warm smile from the court clerk who was happy to stamp me. The judge walked back behind the bench as the court officer announced, "All rise." Everyone stood at his or her own pace. Some people were starting to sit as others were just on their way up. I wondered what it would be like if everywhere I went people had to rise as I entered.

I stepped out of the arena into the warm, fresh air with a sense of the enormous power in my hand. With this document, I was granted the authority to forcibly enter a premise without notice and thoroughly search through everything inside. I had ten days in which to execute the warrant between the hours of 6:00 a.m. and 9:00 p.m. It was classified as a "no-knock" warrant due to the extremely dangerous conditions related to narcotics trafficking and the strong possibility of destruction of evidence. Having that element of surprise could save lives.

I gave Hammer ten dollars to get some food and catch the subway back to Brooklyn. I congratulated him on a job well done and for presenting himself in an intelligent manner in front of the judge and ADA Vernon. He was off to a wonderful start, and I hoped that we could continue to work together.

THIRTY-FIVE

Police, Search Warrant!

Back at the barn, Steve and I informed Sergeant Wilson and Sergeant Cea that we were granted the search warrant for Livonia and Williams Avenue. They were thrilled because no other team had success gaining access to this operation. The bosses reviewed our work schedule, and it was decided that we would execute the middle of next week.

Being granted a search warrant was only the beginning of my work. I would have to gather as much information about the location as possible. It was to our benefit to know the hazards and dangers that we might be presented with: were there any dogs at the location? Did the informant see any guns? What were the possible escape routes, fire escapes? What is the door made of and how many locks does it have? Can you walk into the lobby of the building, or do you have to be buzzed in? How many people are in the location? Are there any children? Does the apartment face the front of the building or the rear?

Over the next couple of days, Steve and I, along with Sergeant Cea, were able to observe the location and gather some intelligence. Steve got out of the car and got a closer view of the building and its lobby. He made it up to the target floor and got an eyeball on our door. He also went to the bodega and got a feel for the inside. I drew a rough sketch of the building and the intersection making notes on the direction of traffic on each block. Steve had a mental picture of the layout of the bodega which I transferred to paper.

As the week grew older and a new one began, my anticipation level rose along with Hammer's. He called me every day wanting to know when the search was going to happen. Even though Hammer was a likeable guy, he was still an informant and not to be trusted. He had to be dealt with at arm's length because I would not risk the safety of my team. He was working off his three pending cases, but his loyalty might still be to the streets. I kept the element of surprise in our favor.

In narcotics at this time, search warrants were scarce, and case work was virtually nonexistent. It was more or less a numbers game with buy and bust being its bread and butter. Case work and warrants usually ate up a lot of time and affected the teams arrest numbers for the month.

Manhattan North, which covered Washington Heights, was considered the narcotics capital and distribution point for the tristate area. Here, thousands of kilos (kilo equals 2.2 pounds) of cocaine and heroin were stored in stash apartments ready to be sold to dealers and brought back to their spots to be cut up and resold. In Manhattan North, it was not uncommon for numerous kilos or "weight" seizures to be made. A kilo of cocaine sold anywhere between eighteen and twenty-five thousand dollars. A kilo of heroin could go for anywhere between eighty and one hundred twenty thousand dollars, depending on supply and demand principles. A Brooklyn dealer might buy a kilo of cocaine or a half kilo of heroin at a time. The kilo would be immediately cut up and packaged for retail. Whole kilos were rarely seized. In Brooklyn, we chased what has come to be known as the Kilo Fairy. The Kilo Fairy was depicted as a dancing cow wearing a tutu holding a kilo above its head.

After days of preparation, a plan of attack was agreed upon. On the day of execution, Steve and I prepared the tactical approach with visions of the Kilo Fairy dancing in our heads. On a large chalkboard, I drew a diagram of the target building and the surrounding streets. I flipped over the board and drew a diagram of the apartment layout as described by the informant and a diagram of the bodega from Steve's recon.

Sergeant Cea called the team together for the tactical meeting in the larger room where we had the chalkboard. Steve and I stood next to the diagrams as Tommy Cea discussed our plan of attack. Copies of the tactical plan were distributed to the team who looked them over as Tommy spoke, "Today, we're finally gonna hit those bastards on Livonia and Williams. Larry got a search warrant for apartment 3G on the third floor. Eddie is going to do a confirmatory UC buy in the bodega to make sure the spot is working. If he gets done, we will give it five minutes or so and then hit the place. If he doesn't get done, we still have a few days to execute, and we will regroup and hit it another day. Sergeant Wilson is going to take a team into the bodega."

Sergeant Sellers Wilson stepped into frame and said, "Okay, my guys are gonna hit the bodega. We need to get in quick and freeze the guy behind the counter before he gets to the buzzer to alert the stash apartment. We're gonna freeze everybody inside and outside the place also until we determine who is who." He glanced back to Tommy as he stepped aside.

Tommy took the ball again. He flipped over the chalkboard to show the layout of the apartment and continued, "My team is going to hit the apartment. We're gonna take the stairs up to the third floor. Steve, you're gonna hit the door, and Craig you're gonna carry the ram up. We are expecting only one guy to be in there but be prepared for anything. Always assume there are guns inside so be on your toes. This place has a power flush toilet, so we have to watch for destruction of evidence. Lieutenant, you got anything to add?"

Lieutenant Lenny Sarter came into the circle and in a deep voice said, "I think you covered everything. Let's move in as quickly as possible and catch them by surprise. Most importantly, let's be safe. I want everyone wearing a vest and raid jacket with your shield out. Let's make no mistake about who we are. Okay, let's get out to the setup location."

The meeting broke up, and everyone descended to the locker room to get ready for the operation. The office was buzzing with excitement. Today was a well-deserved break from working buy and bust, which could be draining to say the least. The search warrant offered us another tool to combat narcotic trafficking. This let us get up close and personal. I thought about the people in the target location right now who were feeling safe and invincible. In about an hour or so, they would be in handcuffs, and their lives will be changed forever.

As I suited up, a minimum of one million thoughts banged around inside my head like cave bats. I was dizzy from thinking and sat on the bench with my head down hoping the angle would settle them. Kenny Velasquez tapped me on the back and asked, "You alright, kid?"

I stammered back, "No, no, yeah I'm good. I'm just going over some things in my head. I'm good. Yeah, I'm good." He seemed to accept that answer and walked out closing the snaps on his dark blue raid jacket with POLICE printed in large block white lettering on the back.

This was a big day for me, and I felt a tremendous amount of pressure. I'm sure a lot of it was self-inflicted because I have a very bad habit of being extremely tough on myself in everyday life. Today, I felt like I was wearing one of those lead vests the doctor drapes over you to protect your body from X-rays. I took a deep breath and said out loud to nobody but myself, "Let's do this."

Working with Stephen Brown as my co-case officer made my life a lot easier. Steve was a well-built black man with a barrel chest who gave off an aura of intimidation. He appeared much larger than his actual frame. Steve was soft spoken and gentle in his demeanor, but I would never want to take a walk on his wild side. Steve ALWAYS did what was asked of him no matter how undesirable the task was without complaint. Through the two and a half years that I worked with him, I fed off of his unwavering, consistent positive work ethic which helped mold me into a better investigator and better person.

Steve and I set up the Kel receiver in the back of the sergeant's auto. I asked Steve if he wouldn't mind driving because I didn't want the added stress of vehicle operation. Without batting an eye, Steve took the keys. The weather was turning a little colder those days, but I couldn't tell that from the furnace burning up energy inside my body. Tommy Cea occupied the front passenger. He was visibly excited as he giggled and rubbed his hands together. I later took notice that Tommy often did this before a big buy or search warrant. To me, he looked like a mad scientist at work marveling over his new creation. With all the checks completed, we headed out to the staging area several blocks away from the target location. We hoped to remain out of range from the "lookout" zone.

Once we were setup a comfortable distance away, Tommy checked the UC Kel one last time. With everything in working order, Tommy gave Eddie the green light to proceed. To his credit, Lieutenant Sarter let Tommy call the operation which helped to keep things simple. Sometimes, too many chefs in the kitchen can spoil the soup. Mark Amos ghosted Eddie and kept us updated along the way. Eddie briefly spoke to someone outside the bodega and was directed inside. Once inside, Eddie struck up a conversation in Spanish. None of us in the car spoke Spanish, but the tone seemed relaxed. I made a mental note to have a translator with us for future operations. Mark remained a safe distance away while keeping a watchful eye on Eddie. After a few moments, Eddie walked out of the bodega and signaled Mark that it was a positive buy. Mark relayed the information over the point-to-point radio, carefully keeping an eye on the bodega, while making sure Eddie was not followed to the undercover auto by a lookout.

The positive buy unlocked the second part of the plan. Once safely back at the UC car, Eddie provided the details of the purchase. He stated, "Boss, it was a positive buy. It is gonna be a two-piece set. The guy in front of the store with the black jacket and black baseball cap directed me inside to the guy behind the counter with a light blue shirt that says New York. New York took my money and went to the right side of the counter toward the back and came back with the drugs. There are two other guys who are just hanging out in the store. I'm not sure what their role is, but they definitely know what's going on. Just make sure you freeze those guys and give them a good toss."

Tommy checked with the lieutenant, and Lieutenant Sarter said, "Looks like a go. Let's hit it when you are ready." Tommy checked with Mark who kept an eyeball on the set.

Mark replied, "Everything's good boss. Nobody seems raised up."

The mad scientist rubbed his hands together again, looked back at me and asked, "You ready?" I swallowed, but my tongue stuck to the roof of my mouth preventing me from using words, so I did the next best thing, I nodded.

Tommy's next words set everybody in motion, "Okay, boys. Move in. Mark, we are on our way."

Mark acknowledged, "Ten-four boss, hit 'em." I sat up straight in the backseat and placed my left hand on the door handle. Our car led the caravan of field team autos toward our target.

Rounding the corner, the building slid into view, and people on the block momentarily froze as we snaked around the curve. Even with the window up, I could hear people yelling, "Five-oh, five-oh!" as a warning. A strong gust of wind caused a herd of leaves to stampede across the street as if they were attempting to escape.

Steve landed the car in front of the lobby door to the building. I yanked the handle, pushed it open, and set my feet on the ground. I could hear the other cars stopping with urgency as doors opened and slammed, unloading their warriors. I was deep in tunnel vision as I rounded the nose of the car, and my feet propelled me to the left. I was gathering speed when I heard my name floating in the air, "Larry!" It was the lieutenant. I looked to my right, and Lieutenant Sarter was waving me over toward him as my field team filed through the lobby door. I was misled by my feet which had carried me in the wrong direction. I readjusted my compass and joined my entry team.

As we charged up the stairs to the third floor, Sergeant Wilson advised over the radio, "He got to the buzzer before we could get to him. You gotta get in there quick." We reached the third floor landing and stood outside the door marked 3G. Not knowing what awaited us on the other side of the door kept us all on high alert. We were going to find out soon enough, as Craig Johnson passed the ram to Steve. Steve took a huge breath and held it as he reared back the ram and sent it forward with all his might into the body of the metal door. The door groaned with pain but still remained closed, valiantly protecting its inhabitants for the moment. A second strike flung the door wide open as the interior doorknob embedded itself in the wall.

I could hear the sound of a toilet flushing as we charged into the apartment yelling, "Police, search warrant!" Don and I reached the bathroom simultaneously. We hurled our bodies at a male kneeling on the floor in his underwear holding the handle down. The toilet was in a constant state of flush. The water violently circled the inside of the toilet and drained down its throat. The toilet seemed to gasp for air once his hand was detached from the handle, and the water leveled off and settled to its normal calm. I had a head lock on underwear-man, and Donald forced his hands behind his back for cuffing. Lying on the bathroom floor, I heard, "All clear" and knew the apartment was now ours.

We left the subject face down on the bathroom floor under the watchful eye of Eddie Narvaez. I stepped out of the bathroom and inspected the rest of the apartment while I tried to catch my breath. Sergeant Cea got on the radio and advised Sergeant Wilson that we had gained entry, and we had one under arrest. Sergeant Wilson advised that they had the bodega under control, and both pieces from the sale to Eddie were in cuffs and were holding two others for investigation. Lieutenant Sarter left our location to check the status of the bodega.

With no threat to our safety, I decided to make myself comfortable. I removed my jacket and vest and placed them on the side. The apartment was clearly a work apartment and had very little furnishings. A single stained mattress lay on the floor in the corner of the bedroom with clothes tossed across it. Dingy curtains barely clung to rods above dirty windows. A boom box was set up near the bed for entertainment. The bathroom paint was chipping off and lay around the floor like dandruff. The mirror was cracked, and the tub had a huge rust spot where water continually dripped from the spout. The living room did not fare any better with a filthy couch pushed against dirty walls. Two low-wattage lightbulbs hung from frayed wires in the middle of the ceiling casting shadows around the room. A makeshift table and chair were against the wall opposite the couch. This was apparently where the subject did his work. There was drug paraphernalia and items used for packaging on the table. Balancing on the edge of the table was a single glassine envelope stamped POISON in black ink with a skull and cross bones. A second glass-ine was found trying to hide under the molding in the hallway leading to the bathroom. Apparently, these two glassines had escaped being flushed down the toilet with the rest of the supply.

Steve was sketching a diagram of the apartment when Lieutenant Sarter's voice came over the radio, "I think we found the buzzer. It appears to be an intercom also. Let me know if you can hear us."

One second later, Papo's voice erupted from the wall, "Larito! Que pasa loco!"

I pushed the button and responded back in a terrible Spanish accent, "Hello, please, who is calling, please?"

Papo fired back, "Let me get a number two with no pickles and supersize it."

I returned volley with, "Thank you. Pull up to the next window please." This was evidence that showed that the two locations were working together. We would remove the intercom faceplate from the bodega, and the faceplate from the apartment, and voucher them both.

I was extremely disappointed with the results regarding the apartment search. The Kilo Fairy had eluded us. Our friend from San Salvador did not speak English and remained mute when questioned in Spanish by Eddie N. About fifteen glassines with the same name brand were recovered from a drawer in the bodega, where Eddie said the seller had gone to retrieve the drugs.

Lieutenant Sarter returned back to the apartment and slowly wandered around. He would stop and examine something, then move on. He tested the floor tiles with his foot, looking for anything unusual. He made his way into the bathroom and stared at the toilet while leaning against the door jam with his hands in his pants pocket. Without changing his posture, he called to Sergeant Cea, "Hey, Tommy."

Sergeant Cea walked over and asked, "What's up, Loo?" (Loo is short for lieutenant.)

With his eyes still focused on the toilet, he asked, "What are the chances that some of the stuff got stuck in the trap of the toilet?"

Tommy thought a moment and said, "I don't know. There is only one way to find out."

Lieutenant Sarter looked at Tommy and smiled, "Then let's find out."

Tommy yelled to Donald, "Don, grab the sledge hammer and give this thing a whack." We turned the water off and drained as much of the toilet as we could.

Don warned, "Watch your eyes," as he delivered a blow to the toilet's porcelain rib cage. Pieces flew through the air and struck the wall, only to fall to the bathroom floor and mix with the dandruff of paint. Water seeped from the wound like blood. Another blow dismantled the toilet for good. I snapped on a rubber glove, knelt in the toilet's blood, and reached down into the unknown. My arm disappeared almost to my elbow as I fished around. My fingers came in contact with something I could not decipher. I prayed to God it wasn't something that would make me lose my lunch.

"I got something. Stand back in case I get sick!" I warned. Holding my breath, I slowly withdrew my arm. Apprehensively, I pulled my hand out and had two bundles of "POISON." Each bundle had ten glassine envelopes. Cheers erupted as I went back in for seconds. As I pulled out three more bundles, my thumb struck a jagged piece of porcelain as the toilet attempted to fight back. A slight gash made my blood drip into the little remaining water turning it pink. I didn't let it deter me as I fished out the last remaining bundles bringing the total to eight or a sum of eighty single glassine envelopes. Now I had something to hang my hat on. We successfully recovered evidence linking both locations together with three bodies. More importantly was the fact that Hammer's information was right on target, and this gave him credibility. It was a small victory in terms of the heroin organization, but it sent a message that they were no longer invincible. For me, this was a tremendous learning experience and would lead to bigger and better things. I called ADA Vernon and reported our findings. She was very pleased and said she would see me tomorrow to draw up the complaint charging the three defendants with sale and possession with intent to sell a controlled substance.

Gathering all our equipment and evidence, we vacated the apartment. I stopped at the superintendent's apartment to let him know that the door and toilet in 3G had to be replaced. We exited the building into the crisp air, and Eddie N. escorted our prisoner out in his underwear. We let him get dressed although I wish we could have sent him through the system in his underwear. The bodega team policed up their gear and had already put their prisoners in the van. As we added ours to the P van (prisoner van), I turned toward the building. There were twenty-five people huddled on the corner who couldn't wait for us to leave. As we caravanned away, the huddled mass moved in unison toward the bodega to get the low down.

THIRTY-SIX

I Want to Kiss You All Over

We had been working very hard and been through some dangerous situations, so we made time to unwind. This was a mandatory unwritten rule of police work. After being in a deadly shootout, fist fights, and foot pursuits with buy subjects, and knocking down doors in search warrants, it was time to crack open some beers and let off steam. For me, this was where never-ending friendships were paved. We went out as a group and ducked into a topless joint just over the border in Queens. Tonight, we were joined by several members of the other teams. It was sort of a family get-together, only grandma wasn't invited.

Heads turned as the front door was pulled open. We entered the bar silhouetted by the remaining sunlight, looking like boxers entering the ring. The energy level changed immediately. About sixteen of us filed in and manned a spot at the back of the bar. There were four or five patrons scattered about the oval bar which surrounded a dance stage. A silver pole stood guard at either end of the stage with another marking dead center. Strategically placed lights aimed at mirrored disco balls sent prisms of colored light dancing off the walls. Seeing fresh money enter the place, both the bar maids and dancers stepped up their game, making their way down to our end of the bar. It was like the place suddenly tilted toward us, sending them sliding in our direction. The bar maid flung coasters around the bar like playing cards, and little fights over who was buying the first round broke out. Agreements were reached as the bar maid snapped off beer caps and placed them on the coasters. Once everyone had a drink in hand, a general toast was made. There is nothing like that first sip of an ice-cold beer.

A dancer wearing a little lavender cut off tee shirt, revealing just a hint of her petite upturned breasts locked on to me. Knowing she had me, she slowly high stepped like a show pony over to my position at the bar. A purple G-string with a matching garter belt made my eyes cascade down her fishnet stockings to her clear spiked high-heeled shoes. The 1978 song "(I want to) Kiss You All Over" by the group Exile pounded in my ears from every direction. She seductively bent over and asked me my name. In my best Barry White voice, I lied, "John, what's yours, baby?" Don't ask me why I lied. It was stupid, I know, but I was feeling mysterious. Or nervous, I'm not quite sure which.

She lied right back, "Candy. You're cute." I think she was talking to the picture of Andrew Jackson lying on the bar in front of me. I complimented her on her purple outfit telling her that I loved the color purple and was a Minnesota Vikings fan. Yeah, I think nervous was more like it. I don't think she knew much about football or where Minnesota was for that matter. At the moment, I couldn't care if she thought that state was a fruit. Her personal geography was well landscaped with perfectly placed hills and valleys. Her gloved hands held her long hair above her head as she lip-synced, "I want to kiss you all over" to me while gyrating her hips. At that moment, we were the only two people in the bar. People were tugging and yelling at me, but I paid no attention to them. My beer was almost finished as I lip-synced, "Show me, show me everything you do" right back at her. As the rhythm of the song and the beer entered my body, I started to gyrate right along with her. She slowly lifted her tee shirt up to reveal two perfectly round breasts with sparkles of glitter which picked up the reflected lights. I grabbed five dollars from my pocket and slipped it into her G-string as she blew me a kiss. Like a tool, I grabbed it and placed it on my lips. AJ was cracking up as he slapped me asking, "What the hell is the matter with you? Are you getting married over here?"

The beers started to go down nice, and Louie decided it was time for the deejay to take a little break. Lou squeezed into the little booth pulling the deejay out. Louie told the deejay he was doing a wonderful job, but that he would take it from here. Once he had that microphone in his hand, it was all over. We acted like Elvis entered the building. Lou started with "Let me hear you say hey…ho" Then he conducted roll call "Tommy's in the house, Sellers' in the house, Larry's in the house, Steve's in the house, etc… He whipped us into a frenzy.

A dancer decided to venture over to our end of the bar to stand in the middle of our shark pool. AJ suddenly morphed into Deney Terrio when he started doing the "bump" as he yelled, "Hey," then did a 180 turn and bumped her again with a "ho." He continued in this fashion going high on some "heys" and low on some "hos." She was trying to conduct a conversation with eight people while AJ thought he was on *Dance Fever*.

An investigator from one of the other teams named John, considered himself an aficionado on strip clubs, claiming he "dated" many strippers. He was conducting a miniclass at the bar as he showed guys how to attract the dancers by displaying a folded twenty-dollar bill in between his fingers. Noting the dollar denomination, the girls would do a little extra dance or show a little extra skin. Then when it came time to deposit the money in the G-string, he did some Criss Angel sleight-of-hand stuff, and the twenty got switched with a one-dollar bill. Technically, I think it could be classified as theft of service or false advertising.

Louie relinquished the music back to the deejay, and a plot was forming in the background. I saw people whispering to one another and laughing. I took my fresh beer over to Tommy Cea and asked him what was going on. He laughed and rubbed his hands together, so I knew it was good, whatever it was. He said a few of the guys were going to grab Albert and tip him over the bar and let the dancer have her way with him. Albert was a straight laced, fair-skinned guy who had an "everything in its place, and a place for everything" attitude. His desk was immaculate. Everything was put there just right, along with his cigarettes and lighter. He won the Martha Stewart award hands down. Kenny Velasquez loved to watch Albert's head turn red like a thermometer by scrambling up his kingdom.

The guys strolled into position near Albert, while a few of us who were privy to the plot tried to contain our excitement. Albert stood quietly near the back wall with a beer in his right hand, his left hand in his pocket. Albert was suddenly attacked, and he put up quite a fight. His beer was dislodged from his hand to protect it from breakage and spillage. He was no match for his attackers. He was sent over the bar head first with a steady cheer of "Al-bert, Al-bert, Al-bert." The dancer, predicting a large reward, strutted over to the helpless Albert. She straddled his head and bounced her G-stringed ass off of his forehead much to the delight of the crowd. He was safely returned to his original spot and handed his beer back. His head was now a painful shade of red. He took it like a man and chugged his beer down.

The festivities continued on as friendships were solidified and refreshed. We learned a lot about each other and fortified our family. There was a genuine love and respect for each other. Color of skin and accents disappeared, and we became one. Inhibitions were also lost as Albert, with glitter all over his forehead, later asked to be hung over the bar one more time!

As the night drew to a close, the bar maids and dancers were sad to see us go. We were very respectful to the dancers and never crossed the line of decency. We had a mutual respect for each other, which made our time spent here almost medicinal. The high energy filed out the door with us, and we returned the club to its steady patrons.

THIRTY-SEVEN

Hammer's World

Work continued as usual while Hammer kept his ear to the ground hoping to mingle with the "right" crowd. He befriended a street hustler named Willie. Willie worked for an organization run by "Boca" that operated on Liberty Avenue in East New York, Brooklyn and also had connections outside the organization. After debriefing Hammer about Willie, I asked Eddie Velasquez his opinion regarding how we could work Willie.

Eddie was the undercover who had made the confirmatory buy before the search warrant on Livonia and Williams. Eddie was small in stature but huge in bravado. He had worked in the Seven-Two precinct before coming to narcotics as an undercover. On patrol in the Seven-Two precinct, he had been involved in armed confrontations and exchanged gunfire with suspects. His five-foot-nothing frame did not deter him from taking care of business.

As an undercover, his work was extraordinary. He told me he would be willing to meet face-to-face with Hammer and discuss what Willie was capable of producing. I arranged for Eddie and Hammer to meet. I was like a nervous parent setting his son up on a blind date. This meeting was important on two levels. First, Eddie had to feel comfortable working with the informant and get a feel for Hammer's personality. Hammer could potentially take Eddie into the belly of the beast and introduce him to some very dangerous people who would be on their turf. Eddie would need to know that Hammer could stand up under stressful situations.

Second, even though we were running the show, Hammer needed to know who he would be introducing to people. If Hammer brought someone who looked and smelled like a cop, there could be some very dangerous repercussions for him and his family. In essence, we were getting ready to put on a play. It was important that we had the right people portraying the right characters. My nervousness was washed away in the first five minutes when these two seemed to hit it off. It took only a few minutes for them to start joking with each other. A relationship was established, and the two agreed that they would work well together.

We decided to ease Eddie into Hammer's world. On our down days (not doing buy and bust), we had Hammer ride with Eddie in the UC auto to meet with Willie. This was to establish Eddie as a friend of Hammer's and to lower Willie's defenses. During the first meeting, no drugs were mentioned. It was a sort of meet and greet. At the next meeting, we nibbled around the edges, planting the seed for later germination and getting the players in the organization comfortable seeing Eddie around. Finally, when we felt the time was right, we attempted to make a purchase from Willie. We started small and wanted to make sure he was selling us quality heroin before we would invest in any larger purchases.

Eddie established himself as a heroin dealer in Staten Island who was looking for a new supplier. We picked Staten Island for two reasons. First was that Eddie was familiar with Staten Island and could answer questions that Willie might have for him. Second, we did not want to pose a threat to the organization that Willie worked for. For the first two buys, Willie kept his distance from Eddie by doing the sale through Hammer. Hammer would set up the day and amount we wanted to buy. Eddie and Hammer would roll up in the UC auto and greet Willie. Willie took Hammer into a bodega and conducted the transaction returning with the narcotics. The heroin purchased was sent to the police lab where it was found to be of good quality.

Things were going well, but we needed to raise the bar. We needed Eddie to establish a direct connection with Willie and eliminate Hammer from the equation. We decided that Eddie and Hammer would stop and see Willie unannounced. Eddie's car was a familiar site on Liberty Avenue and didn't interrupt the workers and lookouts as they went about their business when Eddie pulled onto the block. Willie greeted Eddie and the CI. Eddie told Hammer to take a walk and to give him a few minutes to talk to Willie. Hammer stepped off as requested. Once Willie got into the car, Eddie explained to him that he was looking to purchase a larger amount of heroin. Eddie told Willie that Hammer was a good kid, but he was unreliable and wanted to deal directly with Willie to save him money and time. Willie agreed, seeing Eddie as a potentially steady customer and gave Eddie his phone number. Now we were in a position to deal with Willie on a regular basis without Hammer having to be present.

Now that Eddie had established himself, we needed to purchase a larger quantity of heroin to justify Eddie's story and to obtain the higher criminal charge. Eddie contacted Willie and said he needed to buy a "brick," ten bundles with each bundle consisting of ten glassine envelopes, for a total of one hundred glassines. This was a sign that Eddie's Staten Island spot was slowly growing, and it gave us more time to investigate the organization.

Because of the increase in product, Willie could no longer deal on that level and introduced us to another member known as Carlos. Upon arriving on Liberty Avenue to make the purchase, Willie introduced Carlos. The meeting went well. Eddie explained what he needed and reiterated his Staten Island spot to Carlos. Carlos told Eddie to give him a few minutes. A short time later, Carlos returned with Boca who wanted to get a feel for his new potential customer. A cautious Boca quizzed Eddie as his eyes searched the area around him for anything out of the ordinary. Eddie's skill and ability to submerge himself in his character convinced Boca that Eddie was okay. Boca gave Carlos the nod to do the transaction, and we hit pay dirt, getting the head of the organization involved in a direct sale. On another occasion, Eddie met with Carlos and Boca, and the surveillance team was able to capture Boca calculating a price using a dirty car window for a chalkboard.

Through surveillance techniques and good old-fashioned detective work, we were able to determine that Boca lived in a private house in Queens. We quickly had a pole camera setup, taping his residence twenty-four hours a day. All the team members took turns reviewing the VHS tapes of Boca's home, filling out an activity sheet, making note of the time and people arriving and leaving the household. This allowed us to establish a routine for Boca and would help identify the people that visited the house every day.

As our purchases from Carlos increased in frequency and amount, we wanted to let out a little more net in order to catch more fish. Eddie contacted Willie, telling him that he was having territorial issues with another drug dealer in Staten Island, and that he needed some "heat"—guns—to protect his interests. Willie was a true hustler with connections to everything, and we needed those connections exploited.

All of our telephone conversations were recorded, and it was my job as the case officer to maintain custody of these tapes for evidence. During one of these taped conversations, Willie notified Eddie that he had two pieces he could sell. Eddie asked him if he had bullets for each, and Willie said no. Eddie replied firmly, "What good are they if I don't have bullets? What am I supposed to do throw it at them? Call me back when you get the ammo." Willie said he would work on the ammo and get back to him. If the guns came with ammo, they were considered loaded and carried a heavier charge.

When Willie had the proper ammunition in hand, he called Eddie back and a place and time was agreed upon. Willie lived in the Bronx, so Sergeant Cea, Steve Brown, and I had searched the Bronx for a location that would be to our advantage. We wanted someplace where we could hide undercover officers and members of the field team in order to protect Eddie. With narcotics transactions, you always assume that dealers could have firearms. But with gun buys, you *knew* they'd have them.

We decided on Macombs Dam Park located directly across the street from Yankee Stadium. Tommy and I were both big Yankee fans, and it was the only place in the Bronx that we actually knew how to get to. This park of 44.17 acres was opened in 1899 and named after the Macombs family who operated a dam and mill on the site in the nineteenth century. (Now the home of the new Yankee Stadium.) It was wide open and provided perfect cover to secrete undercover officers for safety.

After doing a recon on the location, Tommy Cea and I decided to take a stroll into Yankee Stadium. With our shields displayed, we had no problem getting in. We walked straight down to the Yankee dugout and sat on the bench while a grounds crew worked on the field. I looked to the end of the bench and imagined Babe Ruth, Mickey Mantle, and Joe DiMaggio sitting there. Any true baseball fan, regardless of what team they cheered for, would have been jealous of us. I also pictured Billy Martin and Reggie Jackson going at it right next to me. Just to be able to see their point of view from the dugout brought goose bumps to my flesh. Tommy is a *huge* Yankee fan, and he sat there with the biggest grin on his face. He started rubbing his hands together as he said, "I want to walk out to the mound. Do you think they would mind?"

I said, "Well, there is only one way to find out." With that, we got up and stepped onto the field. I walked over to home plate while Tommy made his way out to the mound. We were thirteen years old again. You never would have thought that just a few minutes ago, we were planning an operation to purchase illegal guns.

As he got to the mound, I could hear voices getting louder behind us in the stands. Then a voice yelled, "Hey, you're not supposed to be out there." Tommy waved acknowledgement and headed back to the dugout. As we passed through the tunnels behind the dugout, we peeked into the Yankee locker room and found our way out. We walked with a little bit of a swagger, carrying the memory of the dugout with us as we left the stadium.

With an increased potential for danger, we decided do to some risk management. It was agreed that Steve Brown would accompany Eddie on the gun buy. Steve was an investigator and not technically an undercover, but as usual, he accepted his assignment without complaint. We also had new additions to the team. We had acquired three new UCs, Michael Stoney, Rodney Harrison, and Manny Gonzalez. We also had acquired two new investigators, Charley Mackie and Lee Ann Johnson. All fit right in perfectly and were great assets to the team.

We picked a day that the Yanks were on the road to diminish any possible threat to the public just in case things got ugly. We carefully planned out coverage for Steve and Eddie's safety. Stoney, Rodney, Patty, and Mark Amos were our basketball team. Charley Mackie (the old-timer) sat in McDonald's on the corner of River Avenue and E161 Street. We had people walking on the track, sitting in the stands and pedestrians passing by. Steve Zimmerman was going to videotape the transaction from a surveillance van.

We got setup about an hour before the buy was scheduled to let the field team members blend into their surroundings. We kept alert for any counter surveillance. The deal was set to go down on the park side of Ruppert Place and E161 Street. We were buying two 9-mm handguns for three hundred fifty dollars a piece plus ammunition for both guns.

Our basketball team worked up a nice sweat, and now it was time to send in the UCs. The meeting was scheduled to happen in ten minutes, and we wanted to make sure that everyone could get a good eyeball on Eddie and Steve. Sergeant Cea gave Eddie the green light to take his position on E161 Street. The car rolled into view, and the wire was coming in loud and clear. This time I had Papo with us to translate if there was any Spanish conversation. Our people around the area acknowledged that they had the UCs in sight. It now became a waiting game.

Generally, these things never go as scheduled. Most criminals have no concept of time, and it annoys the shit out of me. Is it too much to ask that you sell me my illegal guns and controlled substances at the agreed upon time? As narcotics cops, we are completely regulated by time. We are required to complete a DAR (daily activity report) which accounts for every minute of every day in military time even if we are off duty or on vacation. I generally got mine done on a daily basis and took some flak for it from the rest of the team. The majority waited until the sergeant came out of his office to announce to everybody that he needed their DARs for the past thirty or sixty days. Then everyone would go into a mad scramble fighting for the old roll calls and looking for their notes that they scribbled down on napkins and pads. This was referred to as being in DAR hell. On one of these days, I would ask someone if they wanted to go out for a sit-down meal, and their response was, "Can't. I'm in DAR hell."

Craig Johnson broke radio silence stating, "I think our boy is here, boss. He is in the company of a female Hispanic walking down E161 Street from River Avenue. The female has a knapsack on."

Tommy Cea replied, "Ten-four. Okay, field team, let's be on our toes. We got bad guy plus one female heading to the meet location."

Willie came into Eddie's view as he talked over the hidden microphone, "Okay, boss, he's here and it looks like he has a female with him."

Steve Zimmerman notified us he had the subjects in view and rolling. Eddie exited the UC auto, followed by Steve. Willie slowed his pace once he saw Steve get out of the car. Eddie walked toward Willie as Steve settled against the fence with his arms crossed keeping a watchful eye. Willie gestured for the girl to stop as he cautiously greeted Eddie.

The conversation was in Spanish, so Papo translated, "Willie wants to know who the black guy is. Eddie told him he was cool; he's with me."

Steve stood guard giving Eddie and Willie some space to conduct business. Even though he was off to the side, his presence was powerful. Willie kept a wary eye on Steve, gazing over in his direction every now and then. When Willie felt comfortable, he called over the female with the knapsack. Willie handed it to Eddie who inspected its contents. Eddie made it clear over the wire that the order was complete and passed the buy money to Willie. Willie put the money in his pocket never bothering to check the amount. The two hugged and promised to stay in touch. Willie stole one last glance at Steve and stepped away with his friend heading back in the direction they came from. I followed Eddie's car off the set, giving him a cushion looking for a possible tail. We met at a designated safe area to debrief Eddie and to get custody of the guns.

I felt exhilarated that our meet went as planned. Eddie did an amazing job by remaining true to his character under a very stressful situation. Eddie said, "Piece of cake, boss. This guy will get us anything we want." He turned toward Steve and said, "Willie is scared shitless of this guy. He couldn't stop looking at him."

Steve laughed saying, "That's right. He better be scared of me if he knows what's good for him." I took the knapsack from Eddie and peeked inside to reveal our two 9-mm semiautomatic handguns complete with ammo.

Tommy said, "Great job, guys. Head back to the barn."

THIRTY-EIGHT

ATF

As the case progressed, we got a new lieutenant assigned to SNAG. His name was Jack Walsh. His nickname was Cocktail Jack although he didn't drink. He stood about five foot seven inches tall with pushed back hair and a thick mustache. He was a runner and only carried about one hundred fifty pounds on his small frame. This man never seemed to have a bad day. If he did he never let on, hiding it behind a huge smile which he took with him to the office. In my experience, his demeanor was always pleasant and positive. He brought many years of crime-fighting experience to the unit. His specialty was guns. He was personally responsible for getting hundreds of guns off the streets of Brooklyn South. He was delighted to hear that our team had a gun case running, and he was instrumental in bringing the case to a higher level.

Years ago, working together with Alcohol, Tobacco and Firearms (ATF) Agent William Fredericks, Cocktail Jack targeted Jamaican gun-trafficking gangs. Bill Fredericks was now the supervisor of ATF Group V, which had a few NYPD housing cops assigned. Jack Walsh pulled me and Sergeant Cea into his office and asked us our thoughts about bringing ATF into this case. He explained the advantages of having a federal law enforcement agency involved. Number one was that firearms were their specialty. Number two were the assets that would be made available to us. The ATF had an unlimited amount of funds to buy narcotics and guns. The police department frowned on spending a lot of money. At this level, once you bought narcotics from a subject two times, the NYPD wanted the guy arrested. Joined with ATF, we could use federal monies to continue to buy guns and narcotics to help us keep the case running, giving us time to make a more thorough investigation. We would also be able to access federal databases and trace the life of the gun. For me, it was a no brainer: bring them in.

Lieutenant Walsh set up a meeting with the ATF that would take place at our office in the Brooklyn Navy Yard. Bill Fredericks arrived with Agent Mike Santory and NYPD Housing Police Officer James Dobbins. Agent Santory had been an NYPD cop for three and a half years assigned to the Manhattan South Task Force before leaving to join ATF and had a working knowledge of the police department.

Billy Fredericks was a very relaxed guy with a shaggy hairdo. During our meeting, he crossed his legs while sitting in the chair, and I noticed that he had on one blue sock and one black sock. I felt comfortable enough to bring this to his attention, and he laughed it off, blaming his wife. The oddest thing I learned about him was that he never carried a gun. An Alcohol, Tobacco and Firearms agent who never carried a gun? It was extremely strange to me, but the guy knew how to get bad guys off the streets.

With ATF on our team, the case took off. We were buying guns from Willie on a regular basis. He would take Eddie to different locations in Brooklyn as we purchased guns like the Intratec Tec-9, Ingram Mac-10, and Ingram Mac-11 submachine guns. Eddie also purchased a Tec 22 Scorpion semiauto machine pistol. And on occasion, we continued to purchase heroin from Carlos to keep that end of the case active.

Hammer was very much active in the case even though he was not riding with Eddie. When he was not working as a limo driver, he would periodically show up to visit Carlos and Boca and keep us updated on the organization. Hammer had decided to make a difference working with us. He didn't want to lose his family to prison. Unfortunately, he would be faced with a deadlier battle much larger than any court case or prison sentence. Hammer was diagnosed with AIDS. His years of drug use had finally caught up to him. I was deeply saddened by the news because I genuinely grew to like him. I felt sorry for his wife and son who we had met on several occasions.

Apparently, old habits are hard to break. As much as Hammer enjoyed working for us, he was still a street hustler by nature. I received a call from a cop in Queens asking me if I had a confidential informant who goes by the code name Hammer. I said I did, and the cop told me he had Hammer under arrest for grand larceny. It seems that Hammer was attempting to steal a copy machine from the Queens County Courthouse. I shook my head and asked what happened. I envisioned Hammer lifting a small machine and trying to exit the building. However, that was not the case. This genius, along with another genius, decided to abscond with a commercial, heavy-duty copy machine which they somehow managed to maneuver onto a hand truck. They almost made it out the building under the disguise of repairmen, but an alert court officer stopped and questioned the pair. They obviously didn't have the right answers, and as the saying goes, "Do not pass GO, go directly to jail." He attempted to use his "get out of jail free" card which I vehemently stamped DENIED.

Hammer had managed to take three steps backward, and ADA Vernon was not very pleased with his decision making. While in jail, Hammer was recruited by the Latin Kings, a violent street gang, which pursued members in jail and put them to work upon their release. He became known as King Ray Ray and was given a set of the Latin Kings bylaws which outline the philosophy of the gang along with chants and prayers that are nothing more than brainwashing material. Tommy Cea and I went to Rikers Island where we had a little sit-down with Hammer and basically ripped him a new asshole. He knew he had fucked up and was very remorseful. He handed me an envelope with the bylaws which I turned over to the Gang Unit for intelligence purposes. After a short stay in jail, Hammer was released and eager to continue working with us.

THIRTY-NINE

Don't Lose My Money

Willie had cut his ties with Boca and worked strictly freelance. We decided to test Willie's hustling skills. Eddie called Willie and told Willie that he had an associate who was looking to pick up two kilos of cocaine. Eddie instructed Willie to get the best price possible so that he could make some money on the resale. Willie said he would make some calls and get back to him.

Being the true hustler that he was, a few days later, Willie phoned Eddie and informed him that he had a supplier who was willing to sell two kilos of cocaine for $24,500 each. Eddie agreed to the price, telling Willie that he could resell them for $25,000 a piece and make a quick thousand-dollar profit. Willie said that he was out of town, but the supplier was willing to meet with Eddie and ready to do the deal *now*. Eddie told Willie that he needed a day or two to get the money together and would call him back.

Tommy, Eddie, Steve, and I went to Captain Hickey's office and informed him of the results of the undercover phone conversation with Willie. Captain Hickey said he wanted someone to go with Eddie. Eddie replied, "I'll take Steve with me, boss. Nobody's gonna fuck with me if I got Steve with me." He was extremely pleased and told me to get the necessary paperwork together and run over to headquarters to get the $49,000 flash roll.

Captain Hickey said, "I'll let you, guys, do this, BUT, and listen to me carefully, I want it done someplace where you can cover these two like a blanket. A hundred kilos means shit to me if one of my guys gets hurt. You got me?" We understood completely, and now, it was my job to acquire the funds and find a location that would give us every possible advantage.

After scouting out a number of locations, we decided on the Caesar's Bay Bazaar located on the water in south Brooklyn just off the Belt Parkway. This was a commercial shopping strip which would allow us to stage officers around the area without giving up their identity.

Caesar's Bay Bazaar was right along a pier at the water's edge, and we wanted to cover every possible scenario. One such scenario was that the bad guy could jump into the water and escape. Sergeant Cea arranged for us to have the Aviation Unit give us a ride in the police helicopter to get a bird's eye view of the area and see what kind of options we had.

Tommy, Steve, and I arrived at Floyd Bennett Field off of Flatbush Avenue in Brooklyn and met with our two pilots who would be giving us the ride. Unfortunately, due to weight restraints, only two of us could take the ride and it was decided that Steve would remain behind. Since Steve was acting as an undercover in this scenario, it was advantageous that I take the ride because I was a part of the arresting team. Plus, being the case officer had its benefits too. Steve, as usual, took it like the man he was, without complaining. He's a better man than I because I would have thrown my sippy cup to the ground and would have to be carried away stomping and screaming. We explained the purpose of the flight to the pilots and the area we wanted to cover. With everyone on the same page, we headed out to the airfield.

Once we were buckled in and headsets were in place, we were ready for takeoff. After completing all necessary cross-checks and getting the nod to lift off, the chopper separated itself from the earth. We swayed ever so slightly as the ground pushed away from underneath us. The nose dipped forward and away we went. At that moment, I was transformed into a little boy on a wondrous adventure only a few can say they have experienced. We were all able to communicate to each other through the headsets as I'm sure I voiced a volley of "holy shit" through the airways.

In a matter of seconds, the city, the earth for that matter, had been trans-formed into this canvas of beauty. I shifted from side to side and tried to cap-ture a panoramic view of the world below me. In no time, the pilot informed us that we were above our target location. After several passes of the area, we were satisfied that we could make the necessary decisions to take down our suspects. The pilot asked if we were in a hurry to get back to the base, or if we would like to stay aboard while they completed their aerial patrol. I excitedly looked at Tommy as if to say, "Is it okay? Can we stay, Dad, please?"

But at that point, he was like my older brother and said, "We got all day!"

The pilots pointed the vessel toward Manhattan. We flew so close to the Statue of Liberty that I could say I actually looked her right in the eye. After a couple of loops, we headed toward the southern tip of Manhattan where the majestic kings, the Twin Towers, stood tall and proud as they stretched toward the cloudless blue sky. Being on a level with them gave me a sense of the kind of dominance they had as they looked down on the other structures rooted on the island. Gliding above the Hudson River, our trip was cut short due to a transmission received from the pilots command center indicating that their assistance was requested by units on the ground. We did an abrupt about face and headed back toward Brooklyn.

On the ground and a safe distance from the landing pad, the chopper once again defied gravity and lifted off to render its point-of-view assistance to other officers in need. We graciously thanked the members of the Aviation Unit for their help and joined the rat race back in our neck of Brooklyn.

Armed with all the information we needed, we began to map out our plan of attack. Department of Environmental Protection (DEP) also had an office located in the Brooklyn Navy Yard. The management agreed to allow us to borrow one of their pickup trucks and some equipment for the day of our takedown. Tommy and I wrote out our tactical plan for the operation. We had officers assigned as shoppers. We had officers seated on benches. We even had an officer who agreed to bring his fishing equipment and pose as a fisherman on the pier. We had cops in vehicles in case we had to go mobile. We determined that the "DEP crew" would set up at the mouth of the street that led into the shopping bazaar and would shut it down once the bad guys were on the set.

Having had the tactical plan and request for funds paperwork completed and signed on our level, it was time to bring it over the bridge to Manhattan to the powers that be. We pitched our plan to CHOCC (chief of Organized Crime Control), Chief O'Boyle, who personally signed off on our request for forty-nine thousand dollars in U.S. currency. He made it very clear, "Don't lose my money."

Once I was issued the check in my name, I called the supervisor at the bank to give her a heads up that I would be making a large cash withdrawal. I wanted the bills broken down mostly in hundreds and fifties with a couple of thousand in twenties. Tommy and I gave the bank supervisor some time to get the funds together and then started our walk downtown from One Police Plaza. At the bank, we were greeted by the supervisor who took us to a private room where we recounted the money for accuracy. We bundled up the money in paper bags which I carried under my coat as we walked back toward 1 PP. I was passing hundreds of people with forty-nine thousand dollars in cash just under my coat. I wondered what people would do if they knew. I also started to look at other people and wondered what they were carrying just under their coats. If I was doing it, what's to say that the person who I brushed shoulders with wasn't doing the same!

We arrived safely back at our office in Brooklyn, and I began the tedious chore of recording the serial numbers of all the bills by photocopying them on the copy machine. Steve would fold the bills in half, and then I would align them in rows on the machine. I would hit the Copy button, remove them, unfold them, and start again. Wash, rinse, repeat.

After a few phone calls between Willie and Eddie, a day and time was set for the meet. Willie told Eddie that the guy was Colombian. Willie spoke up for Eddie telling the Colombian that Eddie was "good" people and explained that he had been doing business with Eddie for a while, and he could be trusted. The Colombian was working off the word of Willie and decided to do this deal without first meeting his new customer.

The office was electric the morning of the undercover operation. It was another welcome diversion from the old grind of buy and bust. We had a chance to finally seize some "weight" to bite off a bigger piece of the pie. Eddie was his jovial self, but Steve was a bit more quiet than usual. Eddie didn't want to wear the hidden wire in case the suspect got too touchy. Steve agreed to have the wire taped to his body in the event we lost sight of them for any length of time. This was my case, and I felt totally responsible for the safety of my undercovers and the field team. I would never ask a fellow officer to do something they were not one hundred percent comfortable with. There would always be another way to tackle the situation. Eddie was going to come face-to-face with the suspect, but I felt more nervous than him. His confidence never wavered, which lowered my internal stress level from ten to an eight-point-five.

The tactical plan meeting in the sergeant's office was a little more serious than usual. Everyone knew their assignments and understood how important their role was to ensure the safety of Eddie and Steve. We needed to work as a well-oiled machine to seize the cocaine and unknown suspects without injury to civilians and officers. I invited ATF Agent Mike Santory who was more than willing to help lend his support to the operation.

Sergeant Cea outlined the way the whole operation would go down. The field team would set up at their designated positions. Steve Ziegler would be fishing on the pier. Ernie and Kenny would set up the DEP truck at the mouth of the entrance street to the shopping area. The rest of the officers would be divided up in autos and on foot in the vicinity of the meet location. When the field team was in place, Eddie and Steve Brown would roll into position and await a phone call from the bad guys. Once we knew the bad guys were on the set, we would tighten the net around them. DEP workers would shut down the road, and pedestrian officers would get closer without giving up their identities.

The Colombian might ask to see the money, in which case Eddie would call Sergeant Cea and ask for the money to be sent in. Big Patty and J. C. were designated as the money auto. They would roll up and flash the money to satisfy the bad guy's appetite and immediately leave with the cash to eliminate any thoughts of robbery. Once the Colombian produced the product (cocaine), the ever tightening net would get wrapped around their necks, and these drug dealers would be rewarded with their very own arrest numbers. Thanks for playing.

Everyone took the necessary steps gathering their equipment, supporting their spoke in the wheel. I readied the sergeant's auto and rigged up the receiver. Ernie and Kenny pulled the DEP pickup truck to the front of the office. The pickup certainly wasn't the pride of the fleet, but it would have to do. Beggars can't be choosers, and we were just happy to add another dimension to the field team. It had wooden horses and shovels along with other small bits of wood and tools. Kenny and Ernie each had their very own DEP hard hat and orange safety vest. Steve Z. walked out with his high-water waders on, net, and pole in tow. It was almost as if we were preparing for a masquerade ball. Almost. These guys were going to completely blend into the surroundings.

Sergeant Cea walked to the car with Papo who would again be our Spanish translator if the situation dictated. Tommy Cea carried a small gym bag with the forty-nine thousand dollars, divided into one-thousand-dollar packets for easy verification in case the Colombian wanted to count it. Tommy seemed relaxed and confident as he chuckled at the appearance of our costume wearers saying, "These guys look great." Once the wire on Steve was deemed to be working properly and everyone was ready in their autos, we proceeded through the gates of the Navy Yard en route to the other end of Brooklyn.

We merged into traffic onto I-278, Brooklyn Queens Expressway, heading toward the Verrazano Bridge which would take us to the Belt Parkway. We drove in no particular order or lane. Anyone who lives in New York knows that the Brooklyn Queens Expressway is not one of the city's greatest thoroughfares. It is practically a minefield with potholes big enough to loosen your fillings. Tommy, Papo, and I burst into laughter as we observed the DEP pickup truck up ahead of us. It was sputtering black smoke and would occasionally lose pieces of wood as its wheels thumped through the land mines. I said, "Oh, boy, we are definitely going to generate some sort of complaint for the DEP today."

In spite of the fact that the DEP truck was a little lighter than when it started out, we all arrived safely in the vicinity of the Caesar's Bay Bazaar. It was comical to watch Steve Z. drop a line off the pier wearing his high-water waders. If there was a threat of a tidal wave, Steve was prepared for it. The DEP workers setup shop at the mouth of the street. The nondescript officers blended into the crowd, and we were ready to do business. The UCs stayed off the set, and I remained mobile, checking the area for counter surveillance. I turned the corner off of Shore Parkway, and we couldn't help but laugh as we observed our DEP crew setting up wooden horses around a manhole cover that they had somehow managed to open. After determining that everyone was in their place, I parked the car with an unobstructed view of the area. Now it was only a waiting game.

Something caught my eye to the right. A Con Edison truck had pulled over and stopped to converse with our DEP boys. We all laughed thinking the same thing, "Uh-ho, that can't be good." We were prepared to go over and assist the DEP guys in getting the Con Ed workers off the set when after a few minutes, they pulled away.

When it was safe to transmit, Ernie came over the point-to-point radio, "Did you see that, boss?"

Tommy answered, "Yeah, is everything okay?"

"Yeah, we're good. They wanted to know why DEP was working in one of their manholes."

We were cracking up as Tommy asked, "What did you say?"

Ernie replied, "We fed them a line of bullshit, and they bought it, so we're good."

Laughing, Tommy said into the radio, "Okay, Ernie, good job. Don't get hurt out there."

I could imagine them giving the Con Ed guys a little *The Honeymooners* meets *Back to the Future* bullshit with "Uh, yeah, we are just checking the, uh, armature sprocket which regulates the control of the flow into the dyna flow of the, uh, flux capacitor. Yeah, that's it." God, I love these guys.

Tommy's cell phone rang. It was Eddie telling him that the Colombian called and wanted to meet at the Nebraska Diner on Cropsey Avenue and Shore Parkway. Tommy said, "Get him to meet us here as planned."

Eddie replied, "I did, boss. He said he is not familiar with the area, but he knows how to get to the Nebraska Diner."

God forbid drug dealers stick to a plan! This guy wanted to throw away several hours of my valuable time that I had spent planning this whole thing, just like that. I felt like a housewife who slaves hours over a hot stove, when her husband comes home and wants to go to McDonald's for a number two value meal.

Tommy told Eddie to give us a minute or two. I drove to the Nebraska Diner, just a short drive down the road. On the same side of the street was a large parking area for a supermarket with a number of people coming and going. There was a Burger King restaurant across the street. We could make this location work for us. We felt we could provide a level of coverage that would ensure the safety of Eddie and Steve. Tommy Cea made a command decision to move the operation down to the Nebraska Diner. Steve Z. packed up his tackle box and DEP closed the manhole cover and rerouted to the area of the diner.

Once we were readjusted and in position, we let Steve and Eddie roll onto the set. We observed them park in the diner lot and enter the building. A short time later, Eddie called Tommy and said, "He's here, boss. He said he is pulling into the lot." A black livery type auto entered the diner's lot and parked. A man in his thirties entered the diner and sat at the table with Steve and Eddie. The man carried on a conversation with Eddie in Spanish which Papo translated. All was going well, and the talk was calm. Eddie got up from the table and went outside the diner with the male. Steve remained in the booth and advised us of what was happening.

We could observe Eddie and the male exiting the diner and heading over to the guy's car. We couldn't make out exactly what was happening as the two stood just outside the car. Eddie started walking back into the diner by himself. Tommy's phone rang again. It was Eddie, "Boss, we don't need the money.

I saw the shit. He's standing outside the car, but there is a woman and a kid inside the car. Take him down."

With those words, my body temperature started to rise as my internal control system said, "Here we go again!" Tommy took a deep breath and then commanded into the radio, "Okay, field team, let's take him down. We got the male outside the car and one female inside with a child."

That transmission put all the spokes of the wheel in motion as we closed in on the suspects. Making my way through the parking lot, I could see Big Patty getting to the suspect first. In the blink of an eye, the suspect was gone from my view. I heard a slight crashing noise somewhere behind me as I weaved my way over to the diner's lot. We jumped from our cars, and now I saw the suspect face down on the pavement with his hands cuffed behind his back. The female was taken out of the auto and handcuffed. In the backseat was a small child strapped in a car seat and crying. I crawled into the car and found a diaper bag. I pushed aside some unused diapers to reveal, drum roll please, the Kilo Fairy twins! Yes, two kilo packages of cocaine were officially seized by the Brooklyn North Strategic Narcotics and Guns Unit without incident or injury. Well, maybe just a little lump or swelling, courtesy of Big Patty.

As things were settling down, I noticed ATF agent Mike Santory checking the front grill of his auto. It turns out that the crashing noise I heard was Mike smashing through some shopping carts to get to the arrest location. His car was fine. I'm not so sure about the shopping carts, but our mission was to get to Eddie at any cost. Eddie informed us that he had asked the male subject why they had brought the child along with him. The suspect matter-of-factly replied that they do it all the time so that the police don't get suspicious or stop them.

The husband and wife, along with the child, were charged with 220.43 of the New York State Penal Law, a class A-1 felony, which states that a person is guilty of criminal sale of a controlled substance in the first degree when he knowingly and unlawfully sells one or more preparations, compounds, mixtures or substances containing a narcotic drug and the preparations, compounds, mixtures or substances are of an aggregate weight of two ounces or more.

I had a lot of trouble trying to fingerprint the child because his fingers were so damn tiny. For his mug shot, I had to hold him up and then turn him sideways for a profile shot. It must be pretty cool to be the only one in your pre-k school with an A-1 felony rap sheet. All right, take it easy, settle down. Of course, I'm joking. I do have a heart you know. I only charged him with a misdemeanor.

The husband-and-wife team were processed and brought down to Brooklyn Central Booking. The infant was turned over to family members after notification was made to the Bureau of Child Welfare. Using your child as cover for your narcotics trafficking business says a lot about your parenting skills. I later testified in Family Court regarding the incident, and I can only hope that the child was removed from their custody. More importantly, I was able to return Chief O'Boyle's money back to the bank with a very happy ending. Eddie once again worked his magic like the true professional that he was. His "I can do anything" persona was contagious and gave me the courage and confidence to continue my long-term case.

We reviewed the surveillance tape taken by our observation team of the two-kilo rip. The video was synced with the audio from the hidden wire that Steve had secreted on his body. As we watched the tape unfold, we noticed a steady thumping noise on the tape which baffled us. The thumping noise interfered with the audio and drowned out some of the conversation. It was suggested that we take the monitoring equipment out of service and send to the shop for repair. Steve Brown said, "Wait a minute. Rewind it a little." The tape sped backward for a moment and then began to play at normal speed. We sat quietly and listened again to the steady noise. Steve laughed a second then said, "There's nothing wrong with the tape. That's my heartbeat! I had the wire taped on my chest over my heart!" That gave us a good laugh as we were convinced that that was indeed the case. Steve could save money on his next physical by not getting an echocardiogram. All he would have to do was bring the surveillance tape to his doctor.

FORTY

Ready for Patrol in Baghdad

After the arrest of the Colombian drug dealers and the seizure of two kilos of cocaine under our belts, we decided it was time to reel in Willie. Anticipating that word would travel back that the drug transaction he brokered went bad, we feared Willie might hold Hammer responsible for getting introduced to Eddie and harm Hammer or his family.

Sergeant Cea and I met with Hammer and informed him of what had transpired. As you would expect, Hammer was full of street bravado and claimed not to be afraid of Willie, insisting he could take care of himself and his family. Although I believed Hammer meant what he said, his appearance told me otherwise. The effect of AIDS began to show its presence. His eyes looked hollow, and his once muscular body was diminishing in size. We convinced him to let us put him up at a hotel while things cooled down.

Sergeant Cea and I picked up Hammer, along with his wife and son, and checked them into a hotel on the outskirts of Kennedy Airport. The saddest part was that they believed that they were actually on a vacation. They were truly happy staying in this one-star hotel away from the neighborhood, renting movies and ordering room service. It was a humbling experience for me and let me know how blessed my life has been.

With the Hammer family safely away on "vacation," we began the task of hunting down Willie. Sifting through telephone records, we determined that Willie was residing in Bethlehem Pennsylvania. We narrowed it down to two addresses in the same complex. Since Willie was our link to the purchase of illegal firearms and was charged with federal crimes, we teamed up with ATF Agent Santory for the takedown. Because Willie was out of state, Mike contacted agents in the Philadelphia ATF office for assistance. This was their jurisdiction, and the agents would be familiar with the target area.

Tommy Cea, Steve Brown, Eddie Velasquez, and I packed into one of our cars and followed ATF Agent Mike Santory to a safe location in the vicinity of Bethlehem, PA. We were met by two ATF agents assigned to the Philadelphia office.

These two guys were as serious as they come. There was no play in their game. One agent was about six foot three inches tall with a bald head, and the other was about six foot even with a military buzz cut. Their eyes were hidden behind dark reflective eyewear which added to their "don't fuck with me" attitude. They wore combat boots and commando-style pants with *way* too many pockets.

We briefed them on our case history with Willie, two possible target addresses for him, and supplied them a recent photo. After hearing Willie's involvement in the illegal sale of several guns and numerous drug sales, including a two-kilo seizure, the agents were not about to take any chances. The agents opened up the trunk of their car, which contained an MP5 submachine gun, ammunition, binoculars, sophisticated tracking devices, transmitting and receiving equipment, first aid kit and other new-age surveillance equipment. They strapped their tactical web gear to their waist, which was secured at the thigh. They locked in their 9-mm Sig Sauer handguns with two extra ammo clips and ducked their heads into the heavy-duty body armor. They were ready for patrol in Baghdad.

After watching this process take place, and believe me it was a process, I took stock of myself and my team members. We were all dressed in dungaree jeans with sneakers. Eddie, Steve, and I each had a six-shot .38 caliber handgun tucked in a side holster with no extra rounds and handcuffs hanging out of our back pants pockets. Tommy had a Glock 19 semi auto handgun in his jacket pocket, he had six loose .38 caliber rounds. While the big bad government agents were gearing up to the max, Tommy passed out two extra rounds to the three of us city folk, which I dropped in my jeans pocket. If I popped open the trunk to our car, I would have been very excited to see a usable spare tire. A lug wrench would probably be asking too much.

After the briefing and "gearing up" were complete, we decided that the agents would sit on one location, and we would sit on the other. We were supplied point-to-point radios. If they spotted a person who they thought was the subject, we would drive over, and Eddie would make the confirmatory identification.

While we were in our car, we all had a good chuckle over the immense difference between the two agencies, as I'm sure they did as well. Doing surveillance and sitting on locations can become quite tedious and boring. You could sit for hours at a time by yourself with nothing to report for your efforts. Fortunately this time, we got results right away. Eddie immediately spotted Willie exiting out of our location, walking in our direction. We advised the agents that we had an eyeball on the subject. Willie walked toward our car, and when he was close enough, we calmly got out and placed him under arrest without any fanfare. The agent's car swopped in and skidded to a stop. I think they were a little disappointed it went so smoothly after all the energy they had exerted in preparation.

Being out of our jurisdiction, we had to produce Willie in the nearest federal court (Philadelphia) to have an extradition hearing in order to bring him back to New York. Willie was being charged federally, so Agent Mike Santory took charge of this aspect of Willie's arrest. The suspect was turned over to the U.S. Marshall's office, where his transportation to the Eastern District of the United States Attorney's Office would be arranged.

FORTY-ONE

Detective

In the meantime, Thomas Scotto, president of the Detective Endowment Association (police detective's union known as the DEA) and the City of New York had locked horns in a long drawn out court battle regarding the promotion of police officers to the rank of detective.

The New York Court of Appeals ruled:

IN THE MATTER OF THOMAS J. SCOTTO, &C., ET AL., RESPONDENTS, v DAVID M. DINKINS, &C., ET AL., APPELLANTS:

Any person who has received permanent appointment as a police officer and is temporarily assigned to perform the duties of a detective shall, whenever such assignment exceeds eighteen months in duration, be appointed as a detective and receive the compensation ordinarily paid to a detective performing such duties.

What did all that mean to me? Having been assigned to BNSNAG (an investigative unit) for twenty-two months, it meant that I would be getting promoted to the rank of third-grade detective! Every week, I would come into work and check with the clerical staff to see if a teletype message had come down from headquarters announcing promotions.

One day, I was sitting at my desk catching up on some paperwork when Debbie, one of the police administrative aides, crosses over the threshold into the investigative side of the office with a teletype in hand. She stood at attention, and in a "hear ye, hear ye" manner announced that on April 7, 1995, the following officers will be promoted to the rank of detective third grade:

Stephen Brown
Adam Croom
Michael Girardin
Lawrence Hoffman
Ernest Lentini
Jerome Pugh
Vincenzo Romano
Walter Rossler
Doreen Scrimenti
Steven Swan
Craig Taylor

Congratulatory cheers erupted from all corners of the office, as members from the three teams had cops being promoted. I had an almost out-of-body experience from the amount of joy and pride that radiated from me. I got right on the telephone and shared the news with my parents.

April 7 couldn't come soon enough for me. I felt like a child on Christmas Eve that wanted to go to bed in the early afternoon so the time would pass quicker, and I could just wake up and see what Santa left me. On the morning of the ceremony, I was up early after a restless night's sleep and headed into the office with my dress uniform. My hair was high and tight and mustache trimmed. I slipped into my dress pants, buttoned up my light blue shirt, and slipped on my squeaky shoes. I buttoned up my summer blouse and capped it off with my eight-point hat and white gloves. I walked into the men's room and gave myself the once-over. The smile on the man in the mirror told me he was pleased with my appearance. As I looked straight ahead, I glanced at the chest of my mirrored self and saw the silver shield pinned there. I glanced down to where the silver shield rested. It lay directly over my heart, and for me, that is the only place it could ever be.

We piled into cars driven by other team members in our office and headed over to One Police Plaza. I walked into the first floor auditorium where the ceremony was to take place in about three hours. We lined up in straight rows as a sergeant stepped to each one of us and gave us a thorough going over. A handful of guys failed inspection and were ordered to get haircuts or shaves. Some were ordered to purchase new uniform pants from the equipment section right across the hall. With only about two hours or so to showtime, these guys ran out the door and hit the local barbershop. I am sure the barbers loved promotion days where a handful of cops would come dashing in for last minute touch-ups.

We got in a line to turn in our cop shield and receive our new detective shield. I got to the table and handed in my old shield and identification card and received my gold-and-blue tin with my new shield number: 3081. My new identification card proudly announced DETECTIVE before my name. I stood still, lost in my mind's eye, envisioning myself showing up on a crime scene and saying to the uniform cop on the street, "How you doing? Detective Lawrence Hoffman, what do you got, kid?"

My good friend, Mark Kloiber, who was also getting promoted, grabbed me by the arm and said, "Congratulations, buddy, we made it."

I had met Mark while I was assigned to the Auto Larceny Unit in BNTF. Mark was an active cop assigned to the Seven-Five precinct in East New York, Brooklyn. Mark and his partner had conducted a routine traffic stop when their streetwise intuition alerted them that something was not quite legit about the car. They made a call to my office, and Frank Napoli and I responded over the Seven-Five precinct garage to help investigate.

After a couple of hours of searching, Frank and I were able to find the auto's hidden VIN (vehicle identification number). We determined that the car had been stolen and fitted with an altered VIN plate. Frank and I were sweaty and covered head-to-toe in grease and dirt. I found Mark and his partner, who were resting comfortably in the air-conditioned police officer's lounge, watching television. Mark's car stop turned into an arrest for Grand Larceny Auto (GLA), and he was able to make fifteen hours overtime processing the collars.

Since that day, Mark has remained a very close and dear friend. His friendship throughout the years has allowed both of us to maintain a separation of job and personal life.

"Yeah, we finally made it. Is your family coming?" I asked.

"Yep, they should be here any minute."

There were three sections of seats. The middle section was occupied by the promotees, the left and right was reserved for family. We were arranged by our last names, and I claimed my position in the alphabet. Once we were all seated, we were congratulated and welcomed by a representative of the Detective Endowment Association. Along with the promotion, we were switching unions and were no longer members of the Police Benevolent Association (PBA). Several administrative issues were required. We filled out forms and were explained the new medical and union benefits.

I checked my watch and noticed that two o'clock was rapidly approaching. The auditorium's heavy wooden doors were opened, and family and friends began to filter in. Everyone was rubbernecking to locate their family as seats quickly filled up, and I was no different. My mom and stepdad found seats in the right section almost parallel to mine. We exchanged waves and smiles. Team members crowded into the standing room only section at the rear of the auditorium. Everything was now in place.

Lieutenant Thomas Sandseth, master of ceremony, welcomed family and friends and kicked off the event. We stood as Sergeant Tony Giorgio sang our national anthem. The invocation was done by Rev. Msgr. Joseph Zammitt, and the administration of oath of office was performed by Chief of Personnel Michael Markman. Louis Anemone, the chief of department, was called to the podium. As he took his position, the first two rows of officers were instructed to rise and reposition on the steps to the right of the stage. Chief Anemone put the wheels of promotion in motion by calling the first name, Michael Bell.

As the first two rows on the staircase dwindled down, my row and another were ordered to stand and occupy the space near the wall. Aligned against the wall, I slowly made my way to the staircase. I was on the first step, then the second. Standing on the stage itself now, I watched the person before me proceed to receive his certificate of promotion. All I could think was *whatever you do, don't trip and fall.*

I heard a booming voice, which may have been God, call, "LAWRENCE HOFFMAN." That was my cue. My stiff legs carried me toward the middle of the stage. I stopped ten feet before First Deputy Commissioner John Timoney and snapped a crisp salute then continued forward. I received my certificate in my left hand as I shook the first dep's hand with my right. I could hear the hollering and yelling coming from my family in the rear of the auditorium. I don't remember ever walking off the stage, but I must have. I sat in my seat staring and reading my certificate of promotion. As I sat there, I would hear a familiar name and add my voice to the constant wave of cheers.

Words alone cannot describe the pride I felt on this day. I owned the day and never passed up a chance to whip out the gold and put it on display. Having loved ones there to share in my glory only lifted my spirits higher. The ability and opportunity to share life's accomplishments with loved ones is the greatest feeling in the world.

FORTY-TWO

You Got to Love a Boss Who Stands Up for His Men

Having my dream of becoming a New York City detective realized, it was time to focus my sights on another: the successful takedown of my long-term investigation. This case had been ongoing for thirteen months, and Eddie had done a tremendous job of purchasing seventeen firearms along with numerous amounts of heroin, crack, and cocaine. Working with Mike Santory and ATF Group V made my job a lot easier. The workload of identifying and monitoring the whereabouts of subjects was considerably lightened with additional manpower. The takedown would have to be well thought out and planned, so no other subjects would get a whiff of what was happening, giving them a chance to escape capture.

Since this was a joint effort with ATF, it was decided that we wanted to get the biggest bang for our prosecutorial buck. We agreed that the larger players in the organization would be charged federally, the smaller fish would go state. Agent Santory worked with an assistant United States attorney (AUSA) drawing up federal arrest and search warrants for some of the subjects, and I worked with ADA Vernon drawing state arrest and search warrants for the others.

One concern from ADA Vernon was the amount of time that had elapsed since our last purchase of a firearm from the bodega on Fulton and Warwick Street in East New York, Brooklyn. She needed a "fresh look" to convince a state judge to grant us a search warrant for this location. I immediately put a call into Hammer to request his services. We agreed to meet during the week so that he could walk into the store and get a look around.

We arranged to meet at a predetermined safe location. Tommy Cea, Steve Brown, and I arrived first. Approximately fifteen minutes later, we spotted Hammer heading in our direction. It was hard for me to believe that this was the same person that I had strip searched in the Seven-Five precinct bathroom over eighteen months ago. His frail thin body seemed to expend tremendous amounts of energy just to arrive at my car door. We exchanged greetings, and then I asked him how he was feeling. He said he felt very tired and weak all the time and didn't have much of an appetite.

Fully aware of his assignment, we headed over in the direction of Fulton Street. We told him to take as much time as he needed to try and get them to show him where the guns were kept. We got as close to the store as possible because of his condition. He stepped from the car and labored toward the target corner. He continually needed to pick up his ill-fitted pants and coughed harshly every few feet, marking his way as he spat phlegm to the street. The mood in the car was solemn to say the least. In spite of all his faults and errant ways, we had grown a mutual respect for one another. We all knew with the way the disease was progressing he would not be around much longer. It truly affected me to see him suffer, and my mind drifted toward his wife and son.

Not much time had elapsed when we spotted Hammer rounding the corner en route back to our car. He was out of breath as he opened the rear car door and sat down. He was wheezing, and we gave him a minute or two to catch his breath. He rolled down the window, cleared his throat, and spat out the window, and stated, "Okay, they have four handguns in a pullout drawer underneath where they keep the deli meats."

I replied, "That's my boy. Great job," as I pulled out to return to the original meet location. I had exactly what I needed get a search warrant issued for the bodega. We chitchatted back to where we picked him up, and something he said stuck in my mind. He said he always wanted to take his wife and son to Great Adventure Amusement Park, but because of the way he was feeling, he didn't think that would be possible. He got out of the car, and I told him to stay in touch.

Armed with this new information regarding the bodega, I headed over to ADA Vernon's office on Centre Street where we started working on the arrest and search warrants. I filled her in on Hammer's physical condition, and I could see my words affected her as well.

With the federal and state arrest and search warrants in hand, we planned out our attack. We broke our combined forces down into groups so that we could hit locations simultaneously to avoid word of the takedown being transmitted to another target location. We decided to arrest the main players, Boca and Carlos, at their residence first thing in the morning.

On June 16, 1995, Operation Boca Organization Takedown was in effect. Boca and Carlos were brought into custody without incident, and we moved on to the search warrant locations. My group would be hitting Fulton and Warwick Streets. When all teams were in position, we gave the word. The teams went into apprehension mode and knocked down their respective doors.

My team, along with Captain Hickey, screeched to a halt along the curb just outside the bodega's glass door. We jumped out and ran into the store like a firestorm. Everyone in the store was secured and led outside to sit against the building. Team members identified and searched the men seated against the building, while inside I started my search for weapons and contraband. I went behind the counter and found a pullout drawer underneath the deli meats. I called Tommy Cea over before I opened the drawer. Apprehensively, I slowly pulled on the handles. The drawer roughly slid open but was completely empty. Had the guns been sold, or they were moved to another location or different spot in the store? I tore the store apart, using my legal right to do as granted by the courts, but came up completely empty. I was very disappointed.

Although we had purchased numerous firearms from this particular store, including the Tec 22 Scorpion semiauto machine pistol, I could not place any of its occupants under arrest without recovering evidence at the scene. All of the purchases had been done through Willie and Carlos, and the supplier in the store was never identified. He might be among the men seated against the building right now, but there was no probable cause to arrest him. Today, he would get a pass.

Once we packed up our equipment and vacated the store, the owner wanted someone's name so he could file a complaint against the police for harassment. Without a second's hesitation, Captain Hickey stepped up inches away from the owner's face and said, "You want a name? Take mine. Captain Hickey. And don't embarrass me by spelling it wrong. It's H-I-C-K-E-Y, first name captain!" You got to love a boss who stands up for his men.

All the other locations were taken without incident except for one. Lieutenant Walsh's team, which Steve Brown was assigned to, had the apartment door slammed in their face and held closed. Once they gained access, they chased a male through the apartment that they were able to subdue and place under arrest. The male had a loaded firearm in his possession.

After thirteen months of investigation, my long-term case was brought to an end. Through the combined efforts of Brooklyn North SNAG and ATF Group V, the Boca Organization (a Dominican-based narcotics and firearms group), was completely dismantled. These efforts resulted in the arrests of thirteen major offenders as well as the recovery of twenty firearms (seventeen purchased, three more recovered during the takedown). Also seized were various amounts of heroin, cocaine (including the two-kilo rip), crack, counterfeit money, drug paraphernalia, and two bulletproof vests.

We wanted to get a chance to talk with Boca and see what he had to say about his involvement in the arrest. We let him sit in a room by himself for a while to let his mind go to work on him. After some time passed, we attempted to talk with him. He was still playing his tough guy role and didn't admit too much. We had a couple of tricks up our sleeves which we decided to pull out. First was to introduce him to Eddie. His face lit up with disbelief, but he still didn't give in. Then we decided to have him watch a movie starring himself. We had established a pattern watching the tapes of his residence. His wife would go to work every day, but then, he would have a female visitor come to the house. We asked him what his wife would have to say when she saw this tape. He immediately broke down. Women, as history has proven over time, can be the downfall of men.

Although this was a significant arrest shattering this criminal organization, it can only be viewed as a first step. Due to the strength and seriousness of the charges, there was a strong possibility that many of these offenders would be willing to cooperate and enter into a Proffer Agreement with the United States Government. It was expected that several additional long-term investigations would develop through the testimony of these defendants as well as the solution of numerous previously unsolved violent crimes.

FORTY-THREE

I Felt Death Hanging in the Air

Lieutenant Jack Walsh told me he had been contacted by ATF Group Supervisor Bill Fredericks who expressed a great amount of interest in having me be assigned to Group V to continue to work on this investigation and related cases. Lieutenant Walsh generated an internal letter (UF-49) to my big boss, Deputy Inspector Michael Mandel, stating the recommendation of my transfer to assist ATF Group V and work with the four NYPD Housing police officers assigned there. This letter was endorsed both by DI Mandel and Captain Hickey and forwarded to police headquarters. I was elated with the possibility to move on to bigger and better cases.

I wanted to fill Hammer in on what had transpired. I spoke to his wife who told me that Hammer was admitted to the hospital and was not doing well. A couple of days later, Tommy, Steve, and I headed over to pay him a visit at the hospital. We were greeted in the hallway by his wife. She was visibly upset. I handed her an envelope and told her I was sorry and asked if we could speak with him. She took the envelope from my hand and nodded yes.

His hospital room was very clinical and all business. I felt extremely uncomfortable and wanted to turn around and leave the second I stepped in. Hammer was attached to a machine that stood guard over the bed. As I approached his bedside, I could see that he was on a ventilator. An endotracheal tube was secured to his mouth by white tape. The rhythmic moans of the ventilator accentuated the aura of the room while forcing oxygen into his lungs pushing his chest upward. His arms were twice their normal size. Beige-colored nutrients were being fed to his body by way of a plastic tube that entered his nose. He could not move any part of his body except for his brown eyes.

I took in all the information my senses fed me and tried to disregard what my mind comprehended. I felt death hanging in the air, like stale cigarette smoke, patiently waiting to make its official presence known. I felt his eyes straining to find me. I leaned across the middle of the bed to make it easier for him to see. Although his body appeared lifeless, there was still a light that shined behind his eyes. Strong emotions attempted to surface, and I did my best to keep them at bay. I said, "Guess what? We got him. We got Boca."

His eyebrows arched in surprise as if to say, "Yeah?"

I continued, "But guess what? He cried. Yeah, he cried like a little baby."

He rolled his eyes in disgust. Hammer's wife entered the room with the breached envelope in her hand and said to him, "Papa, they brought us four tickets to Great Adventures!" His eyes shifted back to me. They closed tightly for a few seconds, and then a single tear rolled down his left cheek. When they opened again, I gave him a sincere smile and stepped away from the bed letting Tommy come up to say hello. We had granted his wish, and I knew he appreciated it.

A short time after that visit, Hammer passed away. I took care of the necessary paperwork to deactivate him as a confidential informant. Our team presented Assistant District Attorney Aida Vernon with a plaque entitled "The Hammer Files," commemorating her diligent work and undivided attention, an intricate part of the success behind the cases that Hammer had provided for us.

Early on, I had developed some information regarding two rival drug gangs warring over an apartment building located at 728 Liberty Avenue in Brooklyn. These two gangs wanted exclusive rights to the building, using it as a point of sale for illegal narcotic transactions. Neither group wanted to relinquish control. One organization decided to torch it even though there were families residing inside. On one of the coldest days of the year, the building was set on fire. Numerous fireman and occupants were seriously injured. Using the information I obtained, I worked closely with ATF agents and NYC fire marshalls to make arrests and get convictions. I was awarded a Certificate of Appreciation from the New York City Fire Department for my efforts.

FORTY-FOUR

I'm Hit, I'm Hit!

We had a changing of the guard, and a new captain was assigned to our unit. On September 20, 1995, my team reported for duty at our regularly scheduled time. We were advised by the sergeant that we would be performing a double tour of duty that night with only about four hours in between tours. Based on COMPSTAT (Computerized Analysis of Crime Strategies), a growing number of shootings and shots fired were reported at early morning hours at certain locations, and we were there to address these incidents. I thought to myself, *Um, let's send undercover officers, with no body armor, into locations at a time where shots were most likely to happen. Sounds like a wonderful idea.*

As a group, we were very unhappy about this decision and decided to voice our opinion with the new captain. He invited us into his office, and we aired our grievances. Michael Stoney spoke for the undercover officers and said, "With all due respect, Captain, do we have to be out there at one or two in the morning? At that time of the morning, there are a lot less people on the streets, and it would be harder for us to blend in without raising people up." Mike had come from the streets and knew how they worked, which made him invaluable as an undercover police officer. He continued with, "The same guys carrying and shooting it up at one in the morning are out there at eight or nine o'clock at night, when it would be a hell of a lot easier to blend in." The captain said he understood our concerns but needed us to perform our tour as instructed.

At the completion of my first tour, I was able to grab a bite to eat and relax a little before returning for Act II. I was sitting at my desk as the rest of the crew started to file back in. We should have been home at this time instead of returning to the office. We were, of course, a little grumpy. The other teams had all gone home for the night, leaving us the office to ourselves.

Sergeant Wilson prepared the tactical plan and mapped out our target areas for the night. After making enough copies of the plan for everyone, he called us into his office. We dragged our feet toward his office in defiance. Sergeant Wilson made it clear he was not happy about being here also but said we have to do what we have to do. It was decided that Michael Stoney and Rodney Harrison would be doing the undercover work tonight.

I paired up with Papo and let him know I would drive. I grabbed the keys to the dark blue Nissan Altima and headed down to the locker room to suit up. I secured my gun belt to my waist, popped my head through my Kevlar body armor, and attached the Velcro straps to my chest. I hung my gold detective shield from my neck, letting it rest on my bulletproof vest in the middle of my chest. I slammed my locker closed and headed to the equipment room where I signed out a department radio.

After a short walk, I found the Altima and pulled it near the front of the building to wait for my partner. I popped the trunk for Papo who placed some equipment in the back then took his seat next to me. Papo said, "This sucks, man. We shouldn't be out here tonight."

I replied, "I hear that. You want anything before we set up?"

He stated, "Nah, I'm good."

I looked at the first set on the sheet—Marcus Garvey and Van Buren Street in Bedford Stuyvesant. It was a short drive from the office, and I parked fairly close to the location. I was able to get a legal spot and blend in with the other parked cars with the late hour providing us some protection from look-outs. I turned the car off and set my radio down by the hand brake in between our seats. We shot the shit while I looked at the rear and side view mirrors to observe some of our other cars taking up positions down the block behind us.

After a few minutes, Sergeant Wilson's voice broke the silence, "Condor teams on the air?"

Papo checked us in, saying, "Team two is on the air and set." The rest of the field teams followed suit. Sergeant Wilson informed us that Rodney was going to attempt to buy, and Stoney was the ghost.

Stoney checked his connection to us on his hidden point-to-point radio, "Check one, two. Check one, two."

Sergeant Wilson gave him his confirmation saying, "You're five by five (loud and clear). You guys got the green light to step."

Papo and I continued our conversation, keeping an attentive ear to the radio. It always amazed me how we became trained to listen to the police radio. We could be having an intense conversation with idle chatter and jobs given out by dispatch on division radio, but once your call sign was mentioned, such as Seven Adam or Task Force thirteen eighty-six north, it jumped out and grabbed your attention.

Stoney kept us updated on Rodney's whereabouts and actions. It seemed like nothing was happening on the set, but Rodney was determined to find the "right" people to connect with. Rodney spent what seemed like a lot of time working the set. I expected Stoney to advise the team that it was a "negative," and that the UC was heading back to the car.

Suddenly, Stoney's voice erupted from the radio, putting us in a headlock. He yelled, **"Ten-thirteen, Ten-thirteen, shots fired Marcus Garvey and Van Buren Street. Move in! Move in!"**

My body went from zero to sixty in a half a second as those words tapped into my adrenaline well. My blood vessels opened wide allowing blood to race through my veins at an alarming rate, preparing for the unknown. I dropped the Altima in gear and pulled into the city street. I could see the rest of the team's autos coming to life, joining in behind me. Stoney's words injected me with more adrenaline as he repeated, **"Ten-thirteen, shots fired, move in!"**

With wide open eyes, I drove toward Marcus Garvey. I hung a hard left, hard enough to almost put the car onto two wheels. I could see Michael Stoney standing illuminated under a streetlight. We screeched to a halt and jumped from the car as other team members skidded behind us. Stoney was pointing and informed us that Rodney was chasing the suspect behind us. We jumped back into the cars in an attempt to find Rodney. Not knowing the whereabouts of one of your partners is a frightening experience. At that moment, Rodney was on his own chasing an armed suspect without the protection of body armor.

The cars behind me spun their wheels in reverse, making it to the corner then proceeding up Van Buren Street. I was the last car in the procession as I guided my car in reverse to Van Buren. I dropped the car in drive, and I could see the rest of the field team cars stacked up not far off the corner of Marcus Garvey.

As I stopped our car and prepared to exit, the radio, which was still lying next to the hand brake, emitted words in Stoney's voice that I will never forget. "I'm hit, I'm hit!" I spun my head to the left and observed Stoney on one knee with his head slumped. The streetlight that once illuminated him now seemed to push him toward the ground. After hearing those same words, Papo jumped back into the car, and I raced back to Stoney. Through the windshield, I could see him fighting the weight of the streetlight's rays and finally losing, as he gave in and collapsed onto the sidewalk.

My worst fears were confirmed by the pool of blood that started to collect on the pavement under Stoney. I could see blood saturating the upper left side of his body. I had no idea exactly where or how many times he was hit. At that moment, getting him to the hospital became my life's mission. Papo removed his shirt and made a tourniquet around Stoney's left wrist to stop the bleeding.

Time was working against us, and every second counted. Papo grabbed Stoney under the arms as I picked up his feet. We walked him toward the open rear door of the Altima. Papo laid down in the backseat and pulled Stoney into the car on top of him as I pushed him in with his feet. I slammed the door closed and hopped into the driver's seat. Sergeant Wilson and other members of the field team were now at the corner with us.

A notification was put over division radio that a member of the service (MOS) had been shot. This transmission put cops in motion in Brooklyn and Manhattan. I could hear sirens wailing in the distance as they approached our location. I looked up at Sergeant Wilson from the car. He seemed to be frozen with the police radio at his lips. I smiled at him, giving the impression that everything was going to be okay and said, "I got to get him to the hospital, boss." He remained frozen as I pulled the car away. Papo was lying underneath Michael who wrapped him in his arms to hold him steady.

A marked police van approached me. I flashed my lights and waved my arms in an attempt to get his attention. I wanted to get a police escort to the hospital to ensure a speedy and safe route. Not knowing who or what my cargo was, he passed by us heading to the spot where the incident was reported to have occurred. I was able to get a patrol car to stop. After explaining that I had a cop shot in the backseat, he agreed to lead the way. The patrol car took the lead and then suddenly stopped and pulled to the curb in front of me. At the time, I wasn't sure what he was doing. I determined that I had no time to waste and could not stop anymore. I sped past him on my own to Wyckoff Hospital. I had no police lights or siren and took the most direct route I knew, which involved going down one way streets the wrong way.

Michael Stoney kept repeating the description of the male that shot him over and over again. I didn't care if he was singing "Copacabana." I was just so happy to hear his voice, and when he stopped so did my heart. From underneath Stoney, Papo yelled, "Talk to me, Stoney!"

A second later, Stoney weakly screamed in pain. My heart started thumping with incredible force. I wasn't gonna let him die in the car, so I punched the gas pedal. His screams subsided, and then he repeated the chorus of the suspect's description. His concentration and concern for his partner was heroic. He changed his tune when he announced, "I think I'm going to throw up."

His human seat belt fired back, "Don't throw up on me!"

I turned the car into the ambulance receiving bay. I jumped out to get Stoney from the car and into the hands of medical personnel. We eased him out, and I threw his right arm over my shoulder and started to walk toward the door. We were on the steps when he told me to hold up a second and proceeded to vomit blood and bile onto the step ahead of us, which splashed back onto our legs. Everything and everybody seemed to be frozen in time, and when he finished, time resumed.

Nurses and doctors took Michael from me and laid him on a gurney. I felt like a scared mother refusing to let go of her only child. Other nurses rushed to our car where Papo stood shirtless covered in blood. They were convinced he was shot also. He had to prove he wasn't by moving his appendages all the while insisting that Mike was the only one shot.

I walked alongside the gurney into the hospital until it stopped in some room. The doctors and nurses worked feverishly on him. People were yelling in that unfamiliar language again as they swarmed the room. I laid claim to the left side of the bed against the wall and remained there. There was no way in hell I was going to leave him without a familiar face to connect with.

His clothing was sheared from his body as his scared eyes looked to me for comfort. His left arm near his shoulder had an entrance wound with a matching exit wound underneath. Papo's shirt, which was tied in a knot at Stoney's left wrist, was cut away. I grabbed his right hand and held it saying, "If you need to squeeze, do it! Everything is going to be okay." He screamed as they rolled him onto his right side toward me. A short male in a lab coat moved Mike's left arm which slid away from his body on a bed of blood. The doctor wiped the area just below his armpit with gauze which revealed a small hole filled with blood that quickly spilled onto his chest and collected onto the bed. The doctor then proceeded to stick a finger from his latex gloved hand into this hole. Stoney's body convulsed in pain as if he were being electrocuted, I yelled, "Squeeze, Stoney. Squeeze my hand!"

I can't begin to tell you how frightened I was at this moment, but I couldn't let Stoney see an ounce of this fear. I had to suppress it and try to convince him that everything was going to be okay. He squeezed my hand as instructed until my fingertips were void of blood. They then returned him to his original position on his back, and his grip loosened as the pain level decreased. The medical team continued to poke him, withdraw blood, and set up an IV. We held hands, and I continued to try to put him at ease.

Another doctor entered the room and rolled Mike onto his side and felt the need to stick HIS finger into the hole on his side! Mike screamed and squeezed my hand, forcing the little blood that had recently returned to once again vacate. Mike's pain became my own and to see him contouring in agony again made me voice my opinion. I slammed the doctor by yelling, "Nobody else is going to stick their finger in his side again! You hear me! You get everyone here, and you do the test once! That's it! You're fucking killing the guy!" The doctor just stared into my desperate frightened eyes a second and seemed to understand. He snapped off his glove and deposited it in the metal can on his way out.

Mike asked me to call his wife Maria and let her know what was going on. He had no idea how much damage was caused by the single gunshot, but he made it clear to me to let her know that everything was okay. We broke our death grip as I pulled my phone from my pocket. I had trouble dialing the numbers that he recited to me because my fingers were still white.

I backed up a step into the corner and plugged my ear with the other hand as the phone rang on the other end. Maria answered, and trying to be as nonchalant as I could, I said, "Hi, Maria, it's Larry from work." She immediately wondered why I was calling her and started to question me. I said, "I'm at the hospital with Mike, but everything is okay." The phone suddenly went dead, and I wasn't sure the "everything is okay" part made it through. Now I'm thinking to myself, *Holy shit, what does this poor girl think is going on! She must be going out of her mind!* I tried to call her back and couldn't get a signal.

I stepped back up to the bed to reestablish our hand grip. I could see that he had lost an extensive amount of blood, which lined the outside of his body and seeped through the bed linen onto the thin mattress. The sight of blood does not affect me, but when it is a member of my family, as Stoney is, it shook me to the core. I prayed to God that Papo and I were able to get him to the hospital in time.

I started to ask myself if there was anything more that I could have done. Should I have waited for an ambulance? Was there a quicker route to the hospital? Why did that RMP stop after I asked them for an escort? My thoughts were interrupted when Mike squeezed my hand as he experienced immense pain. "Squeeze, Stoney. Squeeze!" I wanted his pain to transfer between our hands so that his would diminish. "Squeeze!" I yelled through clenched teeth.

Moments later, some of the field team arrived at the hospital to check on their fallen comrade. Donald Bradley came in, and we asked if Rodney was okay. He assured us he was and that they were working with the Seven-Nine precinct detectives searching for the shooter. I explained my failed call to Maria, and Don told me he had spoken to her, and that she was on her way to the hospital. After seeing Stoney in the hospital, my team returned to the streets, determined to find the shooter. My job was to remain at Mike's bedside.

I heard a large commotion approaching the room and looked toward the door. Mayor Guiliani, followed by Police Commissioner Bill Bratton, entered the room. The mayor took a moment to assess the situation. His eyes passed from the beeping machines monitoring Mike's vitals to the hanging bag of plasma that dripped into his arm. He glanced at our locked hands and then brought his eyes up to mine where he smiled and nodded his acknowledgement. He leaned over and placed a hand on Mike's foot and asked, "How you doing, son?"

Mike adjusted himself on the bed using his head for leverage. He squeezed my hand, and, still in his undercover persona, he responded to the mayor's question, "Yo, don't ever get shot. That shit hurt like a motherfucker."

My eyes widened but never left the mayor who stared at him, seeming to ingest Mike's words for a moment. He slowly turned to Commissioner Bratton and said, "My, he's a feisty young man, isn't he? I guess that means he's doing okay." He laughed, which gave the rest of the room permission to join in.

A short time later, Stoney's wife Maria burst into the room. Her face could not hide the emotion she was feeling. She brushed past the mayor and commissioner without a word to get to Mike's bedside. I released Mike's hand and backed away, allowing Maria to take my place. I stood at the top of the bed and started to become emotional as Maria and Mike embraced. She had received one of those phone calls that haunt the mind of every cop's spouse. The anguish of the unknown must be a chilling experience, and my heart went out to her. Mike remained strong as he assured her that he was okay, and the aura of the love that they shared hung above the bed like a protective shield.

Commissioner Bratton said to Maria, "You should be very proud of him. He is a very brave young man." This comment paved the way for Maria to unleash a barrage of statements aimed directly at the commissioner. She let him know exactly what our whole team had been feeling. She told him that this incident never should have happened. She went on to tell him that the team had no business being out there at that time.

The commissioner looked like he could use a hospital bed after the verbal assault Maria hit him with. All he could say was, "If there is anything I can do, let me know."

Maria hit him point-blank in the chest, "You can promote them to detective." Commissioner Bratton nodded.

After the mayor and the commissioner left, I faded into the background and slid out of the room to give Mike and Maria privacy. I found Papo sitting on a gurney in an empty room. He sat shirtless with his arms locked at the elbow and his hands squeezing the thin mattress. His head hung down, his chin resting on his chest which was still smeared with Mike's blood. He was visibly shaken. I sat down on the gurney next to him. I asked him, "Hey, you okay?"

He shook his head never looking up and slowly whispered, "It's too much, man, first the shooting on Glenmore, and now this. It's just too much." Most cops never draw their weapons from their holster. In a matter of months, we had been exposed to two life-threatening incidents. I hadn't had much time to reflect on what we experienced, and as I looked at my bloody hands, I realized he was right. It was too much. We sat in silence, and I stared at the same floor he did for a few moments to collect myself.

After a while, I put my left arm around his bare shoulder and said, "I think we did a good thing tonight. I think he's gonna be okay."

He said, "Yeah, we did."

To break up the mood, I said, "Hey, by the way. Why were you tying your shirt around his wrist when the poor guy is shot up near his shoulder? What kind of Puerto Rican tourniquet is that?"

He laughed as he needlessly defended himself saying, "I just saw all the blood at his wrist and thought that was where he was hit."

I lied and said, "You know, Mike was complaining that his wrist hurt more than where he was shot." Papo laughed as his bright smile returned to his face. I said, "Come on, let's get cleaned up and get out of here."

The shooter was captured a few hours later after some good old-fashioned police work. The streets had spoken, and a suspect was arrested. He confessed to the shooting, stating that he thought that the two guys hanging around the corner were going to rob him and his friends. This was exactly the type of situation Mike had tried to express to the captain at our meeting only hours earlier.

Stoney's condition was stabilized at Wyckoff Hospital, and he was later transferred to Bellevue Hospital in Manhattan.

I arrived home to my empty house and was greeted by my cat Taz, who sat at the window like a worried mother. I opened the door, and he jumped from the radiator cover down toward my feet where he proceeded to rub his body around my legs leaving a film of hair along the way. Normally, I would gently push him aside to avoid the hair, but tonight, it was just what I needed. I checked for messages on my phone, but there were none.

I jumped into the shower to wash this day down the drain. I turned the hot water up as high as I could take it and submerged my head. I stood there with my head hung, breathing from my mouth, as the hot water massaged my shoulders and cascaded down to my feet. My mind's theater played the events of the day and then replayed them like a double feature. The second showing proved too much for me, and I broke down. I dropped down to one knee and held my head in my hands. I sobbed uncontrollably as my tears mixed with the hot water and disappeared into the drain.

The shower proved to be cleansing on many levels. I stepped from the shower onto the floor mat to dry off. I heard running in the living room. A toy mouse jumped into my view followed by a streaking Taz, who somersaulted onto the bouncing mouse, capturing it between his paws and mouth. He lay on his back with the mouse in his claws poised above his body. He looked at me for a moment from his upside down eyes and then launched the mouse into the air giving chase once again. I heard the crash of the fireplace tongs which sent Taz flying back into my view mouseless. He laid there with his head on the carpet and his tail wagging. His eyes reflected the light as he looked at me as if saying, "It wasn't me."

I looked right into those glazed eyes and let go a hearty laugh, which I didn't know existed in me. I shook my head and said, "Thanks, buddy."

FORTY-FIVE

The Greatest Compliment I Could Ever Receive

I awoke the next day to the sound of 1010 WINS radio informing me, "Give us twenty-two minutes, and we'll give you the world." The top story was that an undercover narcotics police officer had been shot in Brooklyn. He was in serious but stable condition at Bellevue Hospital.

I snapped off the radio and said out loud, "No, shit, tell me something I don't know." I washed the sleep from my eyes and dressed for another day in the world of Brooklyn North Strategic Narcotics and Guns. The ride into Brooklyn seemed timeless as memories of the previous day refused to rest in my mind.

I arrived at the office, and instead of the normal "what's up" greeting, we hugged each other, not forgetting that what had gone down could have happened to anyone of us. We recapped the details of the incident, and I learned that the reason the patrol car stopped a second time was to inform me that cops in Manhattan and Brooklyn had blocked off a route for me to get Mike to Bellevue Hospital. Getting Mike to the nearest hospital to stop the bleeding and to get his condition stabilized was my primary goal. My actions would be confirmed as the right decision from information I later gained from my visit at the hospital. Once all of the team made their way into the office, we carpooled to Bellevue Hospital to see Stoney.

At the hospital, I learned the extent of his injuries. He was shot in the upper left arm where the bullet broke his humorous bone in half and then entered his chest. Once in the chest, the bullet broke one rib which punctured his lung causing it to collapse, deflecting the projectile into the tip of his spleen. The doctors said he had lost more than fifty percent of his blood. During surgery, doctors installed metal pins and rods to repair his left arm.

We had a large group of people who were all eager to see Mike. His family was standing around his bedside, so we had to wait before we were allowed to go in one at a time. Sergeant Wilson went in to see him first, and we anxiously waited for his return and the first live report on his condition. Sellers Wilson walked out to the waiting room with his big dimpled smile affixed. He said Mike was in pain but was in very good spirits and couldn't wait to see the rest of team members. I had trouble sitting as I waited for my turn.

Finally it came. I pushed through the first door as I searched for his room down the hallway. I saw his name printed on the outside of the door and took a deep breath before I entered. I poked my head around the corner and saw that Mike had a big grin on his face as he talked with his wife, Maria, and two other women I did not know.

All eyes turned toward me as I stepped fully into the room. His smile lit up my heart because it told me he was going to be okay. I made my way to his beside and said, "Wow, you look a lot better than the last time I saw you, kid. How are you feeling?"

He said, "I'm a little sore, but after the doctor told me how much blood I lost, I'm happy to be alive." He turned to his family and said, "Mom, this is the guy I was telling you about."

The woman stepped from around the bed and walked over to me. She hugged me like a mother would hug her own child, and from her soul, she whispered in my ear, "Thank you for saving my son's life." This was the single most defining moment in my career. This was the reason I become a police officer. I had not given it any thought until that instant. I felt I did what needed to be done. To hear those words reinforced and justified my decision to become a cop. To me, it was the greatest compliment I could ever receive, and it will remain forever in my heart.

The woman Mike had called Mom was actually his Aunt Camille who raised Mike with the help of her sister Aunt Gail, who was also present at his bedside. These women were special to Mike, and he is very blessed to have them in his life. Although I never got to tell them this, I believe they did one hell of job raising a man who I have nothing but admiration for. May God continue to bless you and your family, Mike.

On October 6, 1995, Maria Stoney's last words to the commissioner had been heard. Our entire team was invited to the Blue Room at City Hall for a private ceremony where police officers Michael Stoney and Rodney Harrison would be promoted to the rank of detective third grade. The ceremony was extremely emotional and meaningful for our team.

Due to injuries he suffered on that night in September of 1995, Detective Michael Stoney retired from the New York City Police Department in April of 1997. Rodney Harrison would remain, moving up the chain of command to be promoted to the rank of captain.

FORTY-SIX

OCID? What's That?

In our office in the Navy Yard, there were only three phone lines, one for each team, excluding the boss's phones. At times, it was difficult to find one that was not being used. One day, I was catching up on some paperwork when the phone rang on Donald's desk. He called my name and let me know it was for me.

I picked up the phone and identified myself. There was a female voice on the other end telling me that she wanted to schedule a date for an interview for OCID. I said, "OCID? What's that?"

She said, "Organized Crime Investigation Division." I thought to myself, *I don't want to go to OCID. I want to go to ATF Group V.* She wanted to know my availability over the next few days, so I lied and told her on was on alert for a narcotics buy-and-bust trial and could not give her any dates. She said that was fine and would check back another time to try again.

I thanked her and hung up and repeated to myself, "OCID? I want to go to ATF Group V."

About three weeks later, I received a second call from OCID requesting another available day for an interview. This time, I gave in and made an appointment to see what this was all about. In my heart of hearts, I was not really interested in going because I had my mind set on working with ATF.

Having finalized the tough decision of which of my two suits I was going to wear to my OCID interview, I made my way over to One Police Plaza. I stood by the main elevators among the crowd and waited for my turn to be levitated. I stared at a sign that asked me, "Are you NIS, No Identification Showing?" For some reason, that sign just always pissed me off. First of all, I didn't want to be here today and after reading that sign, I just felt like slapping somebody. I looked to my left for a candidate, but the guy next to me was about six-foot four inches tall, and I decided to give him a pass.

A low dinging noise informed us that the elevator was here. Even before the doors were completely parted people burst out of the elevator like water from a dam. I shuffled my feet with the rest of the people to fill the vacuum left by the exiters. I did an abrupt about face and with my left forefinger lit the button for eleven. Then as a group, we all stared hypnotized at the ever changing numbers above the doors as if they possessed some mystical powers.

When I arrived at the OCID office, I was instructed to take a seat among the other suits and await my turn. The interview process seemed to move along quickly, and I was soon called into the boss's office. The interview panel consisted of Inspector Regan, Lieutenants O'Brien and Coleman, and Sergeant Kerley. They each introduced themselves and then got right into it. I gave a brief history of my career thus far and ended with the conclusion of my long-term investigation. Inspector Regan asked me if I knew how many grams were in an ounce, and I replied that I did not know off the top of my head, but that I had a conversion chart taped to my desk. He seemed to accept that answer. He then asked me what the going price was for a "sixty-two." A "sixty-two" (sixty-two grams) was a common breakdown sold by drug dealers.

I recalled that Eddie had recently purchased sixty-two grams during my long-term case for five thousand five hundred eighty dollars, so I blurted out, "Five thousand five hundred eighty dollars."

Their faces seemed to sour immediately as they exchanged glances between the four of them. Lieutenant Coleman voiced their disapproval, "You paid that much for a sixty-two? No way. That's way too much for cocaine."

I defended myself with, "Cocaine? No, we paid that for a sixty-two of heroin." That answer put the board at ease and seemed to get the interview process back on the right track. They asked me integrity-related questions, which I answered in textbook form. The final inquiry was related to my firearms discharge record which came up in my round-robin check. I went through the whole Snediker and Glenmore shooting, leaving out the Homer Simpson dance done by Big Patty behind the pillar. With the completion of that story, I was free to leave. We all shook hands, and I made my way back out into the fresh air, relieved that it was over.

Lieutenant Jack Walsh always had an open-door policy, which I often took advantage of. His office was a sort of mausoleum. His walls were ornately decorated with numerous photos taken with dignitaries, awards, certificates, and trophies. If I looked hard enough, I wouldn't be surprised to find "the Heisman Trophy" lurking somewhere.

He was very personable and always made me feel welcomed. He seemed genuinely concerned about me, and I felt comfortable enough to talk to him about anything. One day, he was reviewing some paperwork when I popped my head into his office. He stopped everything and invited me in. I took a seat, and he asked me how I was doing. I told him everything was going great. I informed him that I had an interview with OCID the other day. This took him by surprise, and he sat back in his chair, removed his glasses, and asked me how it went. I nonchalantly answered, "I guess it went well, I don't know."

He sat forward in his chair and asked me, "What's the matter? I thought this was something you wanted."

I responded, "I want to work with ATF, not go to OCID."

He looked at me a second and then explained, "Hey, jackass, there is a new federal task force working out of 26 Federal Plaza called HIDTA (High Intensity Drug Trafficking Area); and Billy's ATF Group is merging into it. The four housing cops assigned to the group are being absorbed by OCID." Well, he never used the word "jackass," but he should have. I had no idea about any of this. When I think back now to my "yeah, whatever..." approach,

I took to the interview process and even lying about my availability, I think jackass was quite appropriate.

He went on to explain that the Organized Crime Investigation Division had roughly twenty-six or twenty-seven different teams. They ranged from traditional organized crime, such as the New York Italian Mafia families, money laundering, trademark infringement, to Dominican and Colombian drug organizations. This was where the big boys played. Some of the biggest and most newsworthy cases were generated from OCID.

There was nothing I could do about it now. Not caring about the interview at all allowed me to be more relaxed than if I had known what was really at stake. Who knows, maybe it helped me. I just tried to put it behind me and focused on my work. What's done is done, I thought.

The saying, "Nothing stays the same" rang true at Brooklyn North SNAG. Overtime was being cut down, and we were told to do more with less. Our once free reign of Brooklyn North precincts to pick and choose which sets to target was reduced to designated areas where we could conduct buy-and-bust enforcement. This put undercover officers at risk of being exposed by drug organizations who would take note of arrests after certain customers were sold to.

Morale was low, and we suffered from burnout. So when I got the call in January of 1996 that I was transferred to OCID, it just felt right. Although I was moving on in my career, I felt that I was taking the spirit of my team with me. After all, they were now a part of my life and a necessary piece of the puzzle in my "process" of turning blue. My final days in narcotics were heartfelt and inspiring at the same time. I knew that I had made friends for life here and could only hope that my new experience in OCID would be just as rewarding.

FORTY-SEVEN

Let's Mess with the New Guy

On my first day of my new assignment, I was told to report to the main office at 1 PP to meet with the commanding officer, Inspector Regan. My choice of wardrobe was easy—my final remaining suit. I migrated into Manhattan with the rest of the flock, and with a little bit of luck found a parking spot after completing a grid search of the immediate vicinity. I made sure I wasn't "NIS" and crammed into the elevator. I didn't have to worry about pushing the button because all the floors were lit up. I systematically rose in the building's belly until I reached my destination.

I followed the signs to OCID and was greeted by the girls working in the office. I introduced myself and was welcomed to my new assignment. One of the girls said, "You're one of the lucky ones."

"Oh, yeah? Why is that?"

"Because Inspector Regan has a seven-out-of-eight-kill ratio during the interview process. He is very particular in who he picks up." I felt very fortunate after hearing that news and attributed my success to the well-worded letter (UF-49) written by Lieutenant Walsh requesting my transfer. I had heard that Inspector Regan was a very tough boss, but he went by the book, so you always knew exactly where he was coming from.

He called me into his office and offered me a seat. I sat there with a nervous smile smeared across my face while he glared at me from his side of the desk. I felt like I was in the principal's office for cutting math class and was waiting for my father to come pick me up. Principal Regan spoke, "I know you want to go to the ATF team, but they are new to me. I want to take a look at them and see what they are all about before I put anyone else in the team. In the meantime, you will be assigned to the Trade Mark Infringement Unit. Go next door and see Lieutenant O'Brien, and he will fill you in."

I never got a chance to warm up my seat, and I was out the door into another cold seat in front of Lieutenant John O'Brien. I put my rubber smile on again as the lieutenant looked me over. All I could think of was, *He doesn't like my suit!*

He said, "I hope you have clothes to change into because we are doing a warrant today."

I was expecting a nice easy day, having tea and bagels, and now this guy is telling me I'm going on a warrant! "No, sir. This is all I have to wear. I had no idea about a warrant," I said.

He replied, "The team is already out there doing a buy. Wait outside in the office, and you can drive over with me."

Out the door, I go again. I find another seat out in the main office and wonder how long I will get to sit in this one. I didn't want to be out of the game, so I waited for the music to stop before I sat down.

It's a good thing I wasn't a hen because my eggs would never get a chance to hatch around here. Before I knew it, Lieutenant John O'Brien was out of his office and instructed the staff that he could be reached by pager if needed. With a flick of his head, I was right behind him, headed for the elevator. We rode down to the parking garage and found his unmarked department auto. I had never been down here before and was soaking it all in as we headed up the ramp to the street. We approached a downed gate which lifted just in time as we leveled off to come topside. A uniformed cop snapped a salute as we passed. I gave him a small nod of the head, leaving him guessing who the hell I was.

The drive was short as we pulled up to a self-storage location in Lower Manhattan. We were met outside by some detectives who directed us up to the fourth floor of the building. We took the elevator up and spotted the rest of the team standing in front of small storage rooms which were locked.

The sergeant instructed the lieutenant that an undercover had purchased some bootleg copies of motion picture feature films that were still playing in the movie theaters. The undercover officer was able to get a glimpse inside the two rooms which he believed contained hundreds of additional copies of other feature films. The case officer and the undercover were in the Manhattan District Attorney's Office drawing up search warrant affidavits to be signed by a judge, granting them the right to search and seize the additional copies as evidence.

After some discussion, it was decided that I would be the person to stand guard over the potential evidence until the search warrants were signed and could be executed. I'm sure that somewhere in that discussion, they said, "Let's mess with the new guy and make his suit-wearing ass stand here and watch the locked rooms."

I was instructed not to let anyone go near these two rooms until they came back with the signed search warrants. With a huge smile, I said, "I got it boss. See you later." The second the elevator doors closed, the smile on my face evaporated. I thought to myself, *Oh, this is great. I'm going to be stuck here for hours, all by myself, with no one to talk to and nowhere to sit.*

The rooms were all painted dark-blue while the floor was covered with dusty square foot gray tiles. Long fluorescent lights hung from the gray ceiling like giant upside-down ice trays emitting a low electrical hum.

I stood leaning against the opposite wall staring at these two locked storage units. Time seemed to come to a halt as I checked my watch periodically only to find that six minutes had passed. I kept staring until my eyes lost focus. Without any outside stimulation, my mind would turn to mush in a hurry. I felt like I was doing time in "the hole" in prison, and only ten minutes had gone by.

I needed to keep my mind occupied. My first decision was to see how long I could keep my eyes open before I was forced to blink. Wow, great idea. Let's do it. I took a couple of deep breathes in preparation and then thought,

What the hell is that gonna do? So instead, I fluttered my eyelashes about ten times thinking that would give me some sort of edge. I counted down, "On your mark, get set, GO!"

I looked nowhere in particular and focused on keeping them open. At about twenty seconds, I started to feel my eyes drying out. Forty seconds, it started to hurt. Come on, you pussy, hang in there! Fifty-two seconds, I can't take it anymore! I got to stop! Fifty-six seconds, and it was unbearable; I closed them! Okay, not a bad starting point, but I think I could do better.

I rubbed my eyes, preparing for my second attempt. I took a couple of deep breaths. Doesn't work! I told you that before! Okay, here we go. I kept my eyes squinted to protect them from exposure to the air as I waited for the secondhand to reach twelve. And go! Twenty seconds, the burning started again. As it intensified, I opened my eyes wider hoping that would help. Thirty seconds, come on, you can do it! Thirty-five seconds—felt like being poked with pins.

I had the 1982 Richard Gere movie, *An Officer and a Gentleman,* playing in my head. Lou Gossett Jr. playing Gunnery Sergeant Foley is yelling "I want your DOR, Mayo!" Richard Gere as Zack Mayo fights back, "Don't you do it! I got no place else to go!"

Fifty seconds, and my face started twitching. Come on, hang it there. You can do over a minute! My mouth dropped open as I struggled to fight the urge to blink. The secondhand crossed over the one-minute mark, and it felt like I could hear it thumping out each second. As the thin silver hand marched around the watch face in its glass enclosure, the pain became too much, and I gave in. I slammed my eyes shut and suddenly become out of breath like I ran up ten flights of stairs. Why does that happen? I blinked hard, and a single tear dropped to the floor leaving a clear splash mark in the dust. What am I doing? I'm gonna go blind if I kept this up. First thing I gotta do is get rid of my watch and eliminate the urge to check it every ninety seconds or so. I checked it one last time, and now eighteen minutes has passed. I unsnapped it and put it in my front pocket.

With the Blinking Olympics concluded, I needed to find something else to do. I decided to check the acoustics in the room. "Hello," sounded kind of hollow and tinny. Maybe if I said it a little louder, "HELLO." Not bad. Got a little echo going. How about louder and longer? "HELLOOOOOOOOOOOOO." Ah, better!

I started humming a tune from the band Boston, and before I knew it, I was singing. As my confidence grew and I felt convinced that I was all alone, I decided to reward the locked rooms on the fourth floor with a little vocal rendition of Elton John as well. I threw in some Journey for good measure. I didn't know all the words to most of the songs and had to make up a few verses as I went along. I was feeling pretty good, and my feet decided to join in adding another dimension to my free concert. I used a pen as a microphone as I ran through my playlist of songs.

The concert was going well until I glanced up toward the ceiling and spotted a surveillance camera. OOPS! Oh, boy, that's embarrassing. I envisioned about five employees gathered around the monitor watching my concert. I tried to fool "Big Brother" by modifying my dance moves into stretches. (Come on, I'm not the only one who has ever done that!) I had to get my mind back on my side. *Fuck 'em if they can't take a joke!* I stared at the camera and thought, *Okay, guys, break it up and get back to work. There's nothing to see here.*

I stared at the locked rooms. My legs and back were getting stiff. I needed to move and stretch out. I started walking around swinging my arms from side to side to keep loose. My inquisitive mind wanted to know how long the aisle actually was, so I started at one end and counted the number of square foot tiles on the floor. When I got to the end, my number was one hundred and sixty tiles or one hundred and sixty feet long. I took the time (because I had a lot of it) to convert it to inches which was one thousand nine hundred and twenty. I recounted the tiles on my return trip to make sure my number was right. BINGO! I was onto to something here. Now my brain wanted to know how many strides it would take for me to reach the other side if I walked at my normal pace. How many strides would it take if jogged? How many if I ran? How many steps if I walked heel to toe? How many if I walked on a long angle? The combinations were endless, and I exhausted every one of them.

I was getting thirsty, and my stomach became angry, reminding me that I was hungry. I had configured the dimensions of the floor in every possible scenario and needed to rest. I scraped the dust away on the floor with my shoe and then conducted a test by taking a knee to see how much dust would stick to me and how easily it would brush off. The test was fairly successful, and I decided to take my jacket off and sit down against the wall. Hopefully, my ass wouldn't attract too much dust, and I could slap it off later. Just in case, I had my jacket to cover up the lingering spot.

The relief of being off my feet outweighed the worry of ass dust. My feet thanked me by throbbing, and rigor mortis settled in my back. I closed my eyes, and swiveled my neck to release the tension. My head hung forward with my chin coming to a rest against my chest. I sat motionless with my eyes closed in front of the evil storage rooms.

Time finally ceased to exist as I space traveled within my subconscious. Suddenly hearing voices in my head forced my consciousness to resurface. My eyes opened upon reentry into the now and realized that the voices in my head were actually people getting off the elevator on my floor. I jumped to my feet, arriving there before the blood had a chance to settle, so I felt lightheaded. I leaned against the wall and began spanking myself at an award-winning rate, like an angry nun, while flipping my jacket onto my back.

The voices grew louder as my arm speed increased. Getting caught spanking yourself can only lead to bad things. I completed the task without a moment to spare as the cavalry turned the corner lead by Lieutenant O'Brien. He asked me how I was doing, and I wanted to tell him all about my scientific footage discoveries but decided against it and said, "Great!"

I finally got to meet my new sergeant and team members. After the introductions were done, it was time to get back to business. Bolt cutters rendered the rooms defenseless and exposed their guts to reveal hundreds of copies of movies piled high in each location. The next step was to inventory and package the movies for evidence. This would require getting down and dirty. The lieutenant offered me the option to stay for overtime and help with the process or go end of tour. I decided that I had spent enough time in this concentration camp and wanted to get some fresh air and sit on something soft, so I chose the latter and went home.

This was one of those days when you wished that you could rewind the past few hours of your life to live over again. I didn't just manage to kill time; I assassinated it. The area should have been cordoned off with yellow tape and preserved as a crime scene. I felt like a serial killer trapped in Salvador Dali's *The Persistence of Memory*, where "soft watches" lie dead or dying as they melted on rocks and hung from dead tree branches.

Kevin, a new team member, agreed to give me a ride back to my car by police headquarters. As soon as I exited the self-storage building, I pulled the tie from around my neck like I was starting a lawn mower and undid the top button of my shirt. Talking on the car ride back, we decided to meet at Creedmoor Hospital in Queens the next morning, where we would pick up a category two unmarked auto and continue our commute to our office, located on Broadway in Lower Manhattan. A category two car could be used during working hours but had to be stored within the city limits at the end of your tour. A category one car could be stored at the assigned officer's residence but could only be used during workdays.

I thanked Kevin for the ride and was grateful to be back in the comfort of something I called my own even if it was just a car. I was exhausted from doing nothing all day other than trying to think of ways to keep my mind active. The ride home was arduous and lengthy, but my mind was set on "pause" as the radio's emissions vibrated the air in my car's cabin.

I lazily pulled the car in front of my house. The right front tire squealed like a pig as it rubbed against the curb before coming to a halt. I turned off the ignition and simultaneously exhaled along with the car's engine. I sat motionless for a moment hoping that someone would come to the car and gently carry me into the house. Realizing that was never going to happen, I prepared myself for the forty or so foot journey. I unlocked the front door to the house, and cool air greeted my face. My couch looked like a cumulus cloud at the moment, and I couldn't wait to settle in. I flop onto it like a professional wrestler performing his signature finishing move. I kicked off my leather tape measurers, tucked my knees under my chest, and waited for the referee to count me out, match over. Tomorrow would be a better day.

And it was. I met Kevin in the parking lot of Creedmoor Hospital, and we commuted into Lower Manhattan. It was a delight not to park your own car on the streets of the city and have to worry about meter maids, door dings, and bumper notches.

Our office was on the small side but so was the size of the team. We were five cops and one sergeant. The focus of our team was to combat trademark infringement, which meant going after sellers of bogus sunglasses, pocketbooks, watches, clothing, and motion picture film piracy. A lot of the investigations were focused on Canal Street booths, which are a favorite of tourists and out-of-towners. The knockoffs were hidden from the public view and stored in the back rooms. Venders sat atop wooden ladders on the sidewalk, like lifeguards at a community pool, keeping a watchful eye out for thieves and police.

Two of the members in my team, Harry and Mitch, had done this work for many years and their faces were very recognizable to the local vendors. Whenever Harry or Mitch decided to walk through Chinatown for lunch, the sidewalk lifeguards would send out a distress signal and order everybody out of the pool. Metal gates could be heard crashing to the ground, as if a tornado were approaching. The workers would suddenly close up shop and disappear into the cracks until the coast was clear. I worked here for only three months until I got the internal notification that I was finally transferred to the ATF team.

FORTY-EIGHT

I'm Watching You

Working with the ATF team was a dream assignment. I would finally be working on some high-profile cases with the added ingredient of having federal funding and all the investigative toys that come with it. HIDTA (high intensity drug trafficking area) is defined as "a federally sponsored program which aims at enhancing and coordinating drug control efforts among local, state, and federal law enforcement agencies. The program provides agencies with coordination, equipment, technology, and additional resources to combat drug trafficking and its harmful consequences in critical regions of the United States." This meant a concerted effort among DEA (Drug Enforcement Administration), FBI (Federal Bureau of Investigation), ATF (Alcohol, Tobacco and Firearms), U.S. Marshall's Service, Secret Service, INS (Immigration and Naturalization Service), NYPD, U.S. Military, and the New York State Police.

My wish had been fulfilled. I was assigned to work with ATF Group-V (five) along with four housing cops. Our office was located on the twenty-ninth floor of 26 Federal Plaza in Lower Manhattan. This was the same building I had visited a few years ago when Frank and I had arrested the four males for the robbery of the armored car in Bushwick on Flushing Avenue. This scenic building contained the cologne-wearing suits, clean bathrooms, and working copy machines.

HIDTA was still in transition, and a lot of construction work was under-way. Part of the intelligence gathering group was already set up on the floor, while plans were being made across the hall to accommodate the incoming investigative and enforcement groups.

Because I was assigned to the team late, I had to take one of the remain-ing smaller workstations. I was just happy having a new desk to call my own. The surface was clean and smooth. Two keys hung from the lock of the over-head compartment. My chair was comfortably cushioned and equipped with a spring mechanism which compressed as I sat into it. It even reclined, taking pressure off my lower spine. Four wheels sat atop a protective plastic sheet which allowed the chair to move freely on the even surface. I rolled my chair back and forth around my station, getting a feel for the motion. You have to acquire a good working knowledge of the environment around you. I tried to configure the percentage of roll ability of the chair versus the friction level of the plastic covering so I could come up with the proper amount of thrust psi (per square inch) needed to slide the chair back without it slamming into the workstation directly behind me. Although I knew with time I would be able to figure this out, I was eager to know the formula right away. So, like a crash-test dummy, I sat there pushing myself away from the desk several times under controlled circumstances until I was satisfied with my findings.

Next, I tackled the extremely important and difficult issue of proper phone placement. Does it go on the right-hand or left-hand side? I'm right-handed, so do I pick up the phone with my strong hand, or do I need it to write with? Which side will the cord be less intrusive? Where should it be placed so that I will still have maximum surface area to work with? After some deliberation, I chose the upper left-hand corner.

Looking over the phone, I realized that I now had my very own per-sonal phone number. This particular phone came complete with a hold, mute, conference call, and transfer button. I even had my own voice mail. A small booklet underneath the phone informed me that E-Z step-by-step instructions would walk me through the process of setting up my very own communica-tions center.

As a rule, I generally don't get things done right the first time. I am more of a "trial and error" person, and attempting to set up my voice mail fell right in line with this rule. I made numerous attempts with negative results. As the patience was being sucked out of my body with each failed attempt, frustration began to fill the vacuum and almost forced me to stomp the "new-age technology" right out of it and send it cascading twenty-nine floors to a shattering death. I decided to walk away and come back later with a new attitude and try again. On my way out, I glared at the machine and mumbled the words, "I'll be back."

I walked across the reflective floors to the graffiti-free bathroom and splashed cool water on my face. A paper towel hung from the mouth of the wall dispenser like a tongue in an apparent attempt to mock me. I stood at arm's length from the machine with my head pitched forward so that the droplets of water could fall away from my dry clothing. I thought to myself, *You machines all stick together, don't you.* I then ripped the tongue out of the mouth of the dispenser with a fierce right hook and dried my hands and face. I squeezed it into a tight small ball and slammed it into the garbage can. I walked out of the bathroom, pausing at the door, giving the machine my best John Connor stares (from *The Terminator* movies), mouthing the words, "I'm watching you."

I returned with reinforcements and attempted to tackle the phone once again. Andy Savino was one of the housing cops who had been working with ATF for some time now. He had recently set up his phone and glanced at the E-Z setup instructions as a reminder. Apparently, he was machine-friendly and programmed the phone on the first attempt. He guided me through my voice-recorded greeting. I was all set to receive and retrieve voice messages!

Even though it was still early in the morning, I felt exhausted. You would think that this would be easy, but it's not. My mind was being bombarded with all new information. My brain was working overtime, trying to absorb and sort out the new stimuli.

It was time to get to work, so Andy and I headed out to the pier located at the end of the Rockaway Parkway exit of the Belt Parkway. Andy brought me up to speed, informing me that the team was preparing to purchase additional firearms from two male black subjects in Brooklyn. This was an ongoing long-term investigation in which several firearms had been purchased from these two individuals. What I found strange was that the undercover in this case was a white male in his early fifties, driving an automobile very similar to an unmarked police auto. To me, this screamed "cop," but I guessed that the two subjects were more concerned with making money than going to jail.

Pulling into the lot, I could see a group of men huddled in the rear corner of the parking lot. Andy found a parking spot, and we joined the group. I was introduced to my other teammates, Stevie Johnson, Ricky Nesmith, and Jim Dobbins. Jim had been promoted to sergeant since I last saw him when I was in narcotics and now was the boss of the PD guys. I immediately recognized ATF Agent Mike Santory and then was introduced to the rest of the crew. The attitude was extremely relaxed, especially that of the undercover agent, Sal, who was just moments away from meeting with men who had illegal guns for sale.

With the entire crew present, a tactical plan was given by the undercover case agent, Sal. This meeting had taken place several times in the past and seemed redundant for the other members. This was new and exciting for me, so my heartbeat raced a bit. My concerns about the machines in the office had become a distant memory. The backup teams were given specific locations to park in case things went bad. I didn't take this assignment lightly. Although there had been several meetings and firearms purchases in the past, the chance that the bad guy's intentions could change, and Sal's life could be at risk was always lurking in the background.

After a short period of time, the transaction was concluded. There is always that little sigh of relief when a deal goes as planned. A couple more illegal firearms were taken off the streets of New York City, and the laundry list of federal charges against the two males continued to grow like Pinocchio's nose. The case was later brought down with agents buying approximately fifty handguns which were traced back to Virginia.

At the conclusion of the day, I was given a real gift by Andy. He decided that because I lived on Long Island and he lived in Queens, I should take the category one auto assigned to him. I asked him, "Are you sure?"

He replied, "Of course. It takes me five minutes to get to work by train. You need it more than me. I'll just wait for the next car to come in and take that one."

Not one to argue with common sense, I said, "Thank you very much." The next day, we processed the necessary paperwork so that the gold 1996 Ford Taurus would become my first, very own, work car.

FORTY-NINE

The Bag of Bones

Prior to my arrival, the team had successfully dismantled a sophisticated heroin organization located in East New York Brooklyn on Bradford Street. Two brothers headed the organization in a "New Jack City" fashion. They controlled the corner apartment building, and the residents lived in fear. They had their own surveillance teams keeping a watchful eye open for police and rival drug dealers. They used radios to communicate between each other using codes. The ATF team was able to capture the radio frequency and listen in firsthand to their conversations. They used terms like "proper long" which meant that the avenue was clear, and "proper short" advised that the street was clear. A customer was called a bird. If a customer received his order and was ready to leave, you would hear a radio transmission like "Its proper long and proper short. Let the bird fly." Cameras were mounted at key locations across the street to monitor the building. Guns were concealed around the building for easy access to protect their domain. The front door was made of reinforced steel to prevent unwelcomed entry.

With the help of confidential informants, the team was able to successfully build a solid case against the organization and bring them down. The defendants were charged with Continuing Criminal Enterprise (CCE) under federal statutes, which carried a minimum of twenty years in federal prison.

After the arrest of the brothers and their workers, it was determined that the organization was responsible for several murders. With the brothers facing multiple years in federal prison, they decided it would be in their best interest to cooperate with the United States government.

Willie, one of the brothers, provided information regarding a homicide that had occurred. He suspected that a person close to the family was responsible for stealing fifty thousand dollars in cash from his home. Willie confronted the male, and he agreed to take a ride with Willie and Buffy (an enforcer) to the fortified apartment building. Buffy was eager to make the thief pay.

According to Willie, while he was setting up the workers for their daily shifts, Buffy began to beat and torture the alleged thief in the basement. Willie returned to find the thief badly beaten and bound to a chair with telephone cord and duct tape. Willie became upset with Buffy and told him to get rid of alleged thief. The plan was to steal a car and crash it on Pennsylvania Avenue near the Starrett City apartment complex with the victim in it.

The next day, Willie arrived at the drug location to ready his workers and found the thief still bound to the chair. Willie removed the duct tape from the victim's mouth only to find that he was not breathing. Enraged with a new dilemma, Willie told Buffy, "This is your problem. You get rid of him."

On the third day, Willie showed up to prepare the workers, only to find the room empty and spotless, smelling like ammonia. The problem had been addressed and business resumed as usual.

We needed to locate that body and verify the incident to give closure to the family. To save his own life, the brother agreed to wear a hidden wire on his person and meet with one of the workers, Larry, who was present at the time the body was disposed of. The defendant was given specific instructions on what questions to ask regarding the whereabouts of the victim.

Followed closely by surveillance teams, the brother picked up the worker on his motorcycle, and they discussed the facts pertaining to the victim, as surveillance teams listened in. The defendant told the worker that the police were onto the murder, and the remains needed to be relocated. The passenger went into the details of how Buffy had dismembered the body using a large hunting knife. He also admitted that he was sick to his stomach when he witnessed the knife cut through flesh and bone, as the head, hands, and feet were sliced off. When asked what happened to those parts, the passenger stated, "He put them in a duffel bag and dropped them off the Staten Island Ferry." The rest of the body had been dumped in the vicinity of the Belt Parkway and South Conduit Boulevard near the Van Wyck Expressway. Driving past the area, the worker pointed out the spot where the body was disposed of almost a year ago.

We were given a clue as to the whereabouts of the human remains, and now it was our turn to find them. The area was covered in towering weeds as high as our heads, and the temperature was sweltering. About eight of us ventured into the unknown and were forced back by the natural defenses of the brush and a variety of swarming insects. Going into this roadside jungle unprotected was not going to happen. Andy and I decided to visit a local home depot and purchase two protective Tyveks suits with hoods and gloves. We returned shortly and suited up to do battle with Mother Nature in an attempt to find its well-protected hidden treasure.

My body temperature rose as soon as I was fully enclosed in the suit, and my sweat glands were ordered into work. As I entered the grounds, the head-high weeds fought back against me with its needles and thorns grabbing and poking at my newly shielded skin. My feet crunched under me with every step as if I walked on dry breakfast cereal. Just a few feet away from me, I could hear Andy's footsteps making their way deeper into the brush. I fanned the stalks in front of me away from my face with simulated breast strokes. I brought my knees up to my chest with each step as I advanced into the unknown. Pushing on, I lost all sense of direction. The suit clung to my skin as my body attempted to cool off. I could see numerous mosquitoes of various sizes locked on to my white outer layer in an attempt to pierce the man-made surface. Various other bugs seemed to tag along for the ride.

An unforgettable and unique odor wafted across my path. As I continued further in, the smell became stronger, and I knew death was only a few breast strokes away. A handful of steps more brought me to the source of the odor.

A large garbage bag was at my feet. The tall weeds did their best to hide the bag, but it wasn't enough. "I got something here," I yelled. I stomped the brush away from the edge of the bag, creating a temporary vacuum in the weeds. Kneeling down, I could see countless bugs running across the surface of the bag. With my gloved hands, I ripped through two layers of garbage bag. The smell was intense as it rushed toward my face from the bag like an escaping Jeannie that had been trapped in a bottle for centuries. My breath quickened with anticipation.

An anxious voice yelled to me, "What do you got?"

I pulled the plastic away revealing its contents. "Nah, it's just a dog."

This area proved to be a popular dumping ground for animals. Andy and I collectively recovered five dead dogs. Some appeared to be beloved household pets, while others seemed to be silver medal finishers of illegal underground dog fighting. We concluded the search without finding any human remains. We marched out of the weeds heading back to the team. I brushed away the freeloading bugs from their taxi, along with the predators. I peeled the suit away from my body, and a small warm breeze felt refreshing against my moist skin. I stepped out of the zippered suit and downed a cold bottle of water.

After our grid search of the area resulted in negative results, we went to the local precinct of concern and checked with the detectives. Looking back through their files, we were able to find a case they called the Bag of Bones. Sanitation employees doing a cleanup work detail along the side of the highway made the gruesome discovery of human bones approximately six months earlier. Working together with the detectives, we were able to identify the remains. They belonged to a male who was reported missing approximately one year ago. The open case could now be closed, and the deceased given a proper burial.

Eddie, the second brother, was faced with a long prison sentence. He also decided to cooperate with the United States government. He confessed to an unsolved homicide which happened alongside of the drug apartment building. In the drug business, egos can run high. A "bird" had been dropped off at the building to do business while the driver sat idling outside the location. A cardinal rule of the organization was to keep customer's cars away from the building so as not to draw unwanted attention to the operation. The brother approached the driver and informed him of the rule. Apparently, the driver was unhappy with the level of customer service provided by Eddie, and heated words were exchanged. The car finally drove off only to return a short time later, parking in the exact same spot. Eddie tried to reiterate his point, and a second exchange of words ensued. The driver elaborated his point of view of the circumstances while waving a firearm, using words to the effect of, "Make me move now, motherfucker!"

The battle of egos escalated, Eddie walked to the side of the building and knocked on the first floor window. He told the employee inside to hand him the Mac-10 machine gun. Joined by another worker with a firearm, they walked back to the parking violator. They proceeded to fire forty-some-odd rounds into the "illegally" parked car. In my opinion, he would have made one hell of a traffic agent with that kind of work philosophy.

That day of work ended early, and the operation was shut down. The sudden arrival of four to five police cars will do that to a drug business. I often wondered how the customer inside the building got home after that. I mean, what do you do after your driver has been shot forty times? Do you call for a cab or just walk home?

Eddie confessed to a second homicide of a worker who was accused of stealing drugs from the organization. The worker was brought down near the train tracks, where he begged for his life, saying he never stole anything from the business. He was shot numerous times while he maintained his innocence. The missing drugs turned up later, and Eddie realized he had shot an innocent man.

The investigation was officially terminated resulting in the arrest of numerous defendants. Three previously open homicides were solved. One investigation seemed to end and spin-off into another. We would identify another target and start from scratch in an attempt to dissolve that organization.

FIFTY

I Need a Drink

The formula for drug gang eradication was usually the same. Once an organization was targeted, we would use all of our investigative techniques and resources to establish the players and learn as much about them as we possibly could. We would look through complaint and intelligence reports and computer database systems, such as Department of Motor Vehicles (DMV) and National Crime Information Center (NCIC).

I would try to tap into the department's greatest asset, "The Dinosaur." Scientists say that the dinosaur is extinct. I beg to differ. The dinosaur is alive and well and residing in every precinct detective squad room. The dinosaur was that guy who worked his whole entire career in the same precinct. He's been roaming the same plains and shaking the same trees for thirty years. All that the dinosaur needed was just a nickname, and he could give you a person's entire family tree and associates. The dinosaur had the greatest database system in the world which could not be duplicated: his experience on the job.

Once all the background information was acquired, and we had a clear picture of the people in the organization and how it operated, it was time to infiltrate. We would formulate a plan using confidential informants and undercover officers to gain the trust of the workers and establish them as customers. Through surveillance and other tactical techniques, we learned how the mechanics of the group operated by tracking their movements and locating where they called home. You would be surprised what you could learn about a person after you have gone through their trash. I believe the saying goes, "One man's trash… can be used against him in a court of law" or something to that affect.

Undercover officers and confidential informants would make numerous illegal gun and controlled-substance buys. Hundreds of hours of surveillance film, still photography, and recordings were documented and organized. Once air tight charges could be brought against the organization, we would formulate a plan for the takedown.

What I found to be the most interesting part about dismantling a violent drug gang was what I called the fallout. It was basically the information you acquired once you had somebody in a "prosecutional" hold so tight that they couldn't breathe and would have to tap out to survive. It was like hanging them upside down by the ankles and shaking them, watching all the coins, lint and bubblegum wrappers "fall out" of their pockets. The coins, lint and bubblegum wrappers were information regarding drug suppliers, robberies, and homicides.

Working together with Mike Santory from ATF, we were able to bring down a violent Dominican crack-cocaine organization run by Edwin Ortiz. With the help of his brother, they operated from storefronts in Bushwick and East New York, Brooklyn, using stash houses spread throughout Queens.

Larger organizations do not put all their eggs in one basket. The need for multiple stash houses prevents the entire "product" from being lost to robbery or confiscated by the police at one time. The group can recover from just one of its locations being hit. Stash locations are changed frequently to prevent such losses.

Using confidential informants, we were able to track Edwin Ortiz's movements. At one point during our investigation, we learned that Edwin was at one of his Queen's stash apartments which contained fifty kilos of cocaine, when it was stormed by rival drug members who attempted to rob him. Edwin leaped from the fourth floor apartment and broke his leg but was able to escape with his life. A worker was caught and brutally beaten by the thugs as they claimed the drugs as their own. These types of robberies happen frequently but usually go unreported for obvious reasons. We were able to verify the incident by checking hospital records once we learned the fictitious name used by Edwin.

Edwin had a successful thriving business and would stop at nothing to keep it that way. People played by Edwin's rules or suffered the consequences. During our investigation, information surfaced regarding numerous homicides that were ordered and paid for by Edwin.

Mike and I worked closely with the United States Attorney's Office at Eastern District located in Downtown Brooklyn. The assistant United States attorney or AUSA, who was assigned to our case, was a female attorney by the name of Elaine Banar. Elaine was a slim, attractive, and intelligent woman who combined a great understanding of investigative know-how with excellent prosecution skills. Elaine worked as an agent with the United States Customs Service for ten years before switching to the prosecution side of investigations. With her help and guidance, Mike and I were able to map out an investigative course of action to implode the organization.

Once our investigation was complete with enough evidence to prosecute successfully, we cast a net over the organization and pulled in our prey. An early morning takedown of Edwin Ortiz went as planned. Storming his Bronx apartment, we were able to arrest Edwin, who laid face down, spread eagle in his underwear as his wife used the covers on their bed for protection.

With Edwin now in our custody, NYPD and ATF simultaneously executed numerous search and arrest warrants issued by the U.S. attorney's office. All the people identified in the organization were arrested. Numerous guns, cash, and kilos were recovered.

Faced with the potential of serving many years in federal prison, Edwin Ortiz decided to enter into a cooperation agreement with the United States Attorney's Office. Edwin admitted his involvement in five homicides. Some of the homicides had taken place a few years ago and remained unsolved. Due to heavy case loads and lack of new leads, these homicides were not presently being investigated and had been put on the shelf unsolved.

The Cold Case Squad was formed in January of 1996. It was the brain-storm of three innovative police strategist by the names of Jack Maple, Edward Norris, and Louis Anemone, all under the watchful eye of Police Commissioner William Bratton. The unit sought out aggressive detectives who weren't afraid to walk into any squad room in the city and reactivate cases that no one else was looking at. Mike Santory and I decided to enlist the help of Detective Derrick Parker to help bring these old cases to life again. Armed with infor-mation supplied by Ortiz and confidential informants, Detective Parker was quickly able to locate these old open homicide cases.

Although Edwin Ortiz didn't pull the trigger on his victims himself, he was as guilty as the person who did. Instead of personally pulling the trigger, he'd hire contract killers to do the dirty work. One of those paid killers was a vicious monster named Franklin Frias.

Franklin Frias was already serving twenty-six years to life for murder when I first met him. Derrick Parker and I traveled to upstate New York to pay Franklin a visit. We went on a fishing expedition in hopes that Franklin would shed some light on an open homicide in Queens where a male was gunned down by an unknown passenger on a passing motorcycle. After checking in, we were ushered to a small meeting area, where tables were divided up in cubi-cles. As we waited for Franklin to arrive, Derrick told me that he was going to be very direct with Franklin.

Moments later, Franklin was ushered into the meeting area accompanied by a corrections officer. Derrick and I stood and motioned them over to the table we were occupying. The officer stood nearby keeping a watchful eye. Franklin was wearing an orange correctional jumpsuit with the sleeves rolled up past his elbows. As he approached me, I thought to myself that orange was a very appropriate color for Franklin. Orange meant "caution" or "danger", and Franklin was indeed a dangerous man. Although he was short in stature, his forearms put Popeye's to shame. On the outside, his demeanor was calm, but his build told a different story. His skin was stretched over well-developed muscles, which looked to be carved out of granite. Raised vessels scorched down his arms like raging rivers, as blood surged throughout his body.

He sat at the table with a confused look on his face trying to figure out who we were and why were we there. Derrick sat in a chair across from him, while I half-cheeked a corner of the table. He told us his English was not very good, but he agreed to talk to us without a translator. After introducing ourselves, Derrick got right to business. He took his time and explained the details of the case that we were investigating. Franklin nodded along indicating that he was on the same page with us. Derrick asked him if he knew who the shooter was. Sitting in the chair, Franklin's forehead furrowed as he calmly shook his head and responded that he did not know anything about the case. Derrick paused for a moment studying Franklin's face. Then he shifted his weight toward Franklin, invading his personal space and said, "You were on the back of that bike. Weren't you?"

Franklin retreated in the chair as his eyes seemed to double in size. He became flushed as if Derrick's words had slapped him across the face. He shook his head and offered a vehement, "Nooooooooo" stepping on the "o" like air escaping a deflating balloon.

Derrick continued to jab at Franklin, "I know it was you on the back of that bike. You were the shooter. It was you who killed that kid."

Franklin stood up, and thick veins appeared in his neck to fuel his sudden rage. "NO. NOT ME. FUCK YOU. NOT ME." Derrick remained seated, and I stood up to give us some leverage if we needed it. The corrections officer started to head over to our table to calm things down.

Derrick sat calmly and continued his bluff by stating matter-of-factly, "Yes, it was. I know it was you."

Franklin's eyes glazed over with fury as his body tensed. I pictured those eyes recording his victim's last moments as their lifeless bodies hit the pavement before him. Franklin started heading toward the approaching officer and left us with "NOT ME. FUCK YOU." The corrections officer hooked his arm around Franklin's and directed him toward the heavy metal gate. Franklin looked over his shoulder and whispered, "Fuck you," and was gone.

Derrick and I remained frozen in our positions. Time seemed to hiccup, as it momentarily disconnected then kicked back in. I smiled and said, "Okay, that went well."

Derrick agreed with my sarcastic remark saying, "Actually, it did. We rattled his cage."

I spent only a few moments with Franklin, but I felt that I had aged tremendously. Walking out, I told myself, *I need a drink.*

A few weeks later, Franklin became aware of the fact that the Ortiz brothers were cooperating with the government. He wrote a letter to Detective Parker stating that he wanted to meet again. This time, AUSA Elaine Banar would draft paperwork to have Franklin "produced" or brought down to Brooklyn to be interviewed.

Franklin was temporarily housed with the Federal Bureau of Prisons (BOP) at the Metropolitan Detention Center (MDC) located near the Gowanus Bay between 2nd and 3rd Avenues on 29th Street in Brooklyn. Sensing that he was behind the eight ball, Franklin wanted to come in and cooperate. Derrick, Elaine, Mike, and I sat through numerous sessions with Franklin as he spoke in great detail regarding several homicides he was involved in. Franklin's words were reshuffled and spoken in a different voice from a translator who sat a few feet away from him as he reenacted some of his crimes.

One case he was hired, along with another gunman, to eradicate a problem for a drug lord. Their target was believed to be in an apartment building, and they decided to split up in search of their victim. The second gunman decided to wear a hood on his head when he got into the building to help hide his identity. Franklin, not recognizing the male with the hood, mistook the gunman for the target and shot him dead. When he finished, he shrugged his shoulders as if to say, "Oops. What are you going to do? Shit happens."

After evaluating the information supplied by Franklin, the government decided against entering into an agreement with him but with Derrick's help, we were still able to close out the open homicide cases.

FIFTY-ONE

Q and Q

In the next few months, HIDTA had gone through some administrative changes with Alcohol, Tobacco, and Firearms (ATF) withdrawing from the program. At the end of 1996, the HIDTA administration decided to aim its investigative and enforcement units at New York City's most drug-riddled housing developments. The deck was reshuffled as my team crossed over to the west side of the twenty-ninth floor to unite with the other investigative teams. As a result, our team expanded with the addition of a couple of detectives who came over from the other squads and was renamed the Fox team.

We were given the task of locating and dismantling a successful narcotics organization operating in the Tilden, Brownsville and Van Dyke Housing developments, all patrolled by the Seven-Three (073) precinct in Brownsville, Brooklyn. Having spent most of my career working in Brooklyn North, I gladly took the lead as case officer for this investigation. Having lost ATF as our federal partners, Agent Mike McGarrity of the Federal Bureau of Investigation (FBI) was assigned to our team to help out in any way possible.

We stepped right onto the playing field, and with the help of Detectives Andy Savino and Teddy Jimenez, I met with the housing managers from all of the target developments and tried to gather as much information as possible. The Housing Authority (HA) alerted us to all the potential problem apartments and hazardous conditions in each of their buildings. They were eager to get assistance from the police department in tackling their existing issues. The HA even supplied us with vacant apartments so that we could conduct surveillance around the courtyards and streets where a lot of drug trafficking and other violent crimes were taking place. Dressed as construction workers, we would smuggle up our surveillance equipment and videotape and photograph hundreds of people in an effort to identify dealers.

Sergeant Jim Dobbins worked as a housing cop covering this area and knew a lot of the players by name. We sat down and spoke with detectives from the Seven-Three (073) squad and Housing Public Service Area Number Two (PSA2). We looked through complaint and incident reports to get a feel for what was going on in the streets. Brooklyn North narcotics teams feed off the fertile grounds by snatching up local street dealers during buy-and-bust operations, only to be replaced with pinch hitters waiting in the on-deck circle. Gunshots echoed through playgrounds on a daily basis, as shattered dreams were often carted off by ambulance or in handcuffs.

Our preliminary investigation uncovered a heroin organization run by Rodney Bailey known on the streets as Watson. Aside from his own business, he employed several street dealers who sold heroin independently in the projects and surrounding area with his permission in return for a five percent commission on drug profits. Our investigation revealed that Bailey was believed to be distributing over ten ounces of heroin weekly with profits that ranged between $15,000 and $20,000 per week. It was the intention of the Fox team to bring Bailey's operation to a screeching halt.

Countless hours of surveillance, computer searches, and old-fashioned foot work enabled us to identify the hierarchy of the group and plan our attack. With the help of confidential informants, we were able to insert one of our most dangerous tools: Stevie J.

Detective Steve Johnson was a tall, proud, black man with a booming voice and a contagious laugh. He had one of the essential key ingredients that make an excellent undercover: the gift of gab. Stevie J. could talk the stripes off an elephant. I know that elephants don't have stripes…anymore. Well, now you know why.

Stevie and one of my confidential informants (CI) immersed themselves in the local restaurant on the corner of Rockaway Avenue and Blake Avenue, while we listened in from the car. Detective Rickey Nesmith blended into the background and kept a watchful eye on the undercover. The entire neighborhood virtually passed through this restaurant at some point during the day, and it seemed like a good place to go fishing. While enjoying a nice greasy meal on behalf of the police department, the CI nudges Stevie and points toward the door. Bailey's lieutenant, known on the streets as Pig, entered the establishment and took a seat at the counter. The informant instantly got excited and couldn't sit still like a puppy about to receive his "good boy" treat. Stevie told the CI to relax and stay cool. Once the informant's tail stopped wagging, Stevie told him to invite Pig over to the table.

The CI made contact with the subject, and after a brief discussion returned to the table with Pig. Stevie J. introduced himself, posing as an affluent, expanding heroin dealer doing business in the Bronx, who had been searching for a potent product and a new reliable supplier. Informed by the CI that the group's stuff was the best in Brooklyn, he decided to take a ride and check it out. Pig asked how much Stevie was looking to purchase, and Stevie said he wanted a bundle (ten glassine envelopes) to start. The undercover explained that he was going to hand these out as samples to his clients to see if it met their needs under the guise of making larger purchases in the near future. Pig pondered Stevie's request and said, "I don't know you, but I'll sell to my man here." Stevie shrugged his indifference, and moments later, we had our first buy into the group.

The glassines were sent to the police laboratory where analysts would test the quantity and quality (Q and Q) of the samples. The police department does not like to invest a lot of money toward a low quality product and may force the investigation to come to an early end. To our delight, the Q and Q were exceptional. The high percentage of pure heroin in each glassine envelope made Bailey's product one of the most sought after on the streets of Brownsville.

The investigation went on for weeks as Stevie began to submerse himself in the neighborhood becoming a familiar face on the block. He continued to make larger buys into the organization from other members of the group which we had identified. Although Bailey made his presence known periodically, we had not made a direct connection with the group's leader. We continued to put Stevie in the area in hopes of forcing a chance meeting.

As Stevie's purchases grew larger, so did his waistline and the receipts he handed in from eating at the restaurant. As long as he kept reeling in new subjects and the Q and Q remained high, Stevie could eat like a king. He looked forward to working out on the streets. He even recommended certain days of the week because he was so familiar with the restaurant's weekly specials on the menu. I often had to nibble on cold, disgusting pizza in a cramped auto several blocks away while I listened to Stevie ask the waitress for the dessert menu. When we returned to the office, Stevie would brief us on what was happening in the streets while he rubbed his belly, sucking on a toothpick, as I chewed antacids like candy.

Being employed at HIDTA was much different than working in a police department facility. Yes, the copy machines functioned and the bathrooms were spectacular, but they came at a price. Working with federal money and driving federal cars required us to make monthly progress presentations to the powers that be. I dreaded those days when each case officer and boss would have to dress in suit and tie, cross through the double doors on the other side of the floor, and put on a showcase of their investigation. This presentation required a flow chart of the drug organization and a slide show that was narrated by either the boss or case officer.

These slide shows and charts were usually done at the last minute and were put together by analysts assigned to HIDTA. Analysts Tom Calvert and Dave Noonan were on loan to the HIDTA program from the United States Army and were instrumental in putting together our presentation packages. Tom had a neat and clean Clark Kent aura about him, while Dave was more of the clown who loved to laugh. Their time was much sought after, as each case officer and sergeant fought for their project to be worked on first. Just hours before the presentations were to begin, case officers were notoriously pulling at these men like wishbones to get last-minute adjustments done. To their credit, they always somehow managed to get it all done. Most importantly, they got it done with a smile and never let the stress that we applied to them show. Both of these guys were invaluable to the HIDTA Task Force and vital to every one of our cases.

Once the presentations were done, I would rip the tie from around my neck so fast that it would leave a burn mark. Changing back into my street clothes, I could refocus again on the projects. Getting Stevie on the streets of Brownsville was only one aspect of the case. There were hours of boring computer searches and checks that were necessary for a successful prosecution.

Everyone in the team had a specific job and helped to lighten the load for me. It was an absolute team effort. For example, Bill O'Leary, a New York State trooper assigned to my team, was in charge of organizing any information regarding subject vehicles and compiled a photo album of arrest pictures and rap sheets of all the subjects and associates of the drug gang. Joseph Murphy handled the surveillance van and videotaped buys and meetings with subjects.

Although there was much more we needed to learn about the organization, the case was advancing at a good pace as evidence began to stack up. I was eager to get Stevie out in the street to uncover more information. I looked forward to coming to work and found myself mentally working out a plan on my days off. A simple word or phrase could jump-start the work in my head at any time.

One morning, we sent Stevie into the restaurant for breakfast. After stuffing his face once again, Stevie stepped outside to have a smoke while surveillance teams were embedded around the area. I perked up in my seat when Stevie notified us over his hidden wire that the main subject, Rodney Bailey, was on the set. Stevie managed to meander his way over to Bailey and struck up a conversation using his gift of gab. Stevie managed to persuade Bailey to sell to him after dropping names of other workers that Stevie had been dealing with. Bailey was leery at first and then agreed to make the sale. The case took an aggressive turn when Bailey decided to exchange phone and pager numbers.

With the big guy's contact numbers in our hands, we were able to take the investigation to a new level. FBI Agent McGarrity supplied us with all the necessary documentation so that we could subpoena the phone company for Bailey's telephone records. We combed through hundreds of calls with the hope of identifying additional workers, customers, and suppliers. Detective Daisy Ortiz specialized in telephone analysis and was able to identify individuals that Bailey surrounded himself with. Weaved within this network web were all his associates and his supplier. The case was gathering momentum, but around the end of June 1997, my life suddenly derailed.

FIFTY-TWO

Surf's Up!

While visiting my cousin Augie Stile and his wife Kathy in Pennsylvania, my mother started feeling some pain and discomfort. As the day grew into night, her condition worsened. She was brought to a local area hospital where it was determined that she had a silent heart attack, which diabetics are prone to. It is referred to as "silent" because there are none of the tell-tale signs of a heart attack, such as shooting chest pains that travel down the left arm. She was stabilized overnight and then brought down to NYU Medical Center in Manhattan by ambulance.

Over the past twenty years or so, my mother managed to overcome many illnesses and setbacks related to her diabetes. She courageously survived breast cancer, multiple bypass operations, a stroke, broken hip, and even a botched medical procedure, generating a malpractice suit against the hospital. With a great love and appreciation for life, she fought back every time with every ounce of her soul and managed to maintain a high quality of life. She hid behind a touch of humor and a slightly slanted smile to help disguise her pain from the people who loved her.

The phone call from my stepfather was another in a long list of notifications regarding my mother's health. My reaction was one that said, "Oh, shit. Here we go again." Those phone calls immediately siphoned the existence right out of you. Like a garden hose emptying a swimming pool into the street, you feel as if your life is being pumped from your body and is gushing toward the corner sewer.

I got to NYU Medical Center before the ambulance did and stood on First Avenue like a lost boy looking for his mom, which was exactly what I was. I recognized my parent's black Lincoln trailing behind an ambulance pulling into the hospital emergency entrance. Although it was warm, I felt a sudden chill, as apprehension surrounded me when the ambulance stopped to unload its cargo. As the stretcher was removed from the ambulance and the landing gear hit the ground, I made my way over, expecting the worst. My mother was wrapped head to toe in blankets with two straps buckled across her body. Her slanted smile let me know she recognized me approaching. She managed to wiggle her arm out of the blanket straitjacket and grabbed my hand pulling me in. She asked me, "How are you doing?"

I replied, "Me? How are YOU doing?"

She lied, "I'm fine." Her grip was strong and warm, like a mother's hand should be, and immediately put me at ease. We walked hand in hand as the paramedics rolled her into the emergency room and stayed that way for a long time. After parking the car, my stepfather joined us.

The nursing staff at the hospital knew my mother and stepfather by their first names due the amount of time she had spent at NYU over the last few years. We sat in the emergency room for a while as an undetermined amount of time clinically passed before she was transported to a regular room. Her doctor stopped by to see how she was doing. She boldly told him, "I feel fine. I don't know why I'm still here."

The doctor said, "Well, we are going to do some tests to see what happened, and then we'll take it from there." Two minutes and two thousand dollars later, he was gone.

Over the next day or two, my mother underwent a battery of tests to assess her condition. Although she felt fine, tests showed that her heart had suffered extensive damage that required immediate surgery. As she was prepped for surgery, Pop and I walked on eggshells, while my mother stayed stoic. Two men covered in blue from head-to-toe came to wheel her in to the operating room. We kissed her, and with broken voices, we let her know that we loved her. She responded back, "Oh, will you two stop it? I'm gonna be fine. I'll beat this like I beat everything else." And off she went into familiar territory.

I went down to the main lobby and tried to pass the time. Although the big padded chairs looked comfortable, I was unable to find a suitable position. I people watched for hours, wondering what each passing person's thoughts and dreams were. Were they happy? Were they on track, living the lives they dreamed of? Or were they stuck, letting everyday life dictate their destiny? Or was I really asking myself these questions? Times like these allow us to soul-search and tend to remind us of how vulnerable we really are. Even through her suffering, my mother was teaching me about life. It was up to me to apply these lessons to my own.

Somehow, the hours managed to spin away, and she was finally in recovery. The doctors cornered my stepdad and me, and let us know that the operation was successful, but that they had to extract a vein from her lower leg to repair her heart. Diabetics suffer from poor circulation to their extremities and are at risk of gangrene and amputation. Several years ago, my mother underwent an extensive seven-hour bypass operation in which doctors grafted veins into her thighs to improve circulation to prevent the loss of her toes when gangrene had set in. Before that operation, her toes were dying and looked like little pieces of charcoal. Three months after the bypass operation, her toes miraculously returned to normal. Removing that vein from her leg put her foot in jeopardy. However, saving her life was the main objective now, and caring for her leg became a secondary concern.

Once the operation was behind us, I was able to let myself get back to my case. For several weeks, I visited my mother twice a day at the hospital; once at lunch and again after work. My days became extremely long and taxing. Work became a distraction from my mother's condition.

One morning, Pop called to tell me of a commotion my mother had caused at the hospital. It seemed that in the middle of the night, while my mother was heavily medicated, she removed her hospital gown and started to roam the floor unnoticed. Her night nurse checked her room only to find her missing. The nursing staff went on red alert in an attempt to locate their missing patient. Moments later, my mother was located curled up in bed with an elderly gentleman who failed to notify anybody of this encounter. Apparently, this man thought he was at Club Hedonism Hospital and had just hit the jackpot. He had the biggest smile as if they were headed to the ocean to brush off the sand after winning the two-man naked volleyball tournament. I guess I can't blame him. I can only hope that something like that would happen to me one day.

I visited her the next day to see what the heck was going on in this hospital. I walked into her room and stopped at the foot of her bed. She was talking with my stepfather and turned in my direction. With my arms out at my sides and a surprised look on my face, I said, "What the hell is going on around here? I hope he was a good tipper at least." She immediately burst out in uncontrollable laughter, gasping for air. It gave us all a chance to hide behind some humor. She *claimed* that she had no recollection of the event whatsoever.

I pulled a chair up to the foot of the bed, and we continued to laugh and joke about the incident. We finally got past that conversation when I heard an annoying squeaking sound becoming louder and louder by the second. I turned toward the squeaking noise, which seemed to be right outside the door. A metal IV pole came into view with a bag of clear liquid hanging, and a tube connected to a left arm which was driving the pole. An elderly gentleman, clutching his robe with his right hand, appeared in the frame of the door and stopped. As if being controlled by a remote, he slowly turned his head into the doorway and called out, "Surfs up!", while peering into the room. Or maybe that's just what my demented mind heard. After searching the room, his eyes slowly caught mine and then turned forward as he shuffled his feet, pushing his squeaky IV pole ahead of him, out of view.

A little pee escaped into my underpants as I doubled over in laughter. The old man was out searching for his late-night booty call. He probably had tequila in his IV bag. Come to think of it, I did smell a hint of coconut oil in the air. Seeing the old man gave us a chance to experience more of the best medicine in the world: laughter.

FIFTY-THREE

Killer Monk

As my case progressed, my confidential informants continued to be my eyes and ears in the projects. They notified me of an individual residing in one of the target housing developments who was rumored to have several guns in his apartment. For entertainment, he would fire shots from his window at passing police cars. We immediately took a high interest in this person. And because we cannot work on just rumor alone, I asked the informants to get inside the apartment and get an eyeball on the guns. Two weeks later, I had all the information that I needed to get a search warrant for the apartment.

Once the search warrant was validated by the judge, we set up a day to pay the project sniper an early morning visit. We gained entry into the apartment and handcuffed our subject without incident. A full and thorough search of the residence netted us one shotgun, one rifle, three handguns, a bow and arrows, grappling hook, and one blow dart complete with darts. Why anyone would need a bow and arrows, grappling hook and a blow dart gun in the projects of Brooklyn was beyond me. The answer must lie somewhere between the pages of several *Soldier of Fortune* magazines that were scattered about the apartment. Five guns were safely removed from the deadly streets along with the threat of a random cop taking a sniper's bullet through the windshield.

The analysis of Bailey's phone records indicated that he was using his telephone and pager to further his narcotics trafficking business. With the help of

Agent McGarrity, we were granted a federal court order giving us permission to wiretap his phone and clone his pager. In other words, we would now be able to monitor and listen in on all his phone calls and get the messages on his pager. This was a huge step in our attempt to dismantle this organization. Juries love recorded phone calls and videos. A case is pretty tough to beat when they see and hear defendants engaging in criminal activities for themselves.

We set up shop in an apartment building about one mile from the projects and about three miles from Bailey's residence. This apartment was known as the plant. Because of Detective Ortiz's extensive knowledge of phone analysis and wiretapping, she was designated plant manager. Although I was responsible for all the information and reports generated by the wiretap and cloned pager, I relied heavily on her expertise to make sure that everything was being documented properly and recorded as evidence according to the court's procedures.

Soon after this development, I was deputized by FBI Agent McGarrity's SAC (special agent in charge) in a closed door, raise your right hand, I (state your name), ceremony at 26 Federal Plaza. This granted me the power and responsibility to act as a federal agent regarding this case.

Listening to the subject's telephone calls, we were able to identify Bailey's supplier as a Dominican male, known as Jim. Jim was an elusive guy who changed locations frequently to insulate himself from prying eyes. Surveillance teams were able to document and photograph Jim making deliveries of suspected heroin glassines hidden inside cereal boxes to Bailey at his residence.

Stevie continued to make purchases from Bailey directly. Oftentimes, Bailey would tell Stevie to meet him within walking distance of his home. The role of an undercover is to gather evidence. One way of doing that is to get the subject to make incriminating statements about his criminal behavior. However, Stevie did his part in maintaining that the elephant stayed stripeless. Stevie would go on and on about how he wanted to bang fat chicks and talked about his friends who were stupid and overweight, while Bailey only grunted one word responses. It turned out that those friends were actually people in the field team covering the undercover buys. Stevie used this technique to put him and the officers in the field at ease.

In the recorded videos of the buys, you could see that Bailey's ears were actually bleeding, and he couldn't wait to exchange his drugs for money and get the hell out of the car. After reviewing the tapes, I made a mental note to ask AUSA Elaine Banar, who was prosecuting the case, to give Bailey five years off his sentence for pain and suffering. Whenever I got the chance to arrest Bailey, for his own safety, I would immediately transport him to the nearest hospital to have his prostrate tested for lung cancer after the amount of smoke that Stevie had blown up his ass.

Bailey's business was flourishing until his Dominican supplier, Jim, ran into a dry spell. For some reason that we weren't able to ascertain, Jim was unable to supply Bailey with his high-quality product. There may have been a large seizure at one of the ports which supplied heroin to the East Coast or even a delay in arriving cargo. Whatever the answer was, it knocked Bailey's business offline. As his remaining stash dwindled down, Bailey started reaching out to other suppliers to keep his business running.

While the frequency of recorded phone calls from Jim started to slow, a new voice emerged. The voice belonged to a man known on the streets as Killer Monk. Monk had a thick, muscular physique, and seemed to slither through the streets. When he stepped onto the corner or entered the restaurant, people immediately became uncomfortable. Just his presence made people feel on edge.

With no other alternative, Bailey agreed to do business with Monk. Even though they used the same brand name that was stamped on the glassine envelopes containing heroin supplied by Jim, it wasn't long before the junkies noticed the difference in the quality. The high wasn't as strong, and their escape from life was much shorter.

One day, we intercepted several phone conversations between Pig and Bailey. Bailey had been arrested earlier in the day by TNT narcotics cops for possession of a Billy club (small pipe wrapped in tape) that he had in his car.

He was released a few hours later and given a desk appearance ticket (DAT) to report back to court at a later date to answer misdemeanor charges.

Upon his arrival back home, Bailey called Pig and filled him in on the details of his arrest. He told Pig that the police knew everything about him. They knew his government name, where he lived, how much he made a day selling heroin, and who his workers were. The police told Bailey that they were aware of a recent beef he had with a kid in Brownsville who stole his chains.

Bailey said, "They told me that Shabazz was on the run for a rape… They even asked about you."

Pig responded, "Get the fuck out of here! What did they say?"

"They said, 'Where's your buddy Pig at?'"

"For real?"

"That's my word to my mother! We gotta move out, son…The niggers from Charleston (South Carolina) just beeped me too."

"Let's go down there, man."

"We need the stuff, son."

"Yeah, I know."

"If the niggers could trust us with the stuff, we could go man… and those Spanish kids (Jim) beeped me too."

"Call them back."

"I am, son."

"Let's get this work and get the fuck up outta here, man, fuck it."

"Got to, son… They got a fucking informant out there."

This incident could possibly jeopardize my investigation. Not only had the cops given up more information than they received, but they put Bailey and his crew on high alert. I needed Bailey and his workers to be relaxed and off their guard, so I could be there when they slipped up.

I went to the TNT narcotics division that covered the area and had a sit down with the sergeant. I spoke with him in private about our extensive investigation and needed his team to back off of Bailey and give him enough rope to hang himself. I begged him to keep the circumstances of my case restricted because the less people that know, the less likely word would get out.

FIFTY-FOUR

Looking to Trade for Drugs

My mother's condition had worsened over the last few months as the effects of her disease started to dominate her body. Her eyesight was diminishing, and the wound to her leg, where they removed the vein, was not healing. My stepdad hired an aide to make sure all her needs were attended to. The harder it got for her, the more she tried to protect us from her pain.

Work became a sort of sedative for me. The more I ingested, the less pain I felt. I wore my investigation like a bulletproof vest to help protect me against the inevitable.

Activity on the wiretap started to pick up. The Dominican supplier (Jim) was back in the game, supplying Bailey's business with his high-quality heroin. Monk was being phased out. Pig oversaw the daily operations of the organization, supplying the workers with product and collecting the group's daily earnings. Pig was thrilled that Monk was no longer needed because Pig had immediately sensed Monk's bad vibe and voiced his apprehension to Bailey on several occasions. Bailey's greed and the dependence on Monk for drugs caused him to dismiss his longtime friend's concern. Although Monk was not supplying Bailey anymore, intercepted phone calls alerted us that Bailey still owed Monk about two hundred and fifty dollars.

The boys from Charleston, South Carolina contacted Bailey again and let him know when they were going to be in town with several guns which they were looking to trade for drugs. Firearms were cheap down south and were good currency to exchange with Brooklyn drug dealers looking to protect their territories.

On April 15, 1998, we intercepted a phone call indicating that the boys from Charleston were going to be in Brownsville tonight to trade goods. As a team, we quickly strategized a plan to be an invisible party to their arrival. We submerged eyes and ears into the project environment and just waited. It wasn't long before we saw Pig meet and greet two males who were driving a vehicle with South Carolina license plates. The trunk was opened, and Pig peeked in, while the Southerners keep a watchful eye out for police.

After a brief conversation and some hugs, the two boys were on the move. We slowly pulled away from our camouflaged positions and tailed the car out of Brownsville. We followed the vehicle for a while, allowing enough time and distance so that the occupants had no reason to link us back to Brownsville when it was time to pull them over.

When the vehicle pulled into the Hasidic section of Williamsburg Brooklyn, we decided to make our move. The sergeant engaged the lights of his unmarked auto, instructing the car to pull to the right and stop. They had other ideas and sped off. The car traveled at dangerous speeds down a one-way street before running out of options. The driver was caught inside the car, while the passenger bailed out of the auto and decided to try his luck on foot. Detective Joe Murphy and NYS trooper Bill O'Leary were able to apprehend the male after a brief foot pursuit.

The neighborhood instantly became saturated with hundreds of black coats and hats, as Hasidim emptied their homes to investigate the disturbance. Inside the trunk of the car were three firearms and approximately a half a kilo of cocaine. The masses slowly headed our way, so we decided to put the bad guys in one of our unmarked autos with tinted glass for their own safety.

The Hasidic Jewish community is strong and cohesive. The neighborhood works together and acts as one. Young Jewish males pressed up against the auto, surrounding it with curious faces trying to get a look inside, while methodically banging on the car doors. We quickly rounded up the troops and transported the car and perpetrators into the Nine-Oh (090) precinct where the collars and evidence could be processed.

Tragically, while we were processing the arrests and vouchering the evidence in the Nine-Oh (090), a police officer suffered a heart attack or seizure while working out on a treadmill in the precinct's gym. FDNY is housed in the same building, and they rushed over in an effort to help the fallen officer. In spite of their efforts, the police officer passed away, and the precinct had lost one of its brothers. It was a harsh reminder of how truly vulnerable we all are. A somber mood filtered through the precinct, as officers continued to do their job with heavy hearts.

FIFTY-FIVE

Come Get Your Money, Man ☺

The team worked overtime into the early morning, and only a couple of hours separated us from our next day's work. Detective Daisy Ortiz and Stevie J. had remained at the plant the night before to monitor the wiretap and were able to leave at a descent hour to get some rest.

Stevie was at the plant bright and early the next morning, while the rest of us showed up looking forward to going home as soon as we started. Personally, I don't look or feel well with only a couple hours of sleep. I really wanted to bang in (take the day off), but it was my case, so I told myself to "cowboy up" and get to work. I did although my body was really not pleased with me. I walked in, carrying fatigue around my neck like an anchor, along with two matching Samsonite suitcases under each eye.

Daisy and Stevie handled the wiretap, giving me a chance to catch up on progress reports so that we could continue to intercept "dirty" calls. The wire was relatively quiet in the morning, thank God, so we were able to relax and enjoy some coffee and tea. By the late morning, the phone started getting busy as Bailey woke up.

He checked messages and returned calls and also checked up on workers.

Then Bailey spoke to Jimmy (supplier), telling him that he was going to let his workers finish up what they had.

Pig called, and Bailey told him he was out in Brownsville at 7:30 in the morning to get the workers started. Pig had some compact discs for Bailey: Tupac Shakur's latest jam and another by DMX. Pig complained he wanted to stay out of Brownsville because TNT narcotics were all over the place but then admitted he had to go out there now. Pig thought that it may be the repo man looking for Bailey's car because everywhere he went the same van was around. Bailey reiterated that TNT was always all over the place. Pig cautioned Bailey to walk into the area, instead of driving, so as not to heat up the streets.

After listening to that phone call, I wondered if my conversation with the sergeant from narcotics had gone in one ear and out the other. However, they hadn't approached Bailey after my meeting, so Pig could be acting paranoid after learning what TNT knew about him.

The calls continued to come in:

Monk called looking for his money, and Bailey said, "Come get your money, man."

Monk explained that he "was stuck" and didn't have a ride. He also said that his wife was pregnant, and he had to take her to the doctor because she had been throwing up. Bailey explained he was "stuck" also because his wife had his car.

Bailey then called his wife at work, letting her know that he was still in bed.

Jimmy (Dominican supplier) called and said he was going to come by Bailey's house because he needed to talk to him.

Monk called back again and said he had to go see his PO (parole officer). He was going by cab and asked Bailey if he could meet him halfway. He also asked Bailey if he was watching his kid.

Bailey replied, "In a cab? How the hell am I to meet you halfway? And plus, um, damn."

Monk asks again, "Babysitting, nigger?"

"No, just waiting on somebody (Jim). They supposed to come to the house. Ummm…"

"I'm gonna come to the crib, real quick."

"Alright, man."

Monk signed off, "Chill."

These last series of phone calls meant that we needed a field team to go out to Bailey's residence and cover the meeting between Bailey and his two suppliers. Thank God for Daisy Ortiz because she had to pull people out of their comfortable seats to get them off their asses and into the street. Luckily, I wasn't one of them. I got to hide behind the old "I have paperwork to do" excuse. Detectives Murphy and Duncan, along with Sergeant Dobbins, were kicked out of the apartment by Daisy. She looked at me and said, "Oh my god, what a chore that was. If I didn't physically push them out the door, they would still be sitting here bullshitting."

I laughed my agreement and was thrilled they were gone. That meant more air for me to breathe. I thumbed through several line-sheets (records of incoming and ongoing calls) from the last couple of days, making notations for progress reports that needed to get done for court. Stevie was in early in the morning and left for the day, leaving the job of monitoring the wiretap to Daisy and myself.

Moments later, Sergeant Dobbins advised that they had set up an observation post on Bailey's house to monitor the meetings. Not long after, Sergeant Dobbins advised us that Monk had arrived by cab, spent a short time in Bailey's house and then left the area. He was able to get some photographs documenting Monk's visit.

After the last call from Monk, Bailey's phone continued to ring unanswered with no outgoing calls. Daisy documented the unanswered incoming calls on the line-sheets. Jim's number appeared on the caller ID, and it, too, went unanswered.

Sergeant Dobbins called into the plant to notify us that the field team had ended its surveillance and were going EOT (end of tour) from the field. I asked if Jim had shown up at Bailey's house. Sergeant Dobbins notified us that Jim did in fact arrive at the house but never got out of his car. He stayed a few minutes and left. I informed him that Jim called the house, but nobody answered. In fact, it has been some time since the phone had been in use.

Lieutenant Becker arrived at the plant to check in and get updated on my case. He was aware of the arrests that had been made from information intercepted on the wiretap the night before (South Carolina) and was very pleased with the case's progression and direction. We filled him in on the day's events as Bailey's phone continued to ring unanswered in the background.

Bailey was expecting Jim to show up at his house, so why didn't he take his call? Maybe he was blowing Jim off. Maybe he went back to sleep, or maybe he even stepped out of the house. Daisy and I looked at each other with the same crazy idea, "Maybe Monk killed him for his two hundred and fifty dollars." We laughingly dismissed that thought saying, "Nah, no way. He probably fell asleep again."

I sat on the couch with pink line-sheets surrounding me like a quilt, while my eyes slowly bled. End of tour couldn't come fast enough. The sound of Bailey's ringing phone was beginning to put me in a trance, as my eyelids and head fought the pull of gravity.

Suddenly, the sound of a woman screaming catapulted out of the wiretap equipment, nearly tossing me off the couch. Between screams, the words "oh my god" were heard as she attempted to dial the phone several times. After picking the papers off the floor, I found myself drifting over to where Daisy sat as she scribbled notes on a yellow notepad. Lieutenant Becker and I stood behind Daisy and stared at the machinery as cassette tapes recorded every horrific decimal. A little boy could be heard crying in the background.

It was Bailey's wife, frantically calling 911, trying to explain what happened. She was unable to vocalize as her panic consumed her. The 911 operator tried several times to get her to calm down. Through the screams, you could hear her say, "Just got home... husband in pool of blood... house ransacked."

The operator told her to stop yelling and asked if she needed an ambulance.

She screamed, "He's not moving... He's in a pool of blood... I just got home from work... Somebody please get here. I don't know what to do!"

A neighbor in the background asked, "Is he shot?"

Bailey's wife answered, "I don't know. I didn't look at his face."

Daisy and I looked at each other, as I said, "Holy shit. That motherfucker did kill him."

Lieutenant Becker asked, "Who do you think shot him?"

I answered, "Monk. He was just at the house a little while ago. Matter of fact, Sergeant Dobbins just took pictures of their meeting."

"Do we know who he is and where he lives?" the boss asked.

I responded, "Yes. We have him identified."

Lieutenant Becker said, "Gather all the information that we have on him. Get Dobbins back in here and tell him we need those photos developed ASAP. Get the rest of the team back here also. It's gonna be a long night. I'll notify the inspector."

As Daisy and I paged the team to come back to work, the Seven-Five (075) sergeant's voice came over the wiretap, calling central dispatch to give an update to Operations, "He's DOA, and it's not self-inflicted. There's no weapon at the scene. He's DOA. Tell Operations you're gonna have to hold on until we find out more, okay?"

The plant phone continued to ring, as my team members returned their pages. I put together a folder on Monk with all the information I had, while Daisy notified the rest of the team to come back to work.

Sergeant Dobbins returned to the plant with the undeveloped film and sent Detective Teddy Jimenez over to the Photo Unit at 1 PP with orders to get them done right away. I grabbed my portable radio, the Monk folder, and headed over to the scene of the shooting with Lieutenant Becker and Sergeant Dobbins.

It was dark outside now, and the turret lights from the responding police cars bounced off the face of row housing under the elevated train tracks where Bailey resided. We found a spot on the adjacent block and headed toward the front door, which was manned by a uniformed police officer. We identified ourselves and proceeded toward the crime scene.

Lieutenant Herbert, the Seven-Five (075) squad boss, was on the scene with his detective who caught the case. Sergeant Dobbins and the lieutenant knew each other from working the same area. Herbert asked, "What are you, guys, doing here?"

Sergeant Dobbins replied with a smile, "You're gonna love us."

Pulling out a surveillance photo of Monk, I said, "This is the shooter, and this is where he lives."

Lieutenant Herbert asked, "How do you know that?"

"We've been investigating the victim for several months, and we are "up" on his phone." Lieutenant Herbert smiled from ear to ear. We had just made his job a *whole* lot easier.

While Sergeant Dobbins gave the detective more detailed information about our case, I slipped into the kitchen area, being careful not to disturb any evidence. Crime scene detectives scurried about, doing what they do so well, as I stood staring at Bailey's motionless body. He lay on his left side, back resting against the refrigerator, with his head near the wall. Blood dripped down the white wall like red tears. A massive lake of thick red blood stretched out from his body on the black tiled kitchen floor. His pager rested in the blood, less than two feet from his outstretched hand.

In an odd way, I had grown to know Bailey very well even though we were never formally introduced. I've looked him right in the eye although he has never laid eyes on me. I knew his friends, his family, and even his girl-friends. I knew his dislikes, his likes, his taste in music, and what he ordered when he went to McDonald's. It was definitely a one-sided relationship. I looked forward to us eventually meeting in person when I placed handcuffs on his wrists and read him his Miranda rights.

I stood in the kitchen absorbing the details of the crime scene. EMS was at the apartment and pronounced him dead on arrival from injuries sustained by a single gunshot. The bullet entered at the base of his skull and exited through his left eye.

Although we were on opposite sides of the fence, perusing dreams from different viewpoints, I felt sadness for Bailey and his family. Another child had been exposed to the harsh reality of suddenly losing a parent, and I only hoped that, through his death, he was teaching his son about life.

A tiny piece of lead, fired at close range, had suddenly transposed my role as an investigator. My obligation shifted from building an airtight narcotics trafficking case against Bailey "the subject," to bringing the murderer of Bailey "the victim" to justice with closure for his family. I wasn't going to accomplish that being at the crime scene. The lieutenant, the sergeant, and I returned to the plant to discuss our options.

The rest of my teammates trickled back in and were astonished by the events that had transpired in the last couple of hours. Inspector Kevin McCarthy came out to Brooklyn to help coordinate our next moves. FBI agent Mike McGarrity and members from the other OCID-HIDTA teams were called in to assist in our attempt to locate the killer. Numerous photocopies of Monk were made and distributed to our detectives, including detectives assigned to handle the homicide from the Seven-Five (075) squad. I notified assistant United States attorney Elaine Banar of the recent developments and was told to keep her updated.

Once everyone was briefed and clear on the details of their individual missions, a concerted effort was put together to apprehend Monk. The units headed out to Bushwick where the suspect lived and set up surveillance posts. I remained behind at the plant, which became our temporary command post.

The field teams roamed the streets of Bushwick looking for our shooter. Detective Kevin Bryant (KB) was an extraordinary undercover assigned to one of the other HIDTA teams. He was instrumental in bringing down a number of high-profile organizations. Once a dealer got the deadly "KB hug," they were soon history, sporting their very own arrest numbers. Fighting against the diminishing light of dusk and armed with only a photocopy of the suspect, KB was able to spot Monk among a group of people standing on a corner. KB's radio transmission sent Detectives Joe Murphy and Eddie Benetiz to the corner, and they quickly placed Monk under arrest. The suspect was transported back to the Seven-Five precinct for questioning.

The news of Monk's arrest was called into the plant. I phoned AUSA Banar about the recent developments, and she was extremely pleased with the swift response of the task force. There was more work to be done. We needed to find strong evidence to link Monk to the murder. Elaine Banar decided to meet us at the Seven-Five precinct to lend her assistance and help coordinate our efforts.

The bosses and I, along with FBI Agent Mike McGarrity, rushed over to the Seven-Five squad room where we met up with AUSA Banar. We watched through the mirrored glass as Lieutenant Herbert questioned Monk.

Detective Jimenez arrived at the Seven-Five with the developed photographs that Sergeant Dobbins had taken of Monk's meeting with Bailey. The photographs were nothing short of remarkable. He had captured Monk's arrival in a black livery with the license plate fully visible. The second photo showed Monk waiting on the stoop of the Bailey residence. The third depicted Bailey on the stoop with Monk as he answered the door. The fourth was a clear photo of Monk walking away from the house moments later carrying a child's yellow backpack with a black smiley face: ☺.

Lieutenant Herbert was alerted to our arrival and stepped out of the interview room. We presented him with the developed photographs. He thumbed through them with a look of amazement. He returned to the interview room with the photos to continue the interrogation. I stood behind the mirrored glass as the lieutenant settled back into the room. Monk admitted to knowing Bailey. He also said that he hadn't seen him in about a week or so even though he was wearing the exact same clothing now, as he was in the photos. When Monk was presented with the photos, he stared at them momentarily acknowledging it was him in the pictures. He then asked to speak to his lawyer. The questioning came to an abrupt halt. We had struck a nerve. I could only imagine what was going through his mind when he laid eyes on the pictures.

At this point, my group was brought into the interview room to be introduced to the suspect. Lieutenant Herbert informed Monk that this was a federal case being investigated by a joint task force that consisted of the NYPD and the FBI. Lieutenant Herbert then introduced AUSA Elaine Banar as the prosecuting attorney representing the United States Attorney's Office at Eastern District. Monk dropped his head into his hands and remained silent.

Bailey's widow was able to confirm that the yellow smiley face ☺ backpack belonged to her son. Concrete evidence was contained in that child's backpack, and we needed to locate it. Joe Murphy headed back out to the crime scene with other members of my team and walked the entire route from the victim's house, to where Monk was arrested, checking garbage cans, alleyways, and sewers along the way.

AUSA Elaine Banar, Agent McGarrity, and I returned to her office in downtown Brooklyn. She expressed her delight to the advantages of having such incriminating photos in her arsenal as a federal prosecutor. Recovering the backpack along with the murder weapon would be damaging evidence to Monk's defense. However, I was informed that the area search for the bag was concluded with negative results.

There was a strong possibility that incriminating evidence may be found inside Monk's residence. Therefore, she was going to awaken a federal judge to see if he would grant us a federal search warrant for the house. We needed to secure the house so as not to lose any evidence while applying for the search warrant. Members of my team along with other HIDTA team members surrounded the home to keep a watchful eye.

Elaine Banar contacted a judge at his home and apologized profusely for calling at such a late hour. She explained the events that had unfolded over the past couple of hours, justifying the late disturbance and the need for a search warrant. I pictured the elder statesman sitting in his home office, in his leather chair, wearing his judge bathrobe, judge pajamas, with judge slippers that had little fuzzy gavels on the end of them.

As Elaine sat at her computer with the judge in her ear, my phone rang. It was Detective Mike Donnelly informing me that a plastic bag containing several 9-mm rounds was just thrown from the rear window of the target house. I told Mike to hold on, as I interrupted Elaine to update her on this news. She then passed the information along to the fuzzy gavel slippers.

Once all the information was compiled and an acceptable draft of the search warrant affidavit was completed, the judge granted us permission over the phone to search the target home for evidence. As Mike and I headed out of Elaine's office, she said, "Be careful, guys. And find me something good to work with." I smiled and ducked out the room.

We pulled up to the Bushwick residence, formally announced our intentions to search the home and got to it. The house was huge inside with no less than twenty people living in it. I searched for hours only to recover a white Dutch Masters cigar box, containing a box of .380 caliber ammunition from inside a closet with old rusty electronic equipment and other debris.

Morning yawned on another sleepless night, breaking apart the night's dark blanket. We gathered the equipment and troops together to determine what our next move was to be. I was hoping it involved my own fuzzy slippers and many hours of undisturbed sleep.

As a group, we decided to make one last stop. Monk's girlfriend lived only a few blocks away, so we thought we'd pay her a visit. She was preparing for work as she answered the door. She invited us in, and Agent McGarrity notified her of Monk's arrest and alleged crimes. The FBI can lawfully conduct a search of a premise with the owner's consent. He drafted up a handwritten version of this agreement, which she willingly signed.

As I started searching in her bedroom, Agent McGarrity questioned her about her evening the night before. She admitted that she met Monk at Junior's Restaurant in Downtown Brooklyn for some world-famous cheesecake. Monk had given her some money to hold. She retrieved her pocketbook and turned the money over. I discovered another large sum of cash in her bedroom closet which she had no knowledge of. I asked if Monk had left any property in her house, and she pointed to a white bag on the bedroom room. After removing some of the top layering of clothing, I discovered a black semiauto handgun in a holster.

Within about twelve hours of Bailey's death, we had the suspect, the murder weapon, cash, photos, recorded telephone conversations, and incriminating statements. It doesn't get much better than that folks. After working almost three days in a row, my reward was a hot shower and sleep.

Although the circumstances of this case qualified it as a death penalty case, the United States Attorney's Office declined to prosecute it as such. After testifying for over an hour in front of a federal grand jury, Monk was indicted for, among other things, drug-related murder and drug trafficking. He later pleaded guilty to the murder charge and is doing 360 months to life.

When the target of my narcotics investigation was executed, the need for the wiretap was eliminated, and we focused on picking up the other working parts of the drug organization. We made several arrests and had successfully eradicated one group's negative influence on the neighborhood.

Strong cases against the other defendants lead to more interesting fallout. From information that surfaced, we were able to assist the Joint Bank Robbery Task Force in apprehending two males for bank robbery as well as confiscating over $250,000 of illegal fireworks and an unlicensed handgun.

FIFTY-SIX

I'm Sorry

The last few months had been very rewarding for our team, and my inbox was a strong indicator of just how busy we had been. It was filled with DD-5s, Buy Reports, Tape Receipts, and Arrest Reports. Closing out my major case would be a major pain in the ass.

June 17, 1998 was a pretty slow day around the office on the twenty-ninth floor at 26 Federal Plaza. A lot of the guys from the other teams were just hanging around Michele Rodriguez's desk (receptionist), and it was getting a little on the loud side. I sat at my cubical staring at the blinking cursor on my computer, trying to determine what my next sentence should be. Detective Reports (DD-5s) and Buy Reports lay scattered about my workstation as I tried to organize my case folder. I had only been at work a short time when my phone rang, and I answered with my standard professional greeting when I said, "HIDTA Detective Hoffman, can I help you?"

My stepfather's voice sprung from the phone, and his words fell around me like a net, immobilizing me. "It's over. Come home." My mom had just passed away. There was no need for me to reply, and he didn't wait for one. The receiver remained at my ear momentarily although his voice was gone. I suddenly felt heavy, and my center of gravity seemed to drop.

All the reports that I had been carefully reviewing and organizing suddenly had no meaning at all. They were just objects occupying space. It is amazing how the pecking order of importance can change immediately with the ring of a phone. I finally hung up and slid my seat back away from the desk. My eyes focused on nothing, as an eerie stillness wrapped itself around me like a wool blanket on a cold night as if something or someone was comforting me. I knew this day was coming, but you can never really prepare yourself for it, or know how you are going to react. I sat motionless waiting for something to happen. Nothing did. I felt empty.

I caught Sergeant Jim Dobbins' eye as he walked in the front door, and I waved him over. I let him know that my mom had just passed. He said, "Oh, I'm sorry. Take care of what you need to do. If there is anything that we can do, don't hesitate to call. Are you okay? Do you need someone to drive you home?" I thanked him for his condolences and assured him that I was okay to make the drive myself. I quickly arranged my desk and took what I needed with me. The office noise level began to drop as the news made itself around the office. As I headed out the door, the other detectives and agents wished me well.

I walked down to the Worth Street parking garage and got my car from the lower level. I waved to the attendants as I headed out to my parent's house in North Bellmore. The radio remained off as I made my way east onto Long Island. About a half a mile from the house, I saw my stepbrother walking in the street with a suitcase in tow. I swerved to the curb and picked him up. He was coming from the Long Island Railroad after flying down from Rochester where he lived. He asked me how I was doing and I replied, "Ahhh, okay I guess. What are you going to do?" It didn't dawn on me at the moment, but he had no idea that Mom had just passed away. He was traveling down for a work meeting and a visit. I just assumed he knew. When we arrived at the house two minutes later, he got the news.

I walked to the back bedroom where my mother had spent the last few weeks of her life in a hospital bed provided by hospice. I was greeted by Pop and a hug from the aide that had been tending to my mother's needs. A small shell that had once contained my mother's spirit lay under covers that were pulled up to her neck. Her mouth remained open, frozen in a perpetual silent scream.

I found myself momentarily alone with my mom and stroked her thin gray hair. I wasn't sure of exactly what I should say at the moment other than that I was sorry. "I'm sorry" were the only words that I could vocalize though I wasn't quite sure for what. Sorry for her suffering? Sorry for not being a better son? Sorry for not expressing and sharing my emotions better?

Pop suddenly came into the room, and I quickly withdrew my hand back from my mother's head, as if I were guilty of doing something wrong. Why? I'm sorry...

My cousin Joe on my stepfather's side was a licensed mortician and a detective with the New York City Police Department assigned to the morgue. He took care of all the details necessary for the wake and burial, and I am forever grateful to him. There was an enormous turnout for both the wake and the funeral, which was a great testament to the type of person my mom was. Friends and family made this difficult time bearable. This was a time to find out who your true friends really were, those people who are ready to lend a hand or a shoulder to cry on without hesitation. This was a defining moment in the development and solidification of new and old friendships.

I took my standard death in family (DIF) leave from the department and tried to let life settle back in around me. Although weeks had gone by since my mother's passing, I had not had a chance to grieve. There is no timetable for bereavement, and everyone does it at his or her own pace. I submerged myself in my work which suppressed my need to grieve. Once again, I had internalized by feelings and held them hostage inside. I pushed forward with my case because that was what I felt was important. My investigation was what I thought kept me going, but in hindsight, I now see it was what held me back. Although I hid my grief beneath layers of DD-5s (detective reports), it laid in wait like an abscess looking for its moment to surface.

Late Saturday morning, sunshine invaded my bedroom through two windows, and it took a while for my eyes to adjust to the light. I managed to prop myself up onto my elbows and caught a glimpse of some unknown person staring back at me from the mirrored closet doors. My elbows slid out from under me, and I was back where I started; only now my eyes were at half-mast and staring at the ceiling fan. Dust gave the appearance of ice where it had collected on the edge of each of the blades. I made a mental note to get to that at some point in my life and closed my eyes again.

I finally convinced myself that I had to get up. I flung the comforter against the wall and managed to hang my left ankle off the bed. Okay, that's a start. I continued the process with the other ankle and then hung the left leg off at the knee. As I gained momentum, I pretty much poured myself out of bed like liquid mercury and somehow landed on my feet.

Today was one of those days where I didn't have the strength or willpower to do anything, and it reflected in the way I moved. After a full body stretch and a loud yawn, I was ready to go in motion. I walked with my shoulders hunched forward, arms hanging limp at my sides and chin resting on my chest. My feet never left the low shag carpet as they shuffled along generating mild shocks from everything I touched. I stopped at the mouth of the bed-room door and looked to my right where my cat, Taz, lay in wait in the living room. He loved to play, and his idea of fun was waiting for me to turn my back so that he could silently sneak attack me, embedding his claws and teeth into my Calvin Klein underwear-protected ass. This morning, I locked eyes and telepathically told him, "*Not today, Kato. I will dropkick your cat ass into the radiator cover. Twice!*" He got the message.

I stood in the bathroom, looking myself dead in the eye. Over the past couple weeks, my body seemed to grow more and more tired with each pass-ing day. I felt like I existed with a taut rubber band tied to my waist making everything more difficult, even thinking. This morning, my eyes were swollen and red, and my brain had flatlined. I splashed cold water on my face which didn't seem to help. Everything was a chore. I may have only brushed my top teeth because it was too much work to do the bottom.

I shuffled my way into the living room and flopped onto the couch, but not before I zapped Taz on the nose with my mystical electrical powers while emitting an evil chuckle. I decided that since my mom had recently passed and my last relationship had taken on water and sank, the theme for the day was "fuck it."

Without much brain activity taking place, it wasn't long before my own personal demon opened a chaise lounge chair on my shoulder and started whispering suggestions for fuck it day at my ear:

Demon: *"Old man's bar!"*

Me: "What?"

Demon: *"Let's get drunk. Fuck it!"*

Me: "I can't go out with my eyes looking like this!"

Demon: *"Blame it on allergies or salty Chinese food. Or better yet, wear sunglasses."*

Me: "It's only eleven thirty in the morning."

Demon: *"And?"*

I paused a moment and thought, "Good point. Can't argue with logic like that." Maintaining a sense of integrity, I internally exclaimed, "But I'm not driving!"

Demon: *"Have it your way."*

I wanted to dress the way I felt, so I picked up the closest jeans and tee shirt from the floor and then topped off my ensemble with a baseball cap and sunglasses. The short journey to the bar was unremarkable, and I don't remember getting there. I must have stepped off my stoop and taken a moving walkway directly to the front door of the bar. I may have passed George Jetson along the way. Or was it Elroy? Does it matter?

I pushed through the heavy wooden door, and sunlight charged in behind me. The two vampires seated at the bar winced from the sudden exposure to the light. I may have seen smoke rising from their skin, but I'm not sure. I made my way to the far end of the bar which was vacant. The floor was sticky, and it sounded like I was walking on Bubble Wrap. A mixture of stale cigarette, flat beer, and detergent attacked my nose. The band Queen played on the jukebox, reminding me that fat-bottom girls make the rocking world go round. Ain't that the truth?

I settled into my seat, withdrew twenty dollars from my pocket, and placed it on the bar in front of me. I went with my demon's recommendation to keep my sunglasses on even though the bar was poorly lit. I heard footsteps approach as a shadowy figure appeared in my glasses. I managed to muster up a fake smile and show him my recently brushed upper teeth. A male voiced asked, "How we doing today?"

Demon: *"He really doesn't want to know, does he?"*

Me: "Good, thanks."

Bartender: "What can I get you?"

Demon: *"Whiskey. And leave the bottle. I always wanted to say that."*

Me: "Tap beer is fine."

Demon: *"You pussy."*

The bartender returned with my tap beer in a glass mug and whisked away my twenty, returning with the change. He tapped the currency with his hand and headed back toward the other end of the bar. He was a true professional and could sense that I didn't want any counseling. Just me, my tap beer, and my thoughts. As I reached for the mug's handle, the bar surface grabbed at my skin not wanting to let go. What do they wipe these bars down with, Elmer's glue? Between the floor and the bar, I felt like Jeff Goldblum (from the movie *The Fly*) stuck to a fly strip hanging in a gas station restroom. I kept my forearms against the wooden trim, allowing me to move about less constricted.

Finally wrapping my hand around the ear-shaped handle, I brought the glass to my mouth and drank. There is nothing like that first sip of cold beer, as it slides over your dry tongue and down into your belly where it works its way into your bloodstream like a virus. I licked the foam from my lip as I placed the mug down. I stared into my beer, which looked dark and murky like the East River at night or day for that matter and then realized that I still had on my sunglasses. In here, red swollen eyes were a requirement, and I lost the need to hide them. I lifted them off my nose and rested them on my forehead just above my eyebrows. I glanced back into my pool of alcohol. I have heard that people look into the bottom of their beer glass for answers, but being a more progressive thinker, I looked in both the top *and* bottom. More chances per glass. I stared at my beer like it was a Magic 8-ball, waiting for words of wisdom to rise to the top. Nothing. I chugged down the remainder and looked again. Nothing. I determined that this beer was obviously broken and slid my mug forward, which is the universal sign for a refill.

Right on cue, the bartender strutted back down my end, and I could clearly see that he was a person and not a shadow anymore. He grabbed some money from the bar, returned with the change, and with another tap was gone. I hoped that this beer would be working properly and searched the surface for clues. Nada. A moment later, the glass was empty again, and I remained clueless. I slid the mug forward again, and the obedient bartender yanked on the handle like he was in Atlantic City and refilled my glass with liquid gold. This time, he tapped the bar and said, "This one's on me. Good luck," as if he knew the other two were faulty.

I had not eaten anything, so the beer started to go to work quickly. This was why we were all here to begin with; to escape reality, which sat only inches outside those heavy wooden doors, waiting. In here, we felt safe and protected with the medicine that was distributed by our doctor the bartender. As I sipped from the mug, my body began to relax and feel lighter as if beginning to experience zero gravity in space. I noticed that the smells that had attacked my nose when I first came in had evaporated. A new customer arrived in a halo of light and made me shield my eyes. This kind of scared me for a second and forced me to check if I had grown fangs in the last few minutes. Relief rode down my throat on a carpet of beer knowing that my canines were still the same size as when I came in. The virus was spreading.

Another pull on the slot machine arm and my beer was again full of potential. I continued to feel lighter and lighter and decided to rest my arms on the fly trap surface to prevent myself from floating to the ceiling like a runaway helium balloon. I swirled the beer around in its glasshouse, encouraging it to speak to me. The foam head seemed to dissipate as tiny bubbles popped and died, giving way to the liquid below. I squinted and looked closer as imaginary words began to form. ASK...AGAIN...LATER.

Time became an irrelevant variable. After several more failed attempts, I left. It wasn't a conscience decision, but something that just happened, as if I had no control. Something or someone had made the decision for me. It's like finding yourself in a room with no idea of why or how you got there. I dropped some money on the bar to thank the doctor for the medicine and privacy as I finished up my last mug. I threw a wave over my right shoulder and headed toward the wormhole. I lowered the sunglasses back into place to protect myself upon reentry to the outside world. I lowered my head and shouldered myself through the wooden doors.

The alcohol had shocked my brainwaves back into service, and I became aware of little things around me on my way home. First thing I noticed was that I was drunk. I walked using the entire sidewalk and thought, "Hell, I paid for it, why not use it all?" I watched my feet land on the concrete in front of me and laughed remembering my stepfather always telling me, "Keep your head up and watch where you're going." Chuckling, I answered him out loud, "But I find more money this way." I picked my head up long enough to check for traffic as I crossed over to the other side of the street. I noticed that the pavement had long feathery cracks that looked like mid-August heat lightning.

Taz jumped from the window sill as I got the key in the door on only my second or third try. I was thinking that for moments like this I should invent some sort of funnel device to guide my key directly into the lock to prevent from scraping and chipping the door. I pictured myself hawking it to housewives on a thirty-second commercial break during *One Life to Live* with the energy of Billy Mays or Tony Little. I promised myself that I would work on that right after I cleaned the fan.

Taz rubbed against my leg welcoming me home. As I bent down to pet him, I felt tremendous pressure in my bladder area, which reminded me that I had not used the bathroom since I started my adventure. I tossed my sunglasses onto the couch and unbuttoned my jeans as I headed toward the bathroom. The next thing I knew, I had a cat momentarily attached to my ass. Kato strikes again. However, this time, I was protected by my dear friends, Mr. Levi's and Mr. Budweiser.

During a six-and-a-half-minute piss, I bent at the waist and looked into the mirror and noticed quotation marks (") in the middle of my forehead. I returned my attention to my stream as it mixed with the clear water in the bowl. It looked exactly like the tap beer I was just drinking, complete with the tiny popping bubbles. I flushed the toilet and envisioned it recycling right back into the keg at the bar where someone else would use it to search for their own answers.

I returned to the mirror and rubbed at the unknown markings. I wondered if I had caught some sort of incurable disease from the vampire cave. The answer fought threw my haze and alerted me that it was from the sunglasses I had pushed up to protect my third eye in the bar. A sense of relief filled me as I walked to the bedroom, happy to know that I didn't have to make an appointment with an exorcist. I contently did a belly flop into my bed, landing with my feet still hanging off the side. This would work in my favor when (and if) I decided to get up later.

As I lay there, my head began to swirl like a kaleidoscope. I presumed that my sudden change in altitude from vertical to horizontal was the reasonable explanation. I tried to wait it out and hoped that my blood would settle in the appropriate positions. I started feeling a weird sensation in my belly. I decided to slide my body over to the right so that I could touch the floor, grounding myself in case bed-spins went into effect. But what I was feeling was different from the usual alcohol abuse. I started feeling free, uninhibited and loose, like the rubber band had finally reached its limit and snapped.

My bottom lip began to quiver, and emotions sequestered in my belly began to rise up inside me. As much as I tried to push them back down, there was no stopping them. They bullied their way to the surface, and my defenses were no match for them. I sobbed uncontrollably, sucking in air in short bursts. Hot tears momentarily scorched my cheeks before being soaked up by the pillowcase. I uncaringly wiped my dribbling nose onto the sheets.

The mugs of tap beer were not faulty at all. They were time-released like a vitamin C pill. I had indeed found my answers. Feeling completely exhausted, I muttered into my left arm, "May God rest your soul and release you from your pain. I love you, Mom, and miss you dearly." The last thing I remember were little feet walking on my back, followed by purring in my left ear. Taz's vibrations shook loose a memory in my internal attic. I found myself recalling the sound of a Boog Powell, 1973 Baltimore Orioles baseball card that had been close-pinned to the front tire of my Schwinn bicycle that had no seat, as I pedaled toward our neighborhood pickup baseball game, carrying my glove on my head.

I awoke early the next morning still dressed in the clothes from the day before. Actually, they were really from the day before that. I rolled over onto my back and saw Taz resting near my feet. I craned my neck to look at the clock which read 6:30 a.m. Had I lost an entire day? At least I hoped it was only a day and not more. Taz softly walked up toward me and burrowed his head into my opened hand demanding affection, which I gladly obliged.

I started to recap the events of the day before in my head. After the amount of beer that I drank, I figured that I should really be feeling like shit. However, I felt quite good, excellent in fact. My head was clear, and my body felt rested although my stomach did express its anger for being neglected. As I looked up at the white ceiling, I pieced together the vapors of a dream that I had about my mother in my short sabbatical from life. In my dream, my mother appeared to be about twenty years old and was wearing a stunning dark blue evening dress. With amazement, I said to her, "My god, Mom, you look beautiful."

She calmly responded, "Of course, dear, everyone here looks like this."

FIFTY-SEVEN

Is He Dead?

My life began slowly weaving itself back together as I put the finishing touches on closing my long-term investigation. A new addition to the Fox team, Detective Keith Schiller came to us via a Northern Manhattan Initiative (NMI) narcotics team. Armed with experience, knowledge, confidential informants, and an array of potential targets within Washington Heights, he was able to broaden our area of attack. Washington Heights is located at the northern tip of Manhattan and was considered the main distribution point for various illegal narcotics for the tristate area.

At six foot four inches tall, Keith was a giant of a man, adding a dimension of intimidation to our team on the streets. Having been raised in upstate New York, Keith was given the appropriate nickname of "Big Country." Although Keith only had seven years on NYPD, he was no stranger to law enforcement with several years of experience working as a counselor for New York State Division for Youth (Corrections Department). Keith was able to quickly rise within the police department and landed an interview with OCID as a result of a very successful joint narcotics investigation with the FBI and a bribery collar made while working in uniform.

As Keith patrolled his small territory of land on foot in the Three-Four (034) precinct, he was alerted to a gentleman selling fish and other seafood products out of the back of an unrefrigerated, twenty-foot box truck. Illegal street vending was a large problem in the area and deemed a "precinct condition" that required investigation by officers on patrol. The stench of raw fish became unbearable as crowded sidewalks of pedestrians had to cover their nose and mouths when they passed. Shop owners became angry because the rancid smell consumed their stores and forced potential shoppers to leave.

Keith approached the seafood salesman and inquired about having the proper documentation required to sell on the street. The man offered Keith a couple of hundred dollars to remain in the highly populated area and to overlook his lack of permits. Not influenced by the easy cash, Keith arrested the male and transported him to the precinct for processing.

The Internal Affairs Bureau (IAB) was notified, and the man repeated his offer of cash to Keith and also agreed to "take care" of his sergeant. These incriminating statements were captured on tape as evidence. Keith informed the suspect that he was now not only being charged with the selling of fish without the proper permits but also with attempted bribery of a police officer. As soon as those last few words drifted from Keith's mouth and settled in the suspect's ears, the man vehemently clutched his chest and fell to the ground from an apparent heart attack, right in from of the desk sergeant. The man would survive his attack and have to answer his charges at a later date.

Keith wasted no time in targeting a cocaine organization operating out of a fourth floor apartment on West 184th Street near St. Nicholas Avenue in the "Heights." Undercover Officers Stevie J. and Ray Figaro were able to infiltrate the group with the help of confidential informants and purchase several ounces of cocaine over a short period of time.

After only a couple of buys into the organization, it was determined that we would attempt to take them down. A tactical plan was devised where the undercover officers would order up a kilo of cocaine. When the drugs arrived at the location, the undercover would transmit a predetermined word or phrase alerting Keith and the sergeant that the drugs were present in the apartment. The field team would then be ordered to swoop in, recover the drugs, and arrest all the people working in the apartment.

One obstacle that we faced was the placement of the field team. Because Washington Heights was so saturated with narcotics, numerous teams and agencies targeted the area. These drug organizations were well structured and paid a lot of attention to countersurveillance. They employed an array of individuals, from adults to children, as lookouts. Drug gangs had people on foot, driving in cars, sitting on stoops, and even kids riding bicycles looking out for "five-oh." The field team needed to be far enough out of the range of this area, yet near enough to provide backup for undercover officers nearby.

Keith was very familiar with the area and was able to map out a way that we could get four officers on the roof of the target building without drawing unwanted attention. This way, the undercover officers would have backup just seconds away, and the field team could pull back out of the danger zone of lookouts.

An early morning recon of the building revealed it to be the last of many conjoined buildings with an alleyway on the side of the structure, one story below street level. The target apartment was on the fourth floor with a front entrance. The door to the roof was disabled and could not be locked. Once the undercover gave the signal that there were drugs on the premises, the rooftop officers could gain entry from the broken roof door, come down one flight of stairs to the apartment, which the undercover had been instructed to open. By then, the field team would be well on its way, caravanning onto the block. On paper, it looked like a ground ball. We had done modified versions of this approach hundreds of times before, so we approved the plan.

On the day of the takedown, we huddled into the sergeant's office, and each received a copy of the printed tac plan, outlining each officer's particular assignment. Glancing over the two-page report, I found out that I was one of the four officers to make our way to the roof of the building. I would be joining Keith, Detective Billy LaVasseur, and Detective Teddy Jimenez. The sergeant and Keith went over each officer's assignment of the takedown advising Detective Figaro that the code phrase to be used when he put eyes on the kilo was "Big Country's gonna like this."

When the meeting broke, we suited up in our bulletproof vests, raid jackets, and gun belts. The four of us carpooled out of 26 Federal Plaza over to a gas station on Amsterdam Avenue near West 184th Street. Keith parked his truck and was greeted with handshakes by the owners of the station. We walked through the repair area and into a backroom, where we crawled out of a hole in the wall to get to the first conjoined building.

We entered the first building through a rear entrance and climbed the stairs onto the roof. As we hopped from rooftop to rooftop, we came across an interesting array of items. There was dog shit, human shit, dead birds, empty crack vials, needles, dirty diapers, broken glass, spent shell casings, broken furniture, underwear, and used condoms. There were also plastic lawn chairs for those late-night get-togethers on the roof with good friends. Some of the roof doors were broken and decorated with a variety of bullet holes.

We scaled the last remaining short dividing wall and landed on the target building's black tar roof. We verified that the door was open so that we could gain entry to the floor below. Keith was equipped with a headset allowing him to monitor the radio and keep our position secure from lookouts. We settled into the crouch position so as not to give our location away to onlookers from adjacent buildings. Keith notified the sergeant that we were set up and ready for the undercover officers to make their entry and place the order for a kilo of cocaine.

So far so good, and from here on in it looked like just a waiting game. The sergeant informed Keith that the UCs were on their way into the building. Stuck squatting in one position for a while made us fidgety. Keith, being the case officer and the person monitoring the radio, remained stoic. He had to periodically remind the three of us to keep our voices down so as not to give our position away. He listened in as the sergeant informed him that the UCs placed the order for the kilo and would keep us updated as things progressed.

After what seemed like hours to me, Keith pulled the headset down around his neck and said, "He gave the signal. Let's go!" We stood up stiffly and made our way to the broken door. Keith led the way down the stairs as I followed close behind him. He gained momentum as he rounded the landing, approaching the last set of stairs like a roller derby jammer being whipped ahead of the pack to score points against the opposing team's blockers.

Although the signal was given, the UC had not had the opportunity to open the apartment door. Keith's body became a massive projectile as he slammed into the closed entrance, causing it to bow inward and giving it a slight parenthesis "(" shape.

The door remained closed in its new misshapen form. We needed to cover the fire escape exit to deter any suspects trying to avoid arrest. Like Adam West portraying Batman, Keith exclaimed, "To the roof!"

Like Robin, I followed him back up the stairs. Billy and Teddy remained on the fourth floor waiting for the UC to open the door and the arrival of the charging field team.

The roof door swung open as Keith barreled through it. We hurried to the edge of the building where the rusted fire escape ladder clung to the side wall and snaked its way to the ground, five stories below. Me and heights don't get along so well, so while awaiting my turn to back down the flimsy ladder, my testicles decided to retract inward for protection.

I flipped my hips over the side of the building as my feet found the little metal steps. Keith worked his way below me. I glanced down to the bottom of the alleyway and saw a black male dressed in blue, getting down off an orange ladder propped up against the building wall. As I started to refocus on the tiny steps of the fire escape, sudden movement from the fourth floor window drew my attention to my right. Before I could fully grasp what was happening, I saw this unknown object strike the orange ladder, crumpling it to the ground. Adrenaline raced through my body when I realized that it was a person that had just jumped from our target apartment window and crashed to the ground below.

My entire face managed to stretch open as I yelled, "Holy shit!" as I jumped down to the first metal landing. One second later, another person decided to leap from the window. Realizing that it wasn't one his best ideas, he started clawing at the side of the building on his way down. He crashed down onto the first guy who lay motionless on the broken ladder. Still stretched to the max, my face let go another, "Holy shit!"

Keith continued down the fire escape as I drew my weapon from the holster and yelled down to the black male who was standing next to the two jumpers, "Don't move, motherfucker! Let me see your hands! Now, put your hands up on the wall and don't you **fucking** move!"

Through the screams of the second jumper, I could hear the black male complying with my frantic orders as he slowly walked to the wall with his hands above his head calmly saying, "Okay, but I'm just the cable guy." I covered him with my Glock-19, semiauto pistol as Keith made it safely off the fire escape to the alleyway.

Suddenly, a head popped out the window, and I thought to myself, *"Oh, God, please, not another one!"*

The head belonged to Billy LaVasseur who accessed the situation from the window, looked up at me and said, "Holy shit!"

I holstered my weapon and continued my journey down to the alleyway. Because we didn't know who was who or what was really going on at the moment, Keith handcuffed the black male for our own safety. The second jumper was screaming in excruciating pain as he flopped on the ground. I attempted to handcuff him but was only able to get one cuff on his right wrist because his left elbow was protruding through his arm, blood spilling toward his hand.

The black male was wearing a Time Warner Cable uniform and had a toolbox open on the ground behind him. Realizing he had nothing to do with the situation, I removed the handcuffs as I asked him, "Did you see what happened?" He nodded his head to indicate yes. "What did you see?"

"I was working on the cable wiring and got down off the ladder when the first guy... Is he dead? I think he's dead. Well, he landed on my ladder. I looked up and then that guy (pointing toward the screamer) came out that window up there (pointed upward) and landed on him."

The Calvary came charging down the alleyway led by Mickey, one of the other team's sergeants who were helping out on the takedown. Mickey yelled, "Why isn't this guy handcuffed?"

As I started to say, "His elbow is sticking..." Mickey grabbed the male and twisted his busted arm behind his back and locked the cuff in place. I have never heard a man make a noise like what I heard during that process. Mickey wiped the man's blood off his hands using the bricks of the building as paper.

Someone backed away from the group and called for an ambulance over department radio, as Mickey asked the screamer, "What were you doing?"

Even with a busted pelvis and a compound broken arm, the man managed to concoct a story. Through his tears and moans, he lied, "I was taking a piss right here, ahh! (pain)—in the alleyway—ahh! and I dropped my cell phone. Ahh! When I bent down to pick it up, this guy landed on my back."

I looked at the cable guy who shook his head. To be honest, I was quite impressed with his ability to conjure up an alibi like that after just falling five stories and getting all busted up.

Keith dialed Assistant District Attorney Adam Kaufman who would be prosecuting the case and said, "Adam, its Keith. Listen, we got a problem."

EMS workers made their way to us and stabilized the second jumper as best they could before removing him to the hospital. I walked over to the cable guy who said, "My boss warned me that they throw stuff off the buildings around here, but I never would have thought that something like this would happen."

I slapped him on the back and smiled, "Ehh, you get used to it after a while."

Both undercover officers were able to identify the DOA jumper as the individual who delivered the kilo of cocaine to the apartment.

Mickey told me to stay with the body and guard the crime scene, while other detectives transported the cable guy to the precinct for interviewing. Keith went up to the apartment to take a look around and to recover the kilo of cocaine and other evidence.

I found myself alone in this darkening, tight, five-foot wide alleyway that seemed to be closing in on me as the sun fell in the sky. The body laid facing up toward the heavens, using a mangled ladder as a mattress. He appeared to be in his late twenties or early thirties. Streams of dried blood were frozen on his face in a multiple V formation where it had leaked from his nose, mouth, and ears. His lifeless doll eyes remained half open as they stared at nothing. I looked above me at the roof of the adjacent building, which I figured was my friend's intended target. I shook my head and asked him, "What were you thinking?" His mouth remained slightly open as if he was contemplating an answer to my question.

A crime scene was established, and the field team regrouped at the Three-Four (034) precinct. The deadly incident attracted an array of suits. The commanding officer (CO) of OCID, Inspector Regan, and our integrity control officer (ICO), Lieutenant Coleman joined the party. Several members of Internal Affairs Bureau (IAB) showed up soon after.

The facts of the incident had to be investigated to determine if there was any wrongdoing or reason for criminal charges. General Order #15 (GO-15) of the Administrative Code and Patrol Guide would be in effect. This meant that each officer would have legal representation present from their appropriate union and be asked a series of questions regarding their individual actions and observations. Being GO-15ed meant that the officer would be given immunity for his statements and treated as a witness. These interviews would be recorded for evidence.

IAB set up a room where each officer would be interviewed separately in the presence of the CO and ICO. The officers in the field team sat together in an adjacent room and waited patiently for their names to be called and take their turn in the hot seat.

One detective turned into Sergeant Shultz from *Hogans's Heroes* when he went into the interview room and stated that he didn't see or hear anything, much to the chagrin of the bosses. Lieutenant Ken Becker, who was the supervising officer of the operation, turned completely white after being informed of the detective's statements as he envisioned his thirty-six-plus-years police career suddenly leaping out the window before his eyes. This was an extremely serious situation, and any conflicting statements could shine a negative light on the inquiry.

Keith and I sat together as the interviews continued. One by one, detectives went in and came out. We were the last two left. We stepped into the hallway to get some water and stretch our legs when Inspector Regan exited the interview room. As he passed us in the corridor, he said, "I got good news for you two. You're not gonna get GO-15ed."

My initial thoughts were happy ones. This meant that we would not have to sit in the hot seat and get questioned by Internal Affairs. Wait a minute, on the other hand, this meant that we weren't being considered as witnesses but as subjects of the investigation. We found out that someone stated the men had been thrown off the roof by police. Because Keith and I were the only two on the roof, this meant that this individual suggested that we were responsible.

Keith got on the phone and called ADA. Adam Kaufman who said, "Keith, I'll let you know if you need to get a lawyer." Those weren't exactly the words we wanted to hear. However, the matter was soon cleared up by the testimony given by other individuals who were in the apartment, and the eyewitness statements offered by the cable guy after his near miss.

Detective's Eddy Benetiz and Cesar Ortiz babysat our ailing superhero who later recanted his story about his brokeback phone call adventure. He admitted to being in the apartment and getting high. In his drug induced haze, he thought it was a magnificent idea to exit via the window after watching the first guy leap out as the police raided the joint.

When the smoke cleared and we were able to relax again, I said to Keith, "Welcome to the Fox team."

He replied, "How's that for my first case?"

"Oh, that was just terrific." I slapped him on the back. "Can't wait for the next one!"

FIFTY-EIGHT

Pushing Up Daisies

We continued with several investigations going on at once. We would take time out to work on each of our cases. If you wanted to take some action or do an undercover buy or surveillance, we would make an appointment with the sergeant and schedule a day for that case.

At the end of 2000, I had received information from a confidential source that an associate of the Bonanno Mafia crime family was growing and selling hydroponic marihuana in the Bronx. In Latin, the word hydroponic means "water working." It's the art of growing the plants in a bath or using highly oxygenated, nutrient-enriched water. Along with this water system, it uses HID (high intensity discharge) lighting. The lights allow you to grow plants all year round by providing them with an indoor equivalent to sunlight, which produced more powerful buds for a more intense high.

Although marijuana was low on our target list of illegal substances, the fact that the subject was connected to traditional organized crime made the information more appetizing. The subject was a wannabe mafioso identified as Frank Santoro. Intelligence information had indicated that Frank was a drug user as well as a dealer.

I was able to locate a small warehouse in the Bronx that had no windows, where I believed Frank Santoro was growing the hydroponic weed. The use of the HID lights required a lot of juice, and the last few monthly Con Edison electrical bills reflected my suspicions.

I once again called on the assistance of the Aviation Unit. I requested the use of one of their helicopters equipped with FLIR (forward looking infrared radiometer). FLIR was a thermal imaging system that could detect and measure minute temperature differences. In other words, when the FLIR technology was aimed at my target building, it would light up the monitor like a Christmas tree, indicating intense heat inside the building.

My second adventure in a police helicopter was no less spectacular than the first. This time, I could see New York City at night. From my vantage point in the air, the city glowed in its magnificence. This trip, however, would be strictly business and limited to the task at hand.

As I approached the target area, I could see my field team below as they drove around the neighborhood streets like mice in a maze. I kept in direct contact with them through the point-to-point radio. As the pilot hovered the metal bird in the air, I had one of my teammates stop directly in front of the target building to allow the chopper cops to get an eyeball on the building.

The copilot asked me, "Are you ready?"

I replied, "Absolutely, light it up."

The copilot switched on the FLIR system and aimed it on the warehouse. I anxiously studied the monitor in anticipation. Nothing. The building was stone-cold. The hood of a car parked on the street in front of the building glowed to indicate that it had recently been in use, but the building did not register. The pilot swung around to get different angles, but each attempt was met with the same negative reading.

The investigator in me felt disappointed, but the little boy in me enjoyed every second of airtime above the city as we headed back to the base. I would have to regroup and find another way to gather information about Frank Santoro.

Frank appeared to be a very nervous individual and was extremely surveillance conscience. He was very difficult to follow, making illegal and sudden turns, and then pulling to the curb to check if cars were following behind.

Following him for the short trip to pick up his dry cleaning was a whirlwind affair, as he dodged and weaved through traffic.

I received updated electrical bills for the warehouse in the Bronx, and the usage had dropped down. To me it, meant that he either shutdown the operation or moved it to another location. We put this case on the back burner and concentrated on more active ones. When time allowed, we would occasionally monitor Frank on his erratic driving escapades.

In December of 2000, dizzy from following Frank around the Bronx one afternoon, Sergeant Jim Dobbins got a call from Lieutenant Becker to report back to 26 Federal Plaza forthwith. Jim got on the point-to-point radio and instructed us to meet at a nearby diner. When we got there, Jim told us that we had been ordered to head back to the office forthwith; do not pass Go, do not collect two hundred dollars. Whatever the news was, it didn't sound good.

We arrived back to an office in turmoil. Rumors bounced off the walls that HIDTA as we knew it, was over. The word was that the investigative arm of HIDTA had been dissolved, and we had twenty-four hours to empty out our cubicle, pack up our shit, and get the hell out before the door hit us in the ass. And, oh yeah, clean out your federally funded cars and return the keys along with any government equipment and cell phones that were given out. We had thousands of questions: why? Where do we go? What happened? What about our active cases? Can I phone a friend or buy a vowel?

There were many rumors as to why we were asked to leave. One suggested that NYPD Police Commissioner Bernard Kerik had pulled the plug on the unit after finding out about a police corruption case investigated by the joint FBI / NYPD team about which he had been kept in the dark. Working with the FBI, Detectives John Lawlor and Pete Crespo had uncovered a drug trafficking organization that employed two New York City police officers who were transporting heroin and money for a Dominican drug organization.

Another rumor was that there had been a heated disagreement between the NYPD and HIDTA's boss Chauncey Parker. It really didn't matter to us what the real reason was. The fact remained that we were homeless with no office, and hundreds of investigative hours wasted. Any investigation that was done under HIDTA was over. We had been officially evicted with nowhere to go. Bosses and detectives alike started making phone calls to find us a new home, somewhere.

In the interim, we transported carloads of cardboard boxes containing ongoing case reports, cassettes of video surveillances, photographs, and evidence out to a company located in Westbury, Long Island called Covanta. Covanta turned material waste into energy. We backed up our cars and SUVs to the mouth of a large pit inside the building and then threw the boxes into the hole. A tremendous bucket with sharp teeth dropped into the pit from a crane above and closed its jaws, gathering debris. The bucket raced back up into the air with its mouth full, dropping its contents into an incinerator. The opened jaws once again plunged into the pit to take another bite. Debris clung to the teeth of the open bucket like flesh wedged between the teeth of a killer great white shark.

After unloading our boxes, we sat in the parking lot of Covanta and watched as steam was launched into the blue sky from a smokestack, as all of our hard work was burned. It was very disheartening, and our future together as a team was unknown.

The building adjacent to PSA6 located at 2770 Frederick Douglas Boulevard, between 147th and 148th Street, would become our new home. A vacant office on the second floor had just enough room for both the Fox and Shark teams. Parking in the area was difficult, especially after being spoiled with our own parking garage we had while working with HIDTA. We briefly pissed and moaned but quickly readjusted to our new surroundings. Joe Murphy and Nick Davilla hustled to get us nondescript cars to aid in generating new cases.

Another reshuffling of personnel brought Detectives Ruben DelaConcha, Tommy Grimes, and Biagio Santangelo into the Fox team. We had to start from scratch to get new targets to investigate. We called on our confidential informants to get their asses out into the streets and find out who was doing what.

I decided to take a step back and help my teammates in any way that was needed. Big Country quickly sunk his teeth into a large Dominican cocaine organization operating out of West 141st Street and Broadway while Ruben took us into the Bronx, and Biagio got busy in Coney Island Brooklyn.

In mid-February of 2001, my boss asked me if I still had my case folder on Frank Santoro, the Mafia wannabe suspected of growing hydroponic marijuana. I said I thought I did but would have to dig it out. It was a case that I had not worked with the FBI, so it had survived the big-burn operation.

I located the thin folder in one of my unpacked boxes piled on top of a filing cabinet. I thumbed through it as I walked into the boss' office. I handed him the file and asked about the sudden inquiry. He told me that Frank Santoro was shotgunned to death on February 15 while walking his dog in front of his home in the Throgs Neck section of the Bronx.

In 2007, acting Bonanno crime boss, Vincent "Vinny Gorgeous" Basciano, was convicted of ordering Frank Santoro's murder. Anthony "Bruno" Indelicato and Anthony Donato later pleaded guilty to carrying out the murder after Frank Santoro allegedly threatened to kidnap one of Basciano's sons for ransom. If Santoro had stuck to growing weed like we suspected, he probably wouldn't be pushing up daisies now.

FIFTY-NINE

The Devil's Breath

After having worked my fair share of Labor Days, I decided to make the first two weeks of September my annual vacation pick. This time of the year offered warm sunny days and refreshingly cool nights. And the September of 2001 rang true with my expectations. The day of September 11, 2001 was a spectacular one, and I was out of the house taking care of some early morning errands. I was driving my amethyst colored (I hate calling it purple) Subaru Impreza eastbound on the Long Island Expressway with the radio dial fixed to 92.3 FM, the home of controversial shock jock, Howard Stern. At 8:45 a.m., Howard and Robin were engaged in their usually morning banter when Stuttering John broke in with the odd news that a plane had just struck the north tower of the World Trade Center in Lower Manhattan.

Everyone's first impression, as was mine, was that the pilot of a small plane had lost control due to some sort of sudden illness or inexperience, and struck the massive tower. That was the only logical explanation, wasn't it? At the time, I had no comprehension of the magnitude of this event other than it being a fluke tragic accident. Approximately, eighteen minutes later at 9:03 a.m., Stuttering John and Gary informed Howard and I that a second plane had now crashed into the south tower. Before I flipped to an all-news radio station, Howard surmised that we were under attack from some unknown adversary. It all sounded impossible, but sure enough, 1010 WINS radio was reporting the same facts. I drove with my eyes squinted, not from the sun, but from disbelief. How was this possible?

My girlfriend Yolanda was also a cop at this time. She normally worked in business attire in an office setting in Sunset Park Brooklyn. Today happened to be a primary election day in New York City, and she was detailed to report in uniform to cover an election site in the confines of the First precinct, which covered the Twin Towers. This fact skated on thin ice above my consciousness without any concern on my part. I was still trying to digest that two planes had just crashed into the World Trade Center. It just didn't seem like the truth, but yet, here was my car radio telling me that it was.

I parked the car in front of my Oceanside home and jogged up the walkway to catch the events on television. I aimed the remote at the cable box, and seconds later, live footage of the area was before my eyes. I sat in slow motion with that same squinted, disbelieving face as pictures of heavy smoke billowed from both towers. At 9:30 a.m., President Bush confirmed Howard Stern's assessment when he spoke to teachers and students at a Sarasota, Florida elementary school indicating that the country had suffered an apparent terrorist attack.

The events and information began to seep into my body like blood from a slow intravenous drip. At 9:43 a.m., an American Airlines flight had reportedly crashed into the Pentagon. When will this end? The news reported that there were hundreds of planes still in the air. How many more were hijacked and destined for destruction, and what were their targets?

At 9:59 a.m., the unthinkable happened. In approximately ten seconds, the south tower of the World Trade Center imploded and pancaked down upon itself. As a New Yorker, I thought those buildings were indestructible. That was proven true by the deadly bombing in 1993, wasn't it? All I could think of was the people who were still inside and around the building when it came down. Then the thin ice in my head melted and thoughts of Yolanda consumed me. Oh my god! She was assigned to a public school somewhere in downtown Manhattan.

I grabbed my cell phone and attempted to contact her. Busy. Redial. Busy. Redial. Busy. Fucking cell phones! I tried contacting friends of mine from my team who were working. I called Joe Murphy. Busy. I called Keith Schiller. Busy. Joe Murphy. Busy. Yolanda. Busy.

Frustration took root alongside my fear. I felt helpless as I paced through my house punching numbers on the phone looking for answers. I wanted to throw this useless piece of technology through the window, but I stayed anchored to it knowing it was my only chance of getting information.

My pacing came to an abrupt halt after dialing Keith's number once again, and the phone miraculously started ringing. I was pacing again as the phone seemed to be on perpetual ring. "Come on, answer the fucking phone!"

The ringing stopped, along with my pacing, when I heard muffled voices on the other end. I screamed into the phone, "Hello, Keith! Keith, are you there?" Loud background noise and wind answered me back. "Come on, Keith, say something for Christ's sake."

Passing sirens and screams added to the sounds of chaos surrounding Keith's faint voice on the phone, "Hello?"

"Keith, its Larry. Are you downtown?"

"What? I can't hear you. Hold on a second."

"Wait, Keith, don't go. Ah, for Christ's sake, man. Get back on the phone." I heard wind and noise which pulsated like an approaching locomotive.

"Hello, hello?"

"I'm here, Keith. Have you seen..."

"What? I can't hear you. The fucking Trade Center came down, and it's fucking crazy here."

"Keith, listen to me" (I yelled each word slowly and clearly), "Yolanda had election duty in the First, and I can't get in touch with her. Have you seen her?"

"It's fucking crazy down here bro. I haven't seen her, try Murphy."

"I did, but I can't get him."

"KEEP COMING THIS WAY! This is insane. I got to go."

"Keith, wait..." Dial tone.

"Goddamn it!" I screamed as I threw the phone into the cushioned couch, not wanting to risk disconnecting myself from the world but still needing a release of frustration. I stood feeling angry with Keith for not being able to give me what I craved for: Yolanda's safety.

I couldn't just stand here and stare at the television. I needed to do something. I called my boss, Sergeant Jim Dobbins, who picked up on the first ring, "Jim, its Larry."

"Hey, can you believe what's going on?"

"I know. It's fucking incredible. Where are you?"

"I'm on my way in from Long Island."

"Do you think that you will be able to get through?"

"I'm giving it a try. What are you doing?"

"I'm on vacation, but I want to go in. Yolanda's got election duty somewhere down in the First."

"Oh, shit. Come on in. I'll meet you by the First."

"Okay, I'll see ya."

I tried to flush out my emotions and to get into cop mode. I grabbed my gun and wove the holster through my belt. I deposited my shield and ID card in my rear pants pocket. I walked by the television which updated me that another plane had crashed into a field in Somerset County Pennsylvania. Fucking bastards. I turned off the television and took one last look around the living room before closing the front door.

I started up my work car, a black Ford Explorer, and pulled from the curb. I put on the radio to stay informed. Driving through my town, you would never know that we were under attack. People went about their business like any other day. What else were they supposed to do?

Periodically, I would hit redial on my cell phone in an attempt to reach Yolanda. All attempts failed. I made it onto the Southern State Parkway and was able to put the pedal to the metal. After I merged onto the Belt Parkway westbound, things began to change. For the first time, I noticed motorist driving in the opposite direction with American flags either attached to their car or waving from their hands as they beeped their horns.

At 10:28 a.m., the north tower of the World Trade Center collapsed in eight seconds. Thoughts of Yolanda's safety made my head pulse as if they were trying to make their escape. As I approached the Verrazano Bridge on the parkway, Lower Manhattan came into view. The crippled island emitted plumes of smoke as if a volcano had suddenly come to life and erupted. An ugly charcoal smoke now occupied the air space where the towers once stood.

As the traffic became heavy, I pulled the Explorer onto the shoulder and drove with my police plaque displayed in the window. New York City put a call out over the AM radio requesting that all police, fire, and EMS workers report to their designated mobilization areas. Motorists who were stuck in traffic exited their cars and waved flags while exclaiming, "God bless America."

As I made my way through the streets, I observed people or apparitions of people both walking and running northbound as screaming emergency vehicles rushed southbound. I saw people covered in gray ash, some bleeding, some with no shoes, some crying, and others too stunned to emote. Strangers gathered at intersections and hugged one another for support. I weaved through the walking wounded as I made my way downtown.

I parked as close as I could to the First (001) precinct. I put on my blue raid jacket, hung my detective shield around my neck, and double-timed it over to the building. What struck me immediately as I started to run was this god-awful smell which was different than anything I had smelled before. I had nothing to compare it to. I can only describe it as "deadly." It's what the devil's breath must smell like. Anyone who was down there will know exactly what I mean.

The precinct house was like a hornet's nest that had been disturbed. Cops in plain clothes and uniform ran in and out. I fought my way into the precinct and made my way over to the front desk. Every landline phone was in use as information was being disseminated.

The sergeant behind the desk was standing with reading glasses perched on the end of his nose as personnel scurried behind him. I called to him to get his attention, "Sarg." He tilted his head down as he looked at me from over the top of his glasses. "Has the election duty detail been accounted for?"

With a defeated look, he raised both his arms out to his sides, like Jesus on the cross, and slowly shook his head as he said to me, "I don't know where anybody is."

I had no idea what to do or where to look. Civilians who had run to the precinct for safety sat on hard wooden benches, coughing up black soot, as EMS workers tended to their needs. I made my way outside the building and stood motionless attempting to digest the information that was bombarding me from every direction. I looked to the cloudless sky for guidance. The air was alive with particles of dust and debris, and a constant flow of paper rained down from somewhere. I kept searching faces for a familiar one, as I eavesdropped on conversations going on around me. I listened in as I overheard a group of cops, their uniforms stained with sweat and ash, speak in detail of people leaping from the condemned towers to their death below. They said it sounded like bombs going off as they hit the pavement. I could only imagine what it was like to be trapped above the damaged floors with no way out. What were the conditions like that leaping to your death was a better option?

I stood off to the side waiting. I wasn't quite sure for what. I took notice of a dusty unmarked police car that had pulled up on my left. I started to cough and brought my arm up to my face to use it as a breathing filter while never taking my eyes off the car. The passenger door swung open, and Yolanda stepped out. Her usually crisped ironed uniform was now wrinkled from sweat and blotchy with gray ash. She caught my eye and started to jog in my direction. Her five-foot soul embraced mine, and we stood like that for a while. Tears left track marks as they traveled down her face as if attempting to clear away the dust and pain on their own. I choked back my own tears as I stroked her hair which was pulled back in a ponytail. She told me that she saw the second plane hit the tower, and I wished I could have reached inside her heart and removed that memory because I knew it would never leave her.

Knowing that she was okay, I could get back to being a cop again. I told her I was meeting up with my sergeant and would be guided by his orders. She told me to be careful, which she did every day we were together, but today, it had added meaning.

I met up with Jim Dobbins, who directed me to go north to Canal Street where other members of OCID were assigned to traffic duty. Rumors bounced from cop to cop like a super ball as pieces of information were unveiled. Having just come from the First precinct, I dispelled the rumor that the First had lost all the cops assigned to perform the 8:00 a.m. x 4:00 p.m. tour of duty.

Pedestrians and motorists alike stopped to ask questions that we really had no answers to. All we could do was try to assure them that everything was under control, and that a massive rescue effort was underway.

The ground began to rumble as I stood on Canal Street. Everyone's attention was drawn upward as two United States Air Force fighter jets patrolled the sky. The jets banked slightly to the left in a tight formation reflecting the sun's rays, resembling two sparkling fine-cut diamonds against glass as they etched white lines across the sky. The sight of these symbols of our freedom left my skin rippling with goose bumps as they passed over the area that will forever be known as Ground Zero. Vigorously rubbing my arms to quell my flesh, I whispered to myself, "God bless you, guys."

Assigned to an investigative unit, we were required to keep track of every moment of our day. But since 8:45 a.m., that morning, time seemed to fade away and die. Days and weekends melted into each other, and sleep came only as a necessity. I remember traveling with Sergeant Jim Dobbins to a Bayonne, New Jersey hospital across the Hudson River where we brought clean clothes for Detective Keith Schiller who sat with Lieutenant David Chong who was injured rescuing civilians when the towers came down. Keith was anxious to get out of his contaminated clothes. I noticed a gauze pad taped to the back of his neck and asked him what had happened. Not wanting to elaborate on any of the details, he simply stated that he suffered burns to the area. I did not press.

Lieutenant Chong was laying flat in the hospital bed with white sheets tucked in neatly at his sides as we discussed the ongoing events of this incredible day. He was in good spirits although he had suffered a concussion, fractured ribs, and had injured his ankle. His lungs were burnt making breathing painful and speech difficult. As Keith slipped on clean pants, Lieutenant

Chong tried to piece together the events that had forced him to cross the Hudson River in a barge, landing him in a Bayonne Hospital.

Earlier in the morning, Dave had reported downtown in civilian clothes to Rector Street to answer alleged charges filed against him at the Civilian Complaint Review Board (CCRB). As any cop will tell you this is not a fun way to spend any part of your day, let alone begin one. But if you are an active cop, making arrests and shaking the trees, it just comes with the territory.

At 8:45 a.m., something shook the building, disrupting the proceedings. As the highest ranking officer in the building, Lieutenant Chong gathered officers together and headed out to the street to investigate. Once in the street, the officers felt an intense heat that stopped them dead in their tracks. A human torso lay in the street not far from a deformed jet engine. All eyes were drawn to the sky as fire and smoke billowed from a gaping hole in the north tower. On police department tapes, Dave can be heard identifying himself and advising central dispatch that a plane had struck the north tower.

The street came alive with panic as people started to run aimlessly in search of safety. Sirens grew louder with approaching fire and police autos. Acting on instinct and training and with total disregard for his own safety, Lieutenant Chong began ushering civilians out of the wounded building. Moments later, a second plane struck the south tower. Drawn to the second explosion, Dave made his way over to the south tower to help in the evacuation. Fireman and police officers fought their way through panicked and injured civilians as they made their way up to the damaged floors. Two exhausted, injured office workers descending the stairwell struggled while escorting a severely burnt, semi-conscious woman down the stairs. Recognizing their need for assistance, Dave turned behind him and told a baby-faced fireman, who couldn't have been more than twenty-two years old, to help these men get the woman out of the building. The brave fireman replied, "With all due respect, Lieutenant, I don't want to leave my company, and I'm better equipped to continue up toward the fire. It's better if you escort them out." Dressed in only a business suit, Dave knew the young man was right. He nodded his understanding to the fireman and stepped to the side, allowing the young fireman and other rescue workers to continue upward.

David removed his suit jacket with his lieutenant shield pinned to the front and wrapped it around the woman's shoulders to comfort her, freeing her exhausted escorts to make their own way down and out of the building. Mayhem governed the lobby of the south tower as Dave searched for an exit determined to get the woman to safety. Flashing emergency turret lights guided Dave toward an exit like a lighthouse beacon at night. A charging thunderous vibration grew louder and stronger by the second. Dave suddenly felt the ground rising below him.

Lieutenant David Chong's consciousness broke through, as he found himself buried below the rubble. His head pounded with pain as he struggled with every ounce of available strength, trying to free his imprisoned body. The weight of the debris made it difficult to breathe as he fought against his fears. Not giving up, he was able to extend his arm through the surface of the ruins. Two NYPD Emergency Service officers spotted Dave's arm protruding from the wreckage and grabbed his opened hand, giving him assurance they would get him out.

The two officers struggled to lift and clear debris from around Dave. They supported him as they ushered him to safety in a nearby building. Moments later, the ill-fated north tower began its descent with that same thunderous vibration of a charging locomotive. Dave remembers making his way to the building exit and being held in the grips of a thick, black, hot, choking smoke.

Dave looked up at us from the safety of his hospital bed and said, "It was quiet. No sound at all." He paused looking toward the east-facing window and said, "Everyone was gone."

With a knock, our attention was drawn to a priest, who appeared to be in his late fifties or early sixties, standing at the open door. He walked in and introduced himself. Focusing on David Chong, he asked if we were all here due to what happened across the river. He asked Dave if he was alright, and Dave answered, "No." The room became eerily quiet when the priest asked what was wrong. As the priest came forward, Keith headed toward the door, and I glided out in his wake behind him.

Keith and I waited outside so that the lieutenant could convey his thoughts in private to the priest. The priest came out of the room moments later and said, "Be well and may God bless you all," and walked down the hallway. The nurse later informed us that the priest was also injured during the attack and had received in excess of one hundred stitches. He should have been bedridden but instead insisted on going room to room to offer a kind word and his blessing.

Dave Chong still struggles with the events that took place that day. He often wonders what would have happened if the baby-faced fireman had listened to him and helped that woman on the stairwell instead of giving Dave the opportunity to get out.

Working back over at Ground Zero, we were assigned the task of searching for the black boxes belonging to the two jet airplanes on the rooftops of surrounding buildings. We were given a picture of what they looked like and an area to search. Detectives Joe Murphy, Thomas Grimes, and I traveled deeper into the frozen zone to conduct our investigation. Streets were unrecognizable, and my sense of direction became nonexistent. As we drove toward our target area, I observed a stop sign standing on its corner with a metal window blind draped over it like a shirt thrown across a chair.

Federal authorities claimed that the two black boxes have never been recovered. However, New York City Firefighter Nicholas DeMasi describes the recovery of the devices in a self-published book titled *Behind the Scenes: Ground Zero, A Collection of Personal Accounts.*

The attack had transformed the colorful heart of the world's financial district into a grainy, film noir. Colors were obliterated as gray and black dominated the landscape. I stepped from the van into inches of a powdery dust mixed with paper. I walked with my head down and took stock of what was below me. A doll smiled up at me from the ground as it lay covered in pulverized concrete dust. Family photographs and snapshots depicting memories of good times had been trampled underfoot by responding rescue workers and civilians running for their lives. Pieces of office memos and once important business forms continued to exit the sky looking for a place to rest on the ground.

Land surveyors were called in to monitor wounded buildings for any movement or sign that the site was unstable. If there was any indication of instability or sway in the damaged buildings, a horn would sound alerting personnel in the area to evacuate immediately. One Liberty Plaza, which was situated next to the World Trade Center, was severely damaged during the attacks and in the weeks following it was feared that it may collapse. Brooks Brothers, which was located on the ground floor of the building, was used as a temporary morgue.

A few of us were sitting in Tommy Grimes' van, which he parked in front of One Liberty Plaza. The horn sounded indicating immediate evacuation. People started running in every direction, and Tommy was unable to drive the van out of the area. I leaped from the side door and joined the herd of fleeing workers. I started zigzagging up unknown streets to put distance between myself and the building. I looked back wondering how far I had to go to guarantee my safety. As much as I ran, it never seemed far enough.

A rather large man who was delivering oil to the rescue workers abandoned his oil truck to flee the unsafe area. He fell to the ground and had trouble getting up. Two people stopped and offered their help, trying to get the large man to his feet. Unable to pick the man up and not wanting to leave him behind, the two good Samaritans began to drag the man by his arms like a sled. As they did, the dust began to collect against the man's chest as he snowplowed through the streets. The gray ash built up so much that it caused his pants to peel down to his ankles. The man yelled to his huskies to stop. They did and kept running. The man was able to right himself and started hopping along trying to pull up his pants, now loaded with dust.

When the all clear was given, I stopped to catch my breath. What I witnessed did not register until the fear had escaped my body. Laughter suddenly replaced the fear as a way to cope with the existing conditions. It wasn't funny at the time, but thankfully, we are able to laugh about it later.

Ground Zero was the country's largest crime scene and had to be handled as such regarding the collection of evidence. During that week, my team was scheduled to help in the recovery and rescue dig of the collapsed buildings. Due to the hazardous conditions, each team had to check in at the command post and be assigned to a particular dig site. This way, all personnel could be accounted for, and evidence collected could be recorded properly.

After being outfitted with a paper facemask that was held on by a rubber band, a hardhat construction helmet and gloves, we proceeded out to the dig site. We marched in a semistraight line, stepping through still smoldering debris, toward our sector. A massive pile of rubble stood before us with jagged lines of rescue workers snaked throughout the pile. I joined the end of the line and began passing along white buckets which came down from the top. We were removing two, one-hundred-ten-story buildings and two, 767 airplane jets in white plastic buckets. I gradually made my way up the hill as workers were forced to take a break. There was a constant flow of full buckets traveling down the pile with empty ones returning to the top. A New York City Fire Department chief sat atop the pile keeping a watchful eye over the recovery operation.

My breathing became labored as I slowly ascended the pile. I would occasionally remove my mask, which became bogged down with sediment, to steal a large gasp of the devil's breath. Although we were assured by Christy Todd Whitman of the Environmental Protection Agency that the air was safe to breathe, I chose to wear the breathing filter as much as I could stand.

Looking up to the top of the pile, I could see a constant flow of buckets headed my way. I slid the band back around my head, putting the facemask in place, and continued the bucket brigade. Voices followed one bucket down the hill. They became clearer with each change of hands. The words never changed from one worker to the next. The guy above me repeated them to me, "Human remains." I glanced into the bucket and could see it contained a men's dress shoe with the foot still intact. I sent the bucket along with the same message.

Designated areas were set up to log in any evidence found on the site. Recovered aircraft parts were brought to one area, and human remains were brought to a temporary morgue where they were later sent for DNA testing for identification.

At one point during the dig, our attention was drawn to another bucket brigade to our left. A fallen firefighter had been unearthed. A Stokes basket (wire metal, basketlike rescue stretcher) attached to a guide wire above the pile contained his remains. He was wrapped in an American flag with his misshapen fire helmet resting on top. All work stopped, and hundreds of rescue workers stood in complete silence as the stretcher containing an American hero traveled along on the guide wire, suspended above the wreckage. Work resumed once the basket was secured on the other end. This chilling scenario played out several times during the day for both fire and police officers lost in the attack.

I made it to the top of the bucket brigade and was now one of men filling the bucket under the watchful eye of the fire chief for its travel down the hill. Using our gloved hands, we scraped and clawed at our feet. Large steel beams and iron girders became visible like broken ribs as we cleaned debris out around them.

We were completely exhausted after putting a few hours on the pile and pulled back to the Embassy Suites hotel to recharge. A mess hall was set up so rescue workers could replenish their depleted bodies. We mingled with firemen and police officers from all over the country who unselfishly left their families and friends behind to take part in the recovery efforts on their own time. I chatted with a few firemen from Chicago who had recently gotten off the pile. Our conversation did not end with a handshake but with a heartfelt hug as we shared the pain of the loss of comrades and civilians together. These people didn't have to be here and risk putting their own lives in jeopardy. But they were, and I let them know how I felt with my words and embrace. My hugging these firemen was a symbolic representation of a country pulling together, coming to the aid of a fellow American.

After eating, I walked through hallways of nameless buildings. My gait was much slower as I walked with my mask dangling below my chin with helmet and gloves in one hand. My garments felt ten pounds heavier as if I just exited a pool after jumping in fully clothed. A window blackened with soot possessed a powerful message scratched on it by an unknown rescue worker's finger. I see it as clearly today as I did that day, "NEVER FORGET."

A nurse stood along a wall with vacant folding chairs at her side like a little girl with a lemonade stand. She called me over and invited me to sit down, offering to flush my eyes. Her soft touch and gentle bedside manner were as soothing as the solution that cleared my vision. A makeshift dorm was set up with cots. Sleeping bodies in filthy uniforms with patches representing police and fire departments from all over the country occupied most of the cots, their muddied boots resting alongside them. Curled up in one cot was a dog handler with his faithful comrade asleep at his feet. The black-and-brown German shepherd's paws were wrapped in bloody bandages from cuts sustained from walking on the mangled iron and steel while searching the rubble for survivors. This magnificent animal twitched as it rested in his own thoughts, his wet nose touching his tail. I was able to find an open cot and close my eyes for a short time before regrouping with my team to head back to the office at the end of the day.

Walking back to the car, there was an area set up where restaurants and fast-food chains were giving away food to rescue workers. A gentleman from McDonald's rushed up to me with a huge smile and a bag containing cheeseburgers and fries. He ran back to his stand and returned with the same smile and an ice-cold Coke. I thanked him, and he thanked me before running off to offer food to someone else.

Once in the car, we started to drive out of Ground Zero onto the Westside Highway. Amazingly, thousands of people were lined up alongside the road. As we rode passed them, they cheered, waved, and whistled and proudly displayed American flags, expressing their thanks for the work that was being done. Feeling guilty and undeserving of such a sendoff, I waved back. This unexpected display of gratitude from so many people touched my heart to its

inch above us had been disturbed and was going to collapse onto us. The three of us began to scurry out in fear of being crushed. We were reassured that everything was okay up top, and we settled back to our task at hand. The large bang was an earthmover attempting to straighten out a severed piece of iron so that it could be placed on a flatbed for removal.

As we were clearing the torso of the fireman, we made another gruesome discovery. A left hand had appeared just to the left of the fireman's arm. This hand belonged to a female. Even in his last seconds of life, this brave fireman appeared to have been using his body to protect and shield the woman from the fallen debris.

Through items found on the firefighter's body, we were able identify him and determined that he was a member of FDNY's prestigious Rescue One Squad (RES001). It was customary for members of the same unit to remove the body from the site. Once his fellow firefighters arrived, I exited the hole to give them the courtesy and honor of removing their fallen comrade. Their emotions surfaced as they prepared their friend for his trip out of the rubble. An American flag was brought up along with the Stokes basket.

I was mentally and physically exhausted and made my way down the jagged line to the flat ground below. I found a plastic cooler containing water and helped myself to a bottle. I sat in the dirt against some machinery that was not in use and stared at the still smoldering remains of the towers. I pulled the mask off my face, removed my helmet and gloves, and placed them on the ground next to me. I twisted off the cap and threw it at the pile. In one sip, I managed to finish half of the 16.9-ounce bottle. I tilted my head back, resting it against the side of the machine and closed my eyes. The sun baked the sweat on my face.

Suddenly, the madness became silence as if a switch had been thrown. I leveled my head and shielded my eyes from the sun. Everyone stood motionless and quiet as the two firemen carried the wire basket containing their brother wrapped in an American flag down from my line. I stood up and watched them carefully weave down the treacherous path. They made it to the flat ground and walked past me. The switch was flipped again, and the madness was back in session. I picked up my helmet and gloves and stared back at the rubble for a moment. I suddenly flung the half-full bottle of water at the pile and yelled, "Fucking bastards!" and slowly headed back to the command post.

After about two weeks or so of working down at Ground Zero, our teams were told to get back to normal operating procedures and continue ongoing cases. The transition was a slow one. Criminals did not seem to be affected by 9/11 and probably benefited from the diversion of manpower. Even though we tried to pick up where we left off regarding our investigations, our hearts and prayers remained lying somewhere beneath the rubble with hopes of finding civilians and the remainder of the missing 23 NYPD, 343 FDNY, and 37 PAPD (Port Authority Police Department) officers alive.

As a general rule, cops don't ask for help; we provide it, and any crack in the shield is viewed as a weakness. Seeking counseling through the job was considered career suicide, so we became the best at internalizing our emotions and fears. We are often dispatched to witness and engage the worst scenarios that mankind has to offer, and we gladly do it all, but at a cost to our souls. After all, we ARE humans although family and non-cop friends may beg to differ at times. We are known to sometimes hide behind crude and inappropriate humor and often find solace in a bottle. Alcoholism and divorce rates are *extremely* high for people who do what we do. Tears are shed only in private and behind locked doors. Many cops build a wall around themselves, allowing in the only other people who understand them: other cops. When things get so black and ugly and begin to fester inside of some cops, asking for help is not an option. They turn to their strong side and unlock an instrument that was bestowed upon them to save and protect life, their firearm. In 1995 alone, twenty-six officers chose suicide as their final answer.

Bill Genet walked in cop shoes for thirty-one years and understood cop psyche. He recognized the need to develop a counseling program independent of the NYPD. In 1996, Bill founded an organization known as POPPA (Police Organization Providing Peer Assistance) aimed at giving cops an avenue that was greatly needed and silently craved for.

Bill Genet deployed his volunteer Critical Incident Stress Teams down to Ground Zero, and they remain available to this day. Bill used peer support officers as well as mental health professionals to urge cops to participate in "defusing" sessions.

A couple of months after 9/11, my team received an official notification to attend one of these sessions. We were all cut from the same mold and viewed this as a complete waste of time, and in addition, a severe inconvenience. None of us really knew anything about this POPPY or POPPA thing, or whatever the hell they call it, and didn't want anything to do with it.

It was a mandatory "MUST APPEAR" notification, and we did so begrudgingly. On the trip downtown, we carpooled together and tried to fig- ure out what was going to take place. We guessed we were going to have to listen to some old-fuck retired cop from Piehole Iowa, and he was going to tell us that our mothers never loved us. Get the fuck outta here! Turnaround and let's go to work!

We parked the car close to the downtown office and threw the police plaque in the window to prevent getting parking tickets. We crossed against traffic as car horns blasted their disapproval. Hey, if we were miserable, then everybody else should be. Get over it!

Our attitude walked in a few feet ahead of us as we gathered in the front waiting room. The boss checked us in, and moments later, we were led to the gas chamber for "defusing." We entered a small room with chairs gathered around in an oval circle. We all grabbed a seat and pretty much sat with the same body language; sitting slightly down in the chair with our heads tilted to the side and our arms folded across the chest while the eight-hundred-pound gorilla groomed himself in the corner. Defense shields are up Captain Kirk, good luck getting through.

Two middle-aged men in comfortable clothing introduced themselves to the group. They explained the purpose of the organization, assured us that it was completely independent of the NYPD, and that "anything said here stays here." They were also available twenty-four hours a day, seven days a week if anyone needed to talk. They reiterated that this was very informal, and we were not required to speak if we chose not to. The topic was about our individual experiences on the day of 9/11 and any feelings relating to the events that had transpired since. I sat silent and protected behind folded arms, as my fears and frustrations welcomed the invitation to rush back in and haunt me once again.

They invited anyone who wanted to speak to start the ball rolling. Silence ruled the room as the gorilla started combing through my hair looking for lice. The hairy ape vanished as soon as Keith Schiller raised his hand and said, "I'll start unless someone else wants to go." The room thankfully murmured its willingness for him to go first. He adjusted himself in the chair, took a deep breath, and started.

Keith was also a member of Donald Trump's security team and had worked late the night before. He slept at Trump Towers and had breakfast in the morning with a friend in Upper Manhattan. While eating breakfast, the TV news station broadcasted that a plane had hit the Trade Center. He headed down to the office located on Eighth Avenue in Upper Manhattan. The office was empty when the phone rang. It was Lieutenant Chong requesting for Keith to get downtown and help in any way that was needed. Traffic on the FDR Drive was extremely heavy. An FDNY Battalion truck, ablaze with lights and sirens, cut a hole through the congestion. Keith piggybacked the engine and made his way downtown with his red-and-white escort. He unconsciously parked his pickup truck on a downtown street and headed toward the mayhem. It would be days later before we were able to located his debris covered truck. The NYPD lost over one hundred and thirty police cars that day.

Attired in only jean shorts, work boots, and a tee shirt, Keith threw his police windbreaker across his back and jogged past fleeing civilians. A thunderous roar filled the streets as the south tower collapsed, sending waves of deadly smoke and debris plunging through the streets, appearing to swallow frightened people along its angry path. He removed his shirt and covered his nose and mouth to prevent choking on the hot ashes.

People ran toward him looking for a way out of this unthinkable nightmare. He guided shocked businessmen and office workers into nearby buildings out of the path of the deadly cloud, leaving them with directions to stay inside. A security guard approached with an injured female bleeding from the head. Using his God-given strength and six-foot-four frame, he lifted the woman in his arms and carried her to safety while directing others within earshot of his voice to follow.

I found myself sitting on the edge of my chair as my eyes remained glued to Keith. His guard was down as his hands lay clasped in his lap. His voice was pure, and his eyes grew distant as he brought us all back to that godforsaken day. He continued on, explaining that he often had to ask for directions on how to get to the Trade Center due to the reduced visibility and lack of guiding landmarks. He somehow managed to work his way just a few blocks north of the one remaining damaged tower. He found himself standing on Barclay Street alongside a forty-seven-story building with a red masonry exterior known as World Trade Center, Tower Seven.

This side of Manhattan owned a clear blue sky until an all-too-familiar thunderous roar began to replay and drew his attention upward. The north tower began to implode, sending one hundred and ten floors racing toward the ground as iron and steel buckled. The blue sky evaporated and was instantly replaced with death. Frozen in fear, with no chance or place to run, Keith did what we were taught in elementary school. He dropped to his knees and covered his head and hoped that death would come easily. His eyes focused on the pavement as photographs of his children appeared before him on the ground. Those were the last images that Keith saw when the lights suddenly went out. His body shutdown as it prepared itself for death with his last thoughts saved for his family.

The north tower collapsed onto tower seven, causing extensive damage, leaving a vertical gash spanning ten floors as massive skeletal steel pounded the ground. An angry sky rained down fire. It was only by the grace of God, and the love for his family, that Keith was not struck by the falling debris. He stood up and was unable to see his hand in front of his face because the sun was blocked out by the fallout. He was beyond fear and not sure if he was dead or alive. As his senses began to seep back in, he noticed that it was eerily quiet.

Other than the sound of paper and other small objects continuing to hit the ground, there was nothing. He yelled out for help, but his pleas were no match for the thick black cloud that encased him, forcing his words to fall helplessly to the ground along with the blazing paper. It was as if he were the only living thing on earth.

His instincts told him to move, but his eyes were of no use because the sun had vanished with everything else. His outstretched arms became his eyes as he began to take baby steps. With each step, his foot probed for solid ground with the fear of what lay one small step ahead of him. As he made his way in the dark, he continued to call out for help. Maneuvering through the debris, his hands felt the side of a building. He followed the building line till he came upon a glass door. He rubbed the dust from the glass and pounded on the door. A metal bolt dislodged, and the door opened as an arm pulled Keith inside and shut the door immediately behind him. Keith found himself inside a bank with the security guard who pulled him in and about six other terrified people. The guard ushered Keith to the bathroom where he was able to remove some of the dust that had collected in his nose and throat. His head began to clear as the soot swirled down the drain.

The frightened people bombarded Keith with questions. "What's going on? Are we safe here? What do we do? Where do we go?" He did the best and the only thing he could do. He reassured them that everything would be okay. He urged them to stay inside and await help which he hoped was on its way. Keith knew he had to get back out there and find survivors. The people in the bank pleaded with him not to go back out, but Keith understood what needed to be done.

Emerging back out into the unknown, Keith paired up with an NYPD sergeant and continued looking for survivors. Limited visibility was available as the dust began to settle. The officers heard a faceless voice calling out from somewhere above. The man yelled out his company name, how many people were with him, and what floor they were on. The sergeant and Keith answered back hoping to ease their fears and assure them that help was on the way.

Keith's voice softened with a complete understanding and compassion as he continued the story, recalling a man on a bicycle wearing a psychedelic tie-dye shirt. The man's face was weathered with fear and sorrow as he asked Keith if he had seen his missing little girl. With the vision of his own children still fresh in his mind, Keith knew this meeting of the worried father would remain engrained in his heart forever. The officers promised that they would continue searching for her as the father rode off on his bicycle, dodging the debris as his voice faded away continuing to call out his lost daughter's name.

As Keith made his way to the rubble with the sergeant, they could see firemen working feverishly to unearth a fallen comrade. Keith found himself standing atop a fire truck which had been completely destroyed and buried beneath the tower's broken structure. Keith's work boots filled with water and pulverized concrete as they tossed aside wreckage to dislodge the unconscious fireman. They placed him in a metal stretcher as Keith grabbed an end and lifted it out of the rubble, not knowing if the man would survive.

Keith would later meet up with Sergeant Dobbins who would take Keith over to the New Jersey hospital to support Lieutenant Chong and also get the burns he had suffered on his neck treated.

When Keith finished, it was as silent as when a fallen hero was removed from the pile wrapped in the American flag. The group's body language had changed immensely. No one said a word for several moments as his experience hung in the air above our heads. My eyes glistened as I relived his experience right alongside him. Feelings of guilt and selfishness punched in my heart. I truly felt horrible for experiencing any anger directed at him for not being able to supply me with the information that I desperately needed over the phone on that ill-fated morning. I silently cursed myself for my ability to discount his well-being and fully replace it with my own self-interest.

Keith allowed the rest of the group to lower their guard and reveal a human side that is not often exposed in public. I listened attentively to the others tell their stories, but Keith's story affected me directly and wouldn't let me sit comfortably as if my chair only had one leg. Although Keith had no idea of my frustration, I felt compelled to verbalize my emotions. My chance to speak came, and I prefaced it with a sincere apology to Keith, explaining the feelings I had attached to the other end of that phone call.

The chance to articulate my story and to discover the emotions and experiences of the rest of my teammates was very cathartic. I was able to recognize something that had rooted itself in me and dispelled it using only my ears and my words. I am grateful for the opportunity that POPPA gave me and tried to ease the panic of other officers who would later have the dreaded obligation to "MUST APPEAR."

SIXTY

Powder Puff ADA

Stress can be a dangerous pill to swallow, and unfortunately, it is an unavoidable byproduct of police work. You can only hope to contain it and dispose of it in a healthy manner. Stress comes at you from many different directions and can come in many different forms. Working as an investigator, targeting mid-to-upper-level narcotics organizations, I found out firsthand that stress can come in the form of powder.

Not long after our team therapy session with POPPA, I found myself once again sitting across a table from Internal Affairs officials with a Detective's Endowment Association (DEA) representative seated to my left and a rolling tape recorder dead center.

This visit to IAB was generated from another search warrant obtained by Big Country (Keith Schiller). It was executed at Washington Heights apartment, resulting in the arrest of two defendants with several kilos of crack and cocaine recovered.

The defendants were arrested in the hallway just outside the apartment door by two officers who entered before the caravan arrived so as not to raise suspicion. The apartment had a strong chemical odor in the air that is usually associated with cocaine or heroin processing. Particles of the white powder drifted through the air, attacking our nose, eyes, and throat. Several kilos of cocaine and cut (compounds mixed with the cocaine) were found on a work table. Brown discs of crack cocaine were laid out on tables to dry.

The suspects claimed that they were not in the apartment even though they had white powder all over their clothing and failed the simple heartbeat test. A hand to their chest showed that their hearts were beating a mile a minute and proved they were guilty beyond a reasonable doubt.

Okay, so maybe that test is only good in Russia or somewhere like that so the defendants chose to exercise their right to go to trial in an attempt to convince a panel of jurors that they were not in the apartment and innocent of the charges against them.

Keith was the arresting and recovering officer, and I was assigned as the recorder. My job as the recorder was to sketch a diagram of the apartment and document where every piece of evidence was obtained. When the notification for trial showed up at our office, my name was right alongside Keith's.

We were called down to the assistant district attorney's office for trial preparation to go over all the evidence in the case. The ADA processing the case wanted to clandestinely subject the jurors to the effects of cocaine particles in the air by cutting open the bags of narcotics on the prosecutors table, which would be adjacent to the jury box. With the bags opened, the particles of cocaine would become airborne and could potentially waft over into the jury box affecting the juror's senses, helping to aid in her efforts to link the defendants to the apartment and get a conviction.

As the supervising officer, Sergeant Jim Dobbins would be called in to testify. During trial prep, he strongly objected to the ADA's tactic of opening the evidence bags of cocaine. The evidence was to be kept in the custody of the police department laboratory and taken out for the purpose of trial. The evidence also had to be returned in the same condition after the trial was over and any inconsistencies could potentially become a problem.

A trial starts when a jury is selected. The judge and both lawyers interview a panel of jurors in a process known as voir dire, which means "to speak the truth." Potential jurors are questioned to determine if any of them has prior knowledge, personal interest, or feelings that may make it difficult for them to be impartial in giving the defendants a fair trial. Prosecuting and defense attorneys have the ability to challenge the choice of a juror by the other team. Once both legal teams come to an agreement of the selected jurors, a date can be set for the testimony to begin.

The trial was underway for a couple of days before I was notified of my turn to appear. No matter what or how damaging the evidence is against their client, a skilled (for lack of a better term) defense attorney is masterful at the art of deflection. An excellent defense attorney could, to use the words of Rodney Dangerfield, "Get a rape charge reduced to tailgating." They will use every trick in the book to deflect the jury's attention away from the evidence and pick on minuscule points to make an investigator look stupid or unreliable. It is the job of the prosecuting attorney (ADA) to redeem the officer after the defense team badgered a small inconsistency to within inches of its death.

I waited outside the courtroom's heavy wooden doors by myself after a court officer called for Keith Schiller to step inside to give his testimony. I paced the floor searching through my notes trying to run every possible cross-examination question through my head. After a while, I sat on the hard wooden bench just outside the door and closed my folder on my lap and tried to relax.

Suddenly, the wooden doors flew open, jarring me from my pseudo-relaxed state. Keith's head looked like a cherry blow pop, without the wrapper, ready to explode. He circled around the hallway with his hands on his hips as I stood up and circled after him asking, "What happened?"

"The fucking asshole defense attorney is breaking my balls about some confusion about whether something on a voucher was an item number or an index number or some stupid shit like that, and that bitch just sat there and let him go on and on without objecting or giving me a chance to explain on redirect examination."

To say he was annoyed was like saying World War II was just a little misunderstanding. Before I could say anything else, the doors to the courtroom opened, and a court officer said, "Detective Hoffman."

I stopped in my tracks, but Keith continued his angry flight pattern. "I'll see you in a couple of minutes," I said as I walked through the door held open by the court officer.

The courtroom was quiet. The only sound heard were my patent-leather-dress-shoe footsteps on the tiled floor. I quickly scanned the field to see what I was up against. All the attention in the courtroom was focused on me, clocking my every step. The pews were empty except for a couple of the defendant's family members whose eyes shot disdain-laced arrows at my slow-moving target. I felt the defense attorney's eyes probing me from behind designer glasses as I approached the bench, searching my character for any signs of weakness.

I approached the spring-loaded wooden gate which granted me access into the "arena." As I passed through the gate, the district attorney's table was on my left, next to the jury box, and the defense team was on my right. I circled around the left side of the judge's bench and stood behind my little wooden padded seat. I swore to "tell the truth, the whole truth, and nothing but the truth, so help me God," and then I was seated.

The judge sat in the gold medalist spot while I sat in the silver medal position off to his right, just below him on the podium. A small plastic cup, the size of a shot glass, containing water was at arm's length in front of me. A brown metal container with a black protruding lip stood next to the cup in case I needed another shot or added time to answer a question.

"Officer, would you please inform the court of your name, rank, shield number, and place of employment. And please spell your last name."

"Sure." I shifted in my seat and cleared my throat, "Detective Lawrence Hoffman, H-O-F-F-M-A-N, shield number three-zero-eight-one with the Organized Crime Investigative Division." I stared into the eyes of the court reporter when spelling my name. She nodded her head as she nudged the keys of her machine.

The ADA stood up from her chair and leaned on the table in front of her as she asked the judge, "Has the witness been sworn in, Your Honor?"

"Yes, you may proceed," informed the judge.

I thought to myself, *Okay, buckle up, here we go.*

The ADA asked me to give a little background information regarding my assignment and training in the narcotics field to justify the testimony that I would be providing before the court.

In a loud and clear voice, I rattled off my checklist of info. As I did, I noticed that the ADA had decided to go ahead and open up one of the large bags of narcotics. Just like product placement in feature films, the bag was strategically placed at the edge of the prosecutor's table, its wide yawning mouth aimed at its target audience; the jury. I glanced at the jury to gage if anyone was feeling its effects, but nobody seemed to be wired or uncomfortable.

The ADA asked me if I was familiar with a particular voucher. A court officer delivered a copy of the voucher to me, and I briefly scanned the paper. I stated that I was indeed familiar with the voucher and summarized the printed contents on the form. I was then asked to draw my attention to item number three. As I focused on item number three, the ADA was reading something completely different, and I wondered if I had the wrong document.

I stopped her mid-sentence and said, "I'm sorry. I'm not sure where you are reading from."

The ADA repeated what she said, but much slower, thinking that would help me. The defense attorney was wetting his lips as he listened in on the confusion as he scribbled on his yellow legal pad. I was still confused until I spotted the description of evidence she was describing. I stopped her again and asked her, "Are we talking about index number three or item number three?"

She caught her mistake, apologized, and then corrected herself. I glanced over at the defense table with a look that implied, *Not this time, motherfucker.* He dropped his pen and leaned back in his chair readjusting his expensive frames.

The questioning went on for several minutes, and I took my time to digest each question and burp out a short and concise answer. The ADA shuffled documents around on her table and asked me to explain specific items from various vouchers and laboratory reports.

After asking each question, the ADA would grope around her desk as I answered. She knew the answers were strictly for the jury's benefit, and so her attention became more focused on her desk and the next question than on my answer.

It became a sort of ping-pong match. She would serve up a question, and I would volley back with an answer and explanation. During one of these exchanges, she asked me a question while she pushed her glasses up on her nose. As her hand fell back onto the table, I noticed that there was something new on her face. My chair squeaked as I leaned slightly forward, baffled by this addition. She dropped her head and continued looking over some of her notes. Our volley was temporarily interrupted when I didn't answer her back at our normal steady pace, and the ping-pong ball bounced silently under my chair. She looked up at me with surprise and also with what appeared to be white powder smeared on the tip her nose and cheek.

I stared back with my own look of surprise as I became so distracted that I reached for the shot glass to grant me a few extra seconds to compose myself. Stalling for some more time, I asked, "I'm sorry. Could you repeat the question?" As she reviewed her notes to repeat the last question, I realized that it had to be cocaine on the end of her nose! Apparently, some had spilled from the open bag on to the table, and somehow, she inadvertently placed her hand on the loose powder and transplanted it onto her nose when she adjusted her glasses.

Normally, I would face the jury when giving my answer, but I became obsessed with staring at the tip of her nose. I turned to my left to see if the judge had noticed what was happening. He had his head buried in his notes. I thought to myself, *Am I the only one who sees what's going on here? Who else has this kind of luck: having to testify in a crack-cocaine trial with an ADA who is wearing the evidence as blush!* Suddenly, all I could think of was a quote by Richard Pryor, "I'm not addicted to cocaine...I just like the way it smells." It took all I had, not to break out in uncontrollable laughter. I couldn't wait to be excused from the witness stand to tell Keith.

I finished my testimony without being scarred too badly by the defense attorney. The judge released me from my little wooden padded chair. I glided out in half the time it took me to come in. Keith was still piloting his anger around the tiled floor as I came through the wooden doors.

Keith looked down at me with his jaw hanging open after I informed him of my observations. He said, "Stop. Are you fucking kidding me?"

I shook my head, and I could see his liquid mercury rising again. We waited outside the courtroom until the day's proceedings ended to help with carrying the evidence and case folders back to 80 Centre Street. She emerged from the courtroom drug free as the two of us focused on the end of her nose.

The trial continued on in a less dramatic fashion, and the evidence proved too much for the defense attorney to overcome. The jury found the two defendants guilty of narcotics charges. With the trial over, the narcotics had to be returned to the police laboratory in Queens. Keith and Sergeant Dobbins made the trip over to log them back in. The justice system went full cycle, and we were ready to reload it with our next caper.

Going on trial and having to testify before a jury can push your stress levels to the max. Once the trial came to a successful conclusion, I deleted those files from my head and enjoyed the vacated space. Unfortunately, my stress levels were launched once again after reading a notification that instructed me to appear at Internal Affairs with a small footnote stating, "Bring representation."

When Keith and the sergeant returned the drugs to the lab after the trial ended, it seemed that when the package was weighed back in, it was approximately two ounces short of its initial weight. The police department frowns on these types of inconsistencies and immediately notified Internal Affairs to initiate an investigation. So there I was, standing with this little piece of paper in my hand advising me that I would need a union delegate to represent me at our meeting.

I wasn't the only one going to IAB regarding this matter. Sergeant Dobbins, Keith Schiller, and even Tommy Grimes would be carpooling with me. Tommy did Keith the favor of picking up the drugs from the Property Clerk's Office located in One PP and delivering them to the ADA's office, so now he was a link in the chain of custody and must appear with the rest of us.

We appeared in business attire at Internal Affairs. Our union representatives met us in the waiting room. We briefly went over the particulars of the case and advised IAB that we were ready to proceed.

My turn to be interviewed was announced, and I popped up out of my chair with an eagerness to get the process over with and put it behind me. I strutted into the interview room with a little bit of attitude and took my seat. I sat across the desk from two sergeants from IAB. I noticed that they were each wearing off-the-rack business suits like me while my union rep sported an expensive designer suit. I often wondered where the money that was deducted from my paycheck every two weeks was going, and now I knew: the DEA Suit Fund. I placed my related paperwork on the desk in front of me. Looming ominously in the center of the desk was a tape recorder, ready to capture every decibel.

One of the investigators from IAB explained the reason for the meeting and asked if we were ready to proceed. My biweekly union dues replied that we were. As the sergeant pressed PLAY/RECORD on the recorder, their whole demeanor changed. It was as if those buttons pushed together controlled their behavior. They morphed into an aggressive posture, and their chests seemed to puff up in an attempt to intimidate me. This kind of angered me because I knew I had nothing to do with the missing cocaine. And besides that, these guys apparently didn't know that I took the same class as they did in the three-week CIC (Criminal Investigation Course), regarding interrogation techniques. What was next? Let me guess; good cop/bad cop?

Everyone at the table identified themselves for the record, and the questions began. I explained my participation and role in the case. I expressed my observations regarding the appearance of a mysterious white powder on the face of the Powder Puff ADA during my direct examination on the stand. The two sergeants shot a quick look at each other and then returned their poker faces to me.

After not too long of a time, the pain ended, and the investigators turned off the tape recorder. The STOP button acted as a sort of release valve that returned the investigators to their normal size. One of the sergeants then candidly said that they had already spoken to the assistant district attorney who acknowledged that she had opened the bag and said she claimed responsibility for the shortage. That annoyed me even more. If that was the case, then why were we even here to begin with? And what was with the intimidation factor, did they just want to practice or what? I felt the whole process was a complete waste of our time and energy. This was time that both sides could have used constructively on other issues. Unfortunately, this was part of the system.

We left there thankful that this investigation was officially closed on all accounts. On the way out, I wearily asked Keith if he was done trying to get me fired or indicted. "Do you always have to go for the big bang?"

He shook his head and smiled as he said, "They don't call me Big Country for nothing."

SIXTY-ONE

Susquehanna Hat Company

The one aspect of the job that I really despised was issuing traffic summonses. When I worked as a uniform cop, tickets were a necessary evil. The police department always claimed that there was never a required quota to be filled, but rather there was a target goal. However you want to word it, you had to write to keep your detail. And writing traffic summons usually earned you a trip to traffic court.

I have testified many times before: in Federal Court, Narcotics Grand Jury, Supreme Court, Family Court, and even Landlord Tenant Court. At times I thought that I would rather be subjected to water boarding than have to receive a notification to testify in traffic court. It was torture, and I hated it for reasons I didn't quite understand myself. I sensed the place just had a bad aura about it; it was possessed, in desperate need of an exorcism.

Going to traffic court was much like being at the Big Apple Circus. The judge, acting as the ringleader, would announce each motorist's name and call them to the center of the ring where they would perform for the other "ticket holders," if I may be so bold.

The cast of characters were as intricate and eclectic as any that Stephen King could ever introduce us to in one of his most twisted novels. The motorists came from all walks of life. I've seen all types in there: fat, skinny, tall, short, young, old, well educated, dumb as a nail, well dressed, filthy, dirty, passive, violent, naïve, belligerent, patient, nice, and some who were just downright nasty.

Some of the cops could also fit into a number of the above-listed categories. Add to this, a handful of attorneys trolling around the check-in lines hunting for potential clients. Before the mini-trials began, the attorneys would be as friendly as could be to the officers, but once the hearing was in session, they would try to make you look like one of the circus clowns. There was one attorney, an older gentleman with white hair, who would tell the most god-awful jokes and even went as far as to bring in plastic dog shit for a laugh. You can't make this stuff up, folks.

I would sit quietly off to the side on a short, hard wooden bench reserved for police, and review my memo book entries. My notes were usually extensive and included diagrams that would help refresh my recollection a few months down the road if the motorist decided to fight the summons.

It was amazing some of the excuses that were brought before the court as reasons for running a red light or other moving violation. I have witnessed hearings for a red light summons where the defendant "allegedly" had a witness in the car to provide testimony on behalf of the motorist. The witness is required to step out of the room until the judge calls them back in to give their testimony. The witness returns to the room and "swears to tell the truth, the whole truth and nothing but the truth" and then proceeds to tell the court that his friend the motorist came to a complete stop at the stop sign. Oops, wrong script. Guilty, please pay the cashier outside.

One gentleman defending himself against a red light summons, dug into his pocket and pulled out a piece of a ragged cardboard box that had a diagram of the intersection in question drawn on it. From the other pocket, he pulled out a toy car with Mickey Mouse in the driver's seat, and another with Minnie Mouse, then proceeded to reenact the scenario, moving Mickey and Minnie around the cardboard while the rest of the "ticket holders" broke out in laughter. The judge couldn't contain himself and laughed along with the rest of the room. It didn't faze the motorist who went right on playing with his toy cars like a four year old playing alone in the corner. Finally, the judge couldn't take it anymore and decided to find the gentleman not guilty because of his uniquely creative defense.

Once I was assigned to the Tactical Narcotics Team, my traffic summons writing days were over. However, my responsibility to give cause for issuance of past summons remained. As my career advanced, I continued to appear in traffic court but looked forward to the day when it would all come to an end. The summonses that I issued to young kids, who thought it was cool to throw them out the window as we passed by, now had to answer them to clear their license to get a job. Ripping them up or using them as a coaster for your coffee didn't make them go away. As adults, the tickets would come back to haunt them.

Over the years, I didn't even bother to refer to my memo book for refreshment. I simply made my appearance and issued the following standard statement when asked by the judge to give the facts surrounding the summons: "Due to the amount of time that has elapsed, approximately X amount of years (fill in the X), I have no independent recollection of the incident and cannot honestly say that this is the individual I issued the original summons to."

The judge would reply, "I thank you for your candor. The summonses are dismissed. Have a nice day, Officer." At this point, I would either leave the courtroom or take a seat to reissue that exact statement again for my next motorist, as if I were a trained parrot. I am sure the other "ticket holders" were wishing that they would get to perform in the ring with me. I usually went before the same judges, so as the years pressed on, they had all become privy to my routine and could have recited my mantra for me.

The notifications had dwindled down, and I thought the day had finally arrived making traffic court a thing of the past for me. In 2003 (my nineteenth year on the job), I got a notification to appear for a summons that I issued in 1984 (my first year on the job). Nineteen years later? Are you kidding me? Who answers a summons nineteen years later?

I begrudgingly appeared in court, took my seat on the bench, anticipating the arrival of my motorist after nineteen years. I waited patiently for the ringleader to arrive as the room filled up with motorists and cops, ready to get today's show underway.

After a number of performances were completed, the judge called me and my motorist into the ring. I stood facing the bench on the right side of the judge and the motorist on the left. The judge nodded to me, understanding that this would be a quick hearing. I remained facing straight ahead as the judge began, "Okay, we will be begin proceedings regarding five summonses issued in July of 1984. Wow, these are old. Okay, Mr. Suarez, are you ready to proceed today?"

Mr. Suarez answered, "Who me?"

It was as if he had said, "Susquehanna Hat Company." My body flushed with overwhelming memories as I quickly glanced over to Mr. Suarez. It was indeed him, Mr. "Who Me," my first arrest nineteen years ago on Bergen Street for DWI.

"Yes, Mr. Suarez. I am talking to you," the judge responded impatiently. I chuckled because I knew the frustration of that same answer when I first heard it nineteen years ago. Old habits are hard to break, I suppose.

"Yes, I'm ready."

I stood two feet away from Mr. Suarez, ready to deliver my mantra.

"How do you plea? Guilty or not guilty?" the judge asked.

"Guilty."

The judge was astonished. And so was I. He gave him another opportunity to change his mind, "Are you sure you want to plead guilty?"

"Who me?" I love it!

"Yes, Mr. Suarez. Are you sure you want to plead guilty? The uninsured motorist summons carries a five-hundred-dollar fine alone. You are entitled to have a hearing and listen to the officer's testimony."

"I want to plead guilty."

"Okay, then guilty it is. This concludes this hearing. Pay the cashier out front." He turned to me with arched eyebrows and said, "Thank you, Officer. I don't believe you have any more cases today. You are free to go." I thanked the judge and walked out of the courtroom into the police sign-in room to punch out. I truly wished that Mr. Suarez had elected to have a hearing or even postponed it. I might have been retired by the next court date, and he would have gotten off.

Well, what's done is done. My first arrest was also my last appearance at traffic court.

building. Using the fire department for this step would keep suspicion levels low and at the same time save civilian lives if the information regarding the traps were true.

The operation went off without a hitch, and the team recovered five kilos of heroin and approximately $500,000 in cash. I was extremely impressed with the amount of preparation that was done and learned how important this planning could be in any operation.

Tommy also helped rescue Joe Murphy and I after an operation we were conducting went terribly wrong. I had an informant who was recruited to go to Arizona to pick up several kilos of cocaine and transport them back to Brooklyn. What was supposed to be a one-day trip turned into five. All I can say is, thank God underwear is two sided.

On our return flight, the informant was loaded up with four kilos of cocaine taped to his body, and our field team awaited our arrival at JFK airport. The informant was picked up at the airport by a livery cab with the drugs on him and, as Murphy's Law would have it, a dump truck blocked us from following the car out of the airport. I jumped into the driver's seat of Lieutenant Chong's auto and tried to locate the missing informant and kilos. We knew the area where the car was headed but didn't know for sure where he was going, so I drove like a madman weaving through traffic while Lieutenant Chong screamed like another madman into the radio, "We can't lose those kilos!"

One surveillance car was able to pull near the subject's home in Sunset Park, Brooklyn just in time to see the cab with the informant arrive. As the informant was about to hand deliver the kilos to the target, the surveillance auto screeched its wheels trying to back up out of view. The target got nervous and walked away from the informant like he had the bubonic plague, leaving him stranded with the four kilos.

I continued racing toward the target's house as Lieutenant Chong barked into the radio. When I finally arrived in the vicinity, we regrouped and discussed our options. As I sat there, I noticed a terrible burning smell coming from under our car. I realized that I had driven the entire way from the airport into Brooklyn with the emergency brake on. Of course, I got my balls broken by every member of my team. My defense was, "Who puts their emergency brake on?"

The target never took control of the drugs, so we could not arrest him. He probably believed that the informant was working with the police. The informant was nervous that he or someone in his family would be killed because he would be viewed as a rat, and secondly, because he had lost $80,000 worth of cocaine. Somebody had to answer for that. Tommy was able to come up with a plan that both allowed us to seize the drugs and put enough doubt in the mind of the organization to accept the loss without punishment to the informant or his family. Tommy's quick thinking turned a potentially dangerous situation into one with a safe ending.

Thomas Grimes is currently the founder of New York's Finest Speakers, which conducts Internet awareness presentations for students, business professionals, and parents. He has been featured on "The Today Show" as an Internet safety expert. He has traveled the country educating parents and students alike on the dangers and responsibility of interacting on the Internet. He can be reached at NYFinestSpeakers@yahoo.com or 646-269-8861.

SIXTY-THREE

Let Me See Your Hands

My retirement date was quickly approaching and started nipping at my heels like an annoying, angry Chihuahua. As hard as I tried to suppress its onslaught, the louder it barked. Acknowledging it would mean that I would have to come to terms with the fact that I was now twenty years older. I remember getting sworn in and thinking that I would be retired in the year 2004. That was a new millennium and a lifetime away. Had that much time really elapsed?

I had been through a lot in the last twenty years, both professionally and personally. Was I really ready to retire at such an early age? What would I do with myself afterward?

A day spent sitting in Assistant United States Attorney Dan Braun's office in Lower Manhattan with Detective Tommy Grimes, listening to an inmate who was cooperating with the government helped with my decision to retire. We were strategizing a plan to infiltrate a Dominican drug-smuggling organization. I sat there physically, but I was a million miles away mentally. I saw lips moving but heard no words, as my head nodded like a Derek Jeter bobble head propped up in a backseat window. I was brought back to the office when the inmate asked me, "What do you think?" I had absolutely no idea what was going on and struggled to come up with an answer. I said I basically agreed with what Tommy said, hoping he actually said something.

After that day in Dan Braun's office, I went home and couldn't stop thinking about how I had zoned out during the interview with the inmate. I started to realize that what once made my heart beat faster was now no longer that important to me.

I studied my face closely in the bathroom mirror and noticed that more of my hair was turning gray. Even the hair in my nose was turning gray. Boy, what an uplifting discovery that was. I tested a smile and observed that thin lines had etched themselves around my eyes. I stared into those brown eyes and looked deep within for guidance. Then I said, to myself this time, "Let me see your hands." I held them up in the mirror and examined them. On the surface, they weren't too rough with only a couple of small callous from weight training. As I studied them closer, beyond the surface, I envisioned my hands as they held that young mother's head as she fought for her life, as they pulled the trigger on my service revolver during a deadly shootout, as they held my friends hand as he lay in the hospital bed losing more than fifty percent of his blood from a gunshot. And finally, I watched them dig through the rubble of Ground Zero to unearth the victims of 9/11.

I returned my gaze back into the mirror and ran my fingertips across my face like I had done with my father's picture many years ago. I smiled again, but this time, it was for real and knew at that moment that I was done. Twenty years in the police department was upon me, and in my heart, I was ready to retire. I was at peace with it.

I had the Pension Section "run my numbers" (calculate what I would retire with) and was pleased with the results. Near the end of November, I let everyone know my intentions. Most people were genuinely happy for me and congratulated me on my decision and wished they were in my shoes. Others I'm sure were only happy that I was out of the way on the seniority list, which meant they had a better shot at getting a summer vacation selection. What mattered was that *I* was truly happy with my decision. I chose my anniversary date of February 3, 2004 as my exit date. I would have served twenty years and one day, allowing me to comfortably state that I have been a cop for over twenty years.

Every January, we would be entitled to twenty-seven new vacation days to use in the coming year. I planned on taking my vacation time to carry me straight through to February 3, 2004. New Year's Eve, December 31, 2003 was the next uniformed detail ahead of us. Over the past nineteen years, I believe I worked fifteen of them. I anticipated being home, watching the ball drop in Times Square on TV, with friends and family. However, when the detail roster came down, my name was right there on it. I thought about "banging in" (taking the day off), but that would only piss off the bosses and force someone else to take my spot. Then I thought, *Who cares? I won't be here anymore. I'll be retired.* I thought better of it and wanted to go out on a high note and didn't want to screw up some other poor cop's plans.

At first, I was genuinely disappointed. I mean, how many years do you have to have in the police department before you can get a New Year's Eve off? Isn't twenty enough? Tommy Grimes convinced me that this year would be fun. December 31 would be my last actual date of work before going on vacation till the end. I softened up my attitude and listened to Tommy. I worked fifteen years on New Year's Eve, what's one more, right?

To say it was cold was like saying the atom bomb was a firecracker! No matter how many layers of clothing I had on, the wind managed to find my skin and numb it. We mustered up on Broadway somewhere in the forties and waited to be given our assignments. With my chin tucked down into my chest and waddling side to side to generate heat, I asked Tommy, "Finish this sentence for me, 'I'm here working today because…'"

"You're here working today because…today is your retirement party. New York City is hosting it, and one million people are attending. Surprise!"

"Did they bring gifts? And how will I get them all home?"

Tommy always knew what to say although his verbal judo was less active due to the elements. This was a perfect example of, "If you don't like the answer you're getting, ask a different question." It worked. I viewed this whole celebration as my own. Thank you, Mayor Bloomberg, but you could have picked someplace a little warmer.

New Yorkers never cease to amaze me. As I stood on the corner of Broadway around 48th Street, a man walking his dog approached me from behind. He stood very close to me, much like Robert Deniro as Travis Bickle stood next to the CIA agent in *Taxi Driver*. I turned my rigid body like a robot toward this man and offered a frozen smile. He stood surveying the area as if he had just landed from outer space while his dog's pee gave off a vapor trail as it left its signature on a street pole.

He didn't seem to acknowledge me so I righted my torso, facing Broadway once again. After a moment or two, the gentleman said, "Excuse me, Officer."

Robotically turning back, I asked, "Yes?"

"What's going on here today?"

I chuckled and turned my attention back to Broadway. I didn't hear a return laugh, so I looked back at him. He stared at me waiting for an answer. I sarcastically said, "You're kidding me, right?" He turned and yanked his dog away from the pole in mid-sniff. Under my breath, I said, "It's my retirement party. What? No gift?"

As the evening grew older approaching the New Year, Tommy and I left our post and headed down near the "ball." We passed many cops and bosses we knew and wished them a happy and healthy New Year. With each stop, Tommy announced that I was retiring, and this was my last day. Handshakes turned to hugs, and bosses scratched my memo book with well-wishes. Even if it was two hundred degrees below zero, I still would have had a smile frozen on my face.

The countdown commenced as the seconds exploded down to zero. A thunderous roar welcomed in 2004 as fireworks and confetti littered the black sky. Strangers, friends, and family alike wished each other well in the coming year.

It was officially 2004, the year I would retire. What was once thought of as a lifetime away was now reality. I stood quietly within myself letting this fact absorb in my soul while hundreds of thousands of people roared around me. Tommy shook me from my private moment in public with a hearty hug and said, "Happy New Year, Lorenzo. You made it."

I fitted the card back in my case which closed differently now that the shield was missing. With a small smile, I turned toward the elevator and said in a low voice, "Thank you." As the elevator doors parted, I could see six pairs of eyes looking to see who would join them on their descent to the floors below. Two people entered the elevator in front of me and added their weight to the metal box. Even though there was still room for me to join them, I stepped back and said, "I'll wait for the next one."

Any other day, I would have squeezed myself into the sardine can just to get out of The Puzzle Palace as quick as possible, but today was different. I wanted to stay a little longer because this was the last time that I would be in this building as an active detective. The next elevator came moments later, and I stepped in not looking at its occupants. My head remained down until the doors opened, and I exited on the main floor. People rushed past me, brushing against my arms as they fled the building. I was once one of the fleeing herds, but now, everything was…different.

I broke the seal on the front door of One Police Plaza and a gush of air rushed to greet me. The fresh air engulfed me and then seemed to gently push me away from the building, guiding me in a new direction.

Epilogue

Recently, I found myself leaning against the closed doors of a Long Island Rail Road train heading out to Massapequa, Long Island from Manhattan's Penn Station. Standing to my left was a probationary NYPD police officer. His name tag informed me that his last name was Frost. I was silent as I averted my eyes to shyly steal a glimpse of his crisp academy uniform, which I'm sure he had grown accustomed to over the past couple of months. I was that little boy all over again, as I felt that strong urge to be in uniform and the need to belong.

He appeared to be only about twenty-two or twenty-three years old, and although his hair was blonde and his eyes were blue, I was looking at myself. I did the math in my head and realized that twenty-five years, nine months, and twenty days ago, that was me standing in that same exact spot. What I found interesting was, although the uniform had changed over those twenty-five plus years, the familiar light behind his eyes had not.

My inner voice battled with my curiosity to start a conversation with my former self. The train was nearly halfway to its first stop of Rockville Centre before I suddenly overrode my inner lasso and blurted out, "When do you get out?"

PPO Frost was startled at my sudden projection of words and asked, "Excuse me?"

I intentionally slowed my words down and repeated them, "When do you get out?"

"December 28, just in time for New Year's Eve." He chuckled.

"Wow. My actual last day of work was on New Year's Eve." I paused a moment and then realized that he was not privy to the conversation I had in my head. So for clarity, I added, "I'm retired from the job. Imagine that. I had twenty years on the job and still couldn't get off for New Year's Eve."

Instantly, we were bonded, and I reminisced through his limited experiences. If only I could have injected my twenty years on the job directly into his soul on this short train ride as easily as downloading songs on an iPod. I wanted to save him the pain of living the mistakes that I made over the years.

I passed along those same words of wisdom that were gifted to me in the Seven-Nine (079) precinct many years ago, saying to him, "This may not make any sense right now, but trust me, it will. If you find one gun, look for two. If you find two guns, look for three."

As we exited at the same stop, I turned to him and said, "Remember this conversation we just had because the years go by amazingly fast. And twenty-five years from now, you'll find yourself sharing similar words with a wet-nose rookie who will remind you of yourself back in the day. You have the ability to change people's lives. It's a great job. Honor the shield and may God bless you." Then I parted his company offering, in my opinion, what are the greatest two words you could ever say to a cop, "Be safe."

Since being retired, the question I am most asked is, "Do you miss the job?"

I have put much thought into my answer, and can only say this in reply, "I miss the clowns, but not the circus."

For those of you who choose to wear the uniform of a police officer, from my heart, I would like to offer you the same two greatest words, **"BE SAFE."**

The Final Inspection

The policeman stood and faced his God,
which must always come to pass.
He hoped his shoes were shining,
just as brightly as his brass.

"Step forward now, policeman.
And how shall I deal with you?
Have you always turned the other cheek?
To my church have you been true?"

The policeman squared his shoulders
and said, "No, Lord. I guess I ain't.
Because those who carry badges,
can't always be a saint."

"I've had to work most Sundays,
and at times my talk was rough…
and sometimes I've been violent
because the streets are awful tough."

"But I never took a penny,
that wasn't mine to keep…
though I worked a lot of overtime
when the bills got just too steep."

"And I never passed a cry for help,
though at times I shook with fear.
And sometimes, God forgive me,
I wept unmanly tears."

"I know I don't deserve a place
among the people here.
They never wanted me around
except to calm them in their fear."

"If you've a place for me here, Lord,
It needn't be so grand.
I never expected or had too much,
but, if you don't…I'll understand."

There was silence all around the throne,
where saints had often trod,
as the policeman waited quietly
for the judgment of his God.

"Step forward now, policeman.
You've borne your burdens well.
Come walk a beat on heaven's streets.
You've done your time in hell.

—Author Unknown

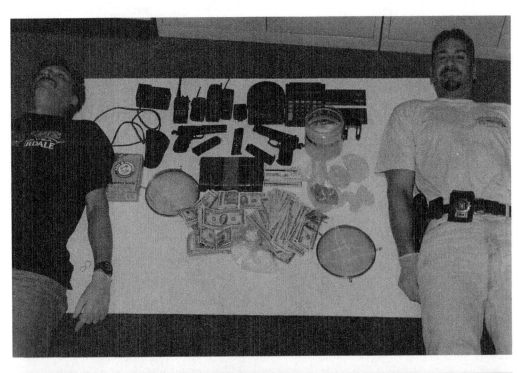

Remember the Heroes

September 11, 2001

About the Author

Lawrence Hoffman was born and raised on the south shore of Long Island, New York. He joined the New York City Police Department in 1984 and retired with the rank of detective after twenty years of service in 2004. He is a member of the NYPD Honor Legion and has received over twenty-four departmental awards and medals of recognitions along with letters of commendation from the Eastern District of United States Attorney's Office in Manhattan, the Federal Bureau of Investigation (FBI), and the New York City Fire Department. Lawrence is also a member of the Screen Actors Guild and can be seen in several blockbuster feature films and television shows such as *Law and Order, Life on Mars, A Beautiful Mind, The Bounty Hunter, Break the Stage,* and *The Taking of Pelham 123.* He continues to pursue his dreams in acting and writing and currently works in the public safety field in Florida where he resides with his wife Jeanette.

CPSIA information can be obtained at www.ICGtesting.com
Printed in the USA
BVOW11s2017200116

433310BV00005BB/76/P